Sources of Unofficial UK Statistics

Fourth Edition

Compiled by
David Mort and Wendy Wilkins
Information Research Network

Gower

First edition published 1985

Published by
Gower Publishing Limited
Gower House
Croft Road
Aldershot
Hampshire GU11 3HR
England

Gower
Old Post Road
Brookfield
Vermont 05036
USA

British Library Cataloguing in Publication Data

Sources of unofficial UK statistics. - 4th ed.
 1.Great Britain - Statistical services
 I.Mort, D. (David), 1952- II.Wilkins, Wendy
314.1'07

ISBN 0 566 08236 5

Library of Congress Cataloging-in-Publication Data

Mort, D.
 Sources of unofficial UK statistics / compiled by David Mort, Wendy Wilkins.--4th ed.
  p.cm.
 Includes indexes.
  ISBN 0-566-08236-5
 1.Great Britain--Statistical services--Directories. I.Title: Sources of unofficial United Kingdom statistics. II. Wilkins, Wendy.

 HA37.G7 M665 2000
 016.3141--dc21   99-049655

Typeset in Palatino and printed in Great Britain at the University Press, Cambridge.

SOURCES OF UNOFFICIAL UK STATISTICS

Fourth Edition

Contents

Introduction

Published statistical series and marketing data play an important role in the provision of information for business, industry, economic analysis and academic and other research. In the United Kingdom, Central Government is the main supplier of statistical information. These statistics are usually referred to as 'official statistics' and details of the range of official statistics available can be obtained from the Office for National Statistics (ONS). However, there are many other organisations involved in compiling and disseminating statistics and these include: trade associations, professional bodies, market research organisations, stockbrokers, banks, chambers of commerce, economic research and forecasting organisations, consultants, academic institutions, limited companies and PLCs particularly in consumer markets, and commercial publishers. Sources from these publishers form the basis of the entries in this directory, and these resources are usually referred to as 'unofficial statistics' or sometimes 'non-governmental statistics'. Traditionally, these two areas of statistical publishing – official and unofficial – have been largely separate from each other, although some trade association data has been used in selected official series, and various non-governmental bodies often lobby and advise government statisticians on statistical matters. In recent years, however, the line between official and non-official sources has become increasingly blurred, with more and more official series distributed and sold through private sector agents. These agents are included in this directory alongside more conventional non-official publishers.

This fourth edition of *Sources of Unofficial UK Statistics* provides details of almost 900 unofficial statistical titles and services, and is a unique source of information on an important area of business information.

Unofficial statistics

Central Government may be the major producer of statistics but, for various reasons, these statistics do not always provide sufficient detail on specific markets, sectors and products. Unofficial sources can cover product areas and sectors excluded from Central Government data, and also different types of data not usually included in official sources: for example, end-user statistics, salary surveys, opinion surveys, product price information and forecasts. In some cases, unofficial sources simply repackage and comment on official data, but these commentaries often provide a useful analysis of the major trends in official statistics. Many of the private sector agents now selling detailed time series from Central Government are also adding value to the data with commentaries, ratios and calculations from the original figures.

Prices of unofficial statistics vary from a few pounds to thousands of pounds for detailed market research, but a considerable proportion of the UK titles are still available free of charge.

One disadvantage of unofficial statistics is that, in many cases, the material is not available generally. Many trade associations and professional bodies, for example, only circulate material to members while other organisations limit access to clients, survey participants and so on. However, the percentage of the total non-official output restricted to only a limited group of users is relatively small and, even where detailed statistics are confidential, an executive summary or synopsis of data may be available generally. Another problem is that the reliability and accuracy of the data can vary considerably from one unofficial source to another. The amount of resources devoted to statistical activity, and the level of statistical expertise, can vary from one organisation to the next and this is likely to have an effect on the statistics produced. Few sources give any details on how the figures have been compiled and the specific methodologies used. Most of the items included are clearly statistical publications but non-statistical sources, such as trade journals, are included if they contain a regular statistical series or feature. Examples of these sources are included in the directory. This edition of the directory also includes details of Internet sites and, where possible, there is an indication of whether statistics are available on these sites.

Sources included in the directory

Over 880 statistical titles and services produced by around 460 organizations are included in this directory, based largely on information supplied by the publishing organisations in mid-1999.

Statistics of interest to business and industry, which are produced regularly, are included. For a source to be considered as 'regular' it must be produced at least once every six years. Most publications included are either annual, monthly, quarterly or biennial (once every two years), and one-off surveys or market reports do not qualify.

Only sources issued in, and concerning, the United Kingdom or Great Britain are covered. Material with international coverage has generally been excluded.

Some regional sources, relating to Scotland and Wales, and some local material covering the capital city, London, have been included but other local statistics on very specific local areas have been excluded.

Sources are included even if they have a restricted circulation but, in some cases, the publishers have asked to be excluded from the directory and we have agreed to this request. As well as the standard time series statistics, forecasts, trend surveys and opinion surveys are included, but data dealing with only one corporate body, such as company annual reports, has generally been excluded. Most of the items included are clearly statistical publications, but non-statistical sources listed in the previous section are included if they contain a regular statistical series or feature.

Finally, the sources listed cover a range of physical formats including the standard book form, those which are produced on one or two sheets of paper such as press releases and pamphlets, through to electronic data available on-line, on CD-ROM, via the Internet or on diskette or tape.

Structure of the directory

This directory is divided into three Parts. A brief synopsis of each is given below.

Part I   The Statistics

In this Part, the entries are arranged alphabetically by publishing organisation, and numbered consecutively. The entries have been based on responses from the publishing bodies themselves, supplemented, where possible, by a scanning of the source document. Usually if an organisation publishes more than one title, each has a separate entry. The exceptions are regular market research surveys produced by one publisher on various topics. As most of these surveys follow the same format, they are included in one general entry rather than listed separately.

The 'ideal' entry contains information for each of the categories listed below:

- **Name** of the publishing body
- **Title** sources
- **Coverage**, including details of any commentary, analysis accompanying the statistics and the sources of the statistics
- **Frequency** of source
- **Availability** of source and any restrictions on use
- **Cost** per annum and/or per issue
- **Comments** about the publication, including availability of data in machine-readable and other publications
- **Address** of publisher
- **Telephone, Fax, e-mail** and **Website** details of publisher.

However, some entries are incomplete due to information not being available or applicable to that particular source.

Part II   Title Index

All the specific titles covered in this directory are listed alphabetically here. Titles beginning with numbers such as '31' are listed at the beginning of the sequence. Annual reports are listed individually under 'Annual Reports' followed by the name of the organisation publishing a particular annual report. The numbers given are entry numbers, not page numbers.

Part III   Subject Index

This index contains references to the relevant entry number in Part I.

Part I
The Statistics

1

Title	3I PLC **Enterprise Barometer**
Coverage	Based on an opinion survey of its companies, 3I produces a regular report on likely trends in turnover, profit, investment, employment etc. A commentary supports the statistics.
Frequency	Regular
Availability	General
Cost	On application
Comments	Published by Bannock Consulting at the address below.
Address	47 Marylebone Road, London W1M 6LD
Tel. / e-mail	0171 535 0200
Fax / Web site	0171 535 0201

2

Title	ABACUS DATA SERVICES (UK) LTD **UK Import and Export Statistics**
Coverage	Import and export data, from 1987 onwards, for any traded product with basic data available by value, volume, month or year to date, country of origin, country of destination, port of entry or departure, flag or carrier used. Abacus is an officially appointed agent of HM Customs and Excise.
Frequency	Monthly
Availability	General
Cost	Depends on information required
Comments	Data available in various machine readable formats.
Address	Waterloo House, 59 New Street, Chelmsford CM1 1NE
Tel. / e-mail	01245 252222 abacusuk@aol.com
Fax / Web site	01245 252244 www.abacusuk.co.uk

3

Title	ABSA **Business Support for the Arts**
Coverage	An annual review of business sponsorship of the arts broken down by type of sponsorship, type of art form, regions. Based on data collected by the association.
Frequency	Annual
Availability	General
Cost	£40, £20 to members
Comments	ABSA is the Association for Business Sponsorship of the Arts. Basic statistics from the annual survey freely available on the web site.
Address	Nutmeg House, 60 Gainsford Street, Butlers Wharf, London SE1 2NY
Tel. / e-mail	0171 378 8143 info@absa.org.uk
Fax / Web site	0171 378 7527 www.absa.org.uk

4

Title	**State of the Nation**
Coverage	Information and statistics on the grocery trade with details of shop numbers and turnover trends by type of outlet, region. Based on Nielsen's own research.
Frequency	Annual
Availability	General
Cost	£950, £50 additional copies
Comments	Various other reports on the retail sector are available.
Address	Nielsen House, Headington, Oxford OX3 9RX
Tel. / e-mail	01865 742742
Fax / Web site	01865 742222 www.acnielsen.com

AC NIELSEN

5

AC NIELSEN MEAL

Title	**Summary of Brands and Advertisers**
Coverage	Total advertising expenditure for all brands spending over £150,000 per annum. 550 product groups are included. Data covers the latest quarter, a monthly breakdown within the quarter, and a moving annual total. Based on a monitoring of advertising in the press, television, satellite TV, radio, outdoor, and the cinema.
Frequency	Quarterly
Availability	General
Cost	£880
Comments	–
Address	2nd Floor, Kings Court, 185 Kings Road, Reading RG1 4EX
Tel. / e-mail	0118 956 9165
Fax / Web site	0118 959 6579 www.acnielsen.com

6

ACCOUNTANCY PERSONNEL LTD

Title	**Guide to Salaries in Accountancy**
Coverage	Covers accountancy salaries and banking salaries. Information based on surveys carried out in various regional centres.
Frequency	Twice yearly
Availability	General
Cost	On request
Comments	–
Address	141 Moorgate, London EC2
Tel. / e-mail	0171 678 4456
Fax / Web site	

7	
	ADECCO ALFRED MARKS
Title	**Survey of Secretarial and Clerical Salaries**
Coverage	A survey of salaries based on 11 job categories and covering over 6,000 specific jobs in industrial and service sectors. Based on data collected by the company.
Frequency	Annual
Availability	General
Cost	Free to clients, price to others on request
Comments	–
Address	Adecco House, Elstree Way, Borehamwood WD6 1HY
Tel. / e-mail	0181 207 5000
Fax / Web site	0181 236 0253

8	
	ADMAP
Title	**Adstats**
Coverage	Statistics on various aspects of advertising and the media including total expenditure, expenditure by media, expenditure in selected product categories. Most of the data is from Advertising Association surveys.
Frequency	Monthly in a monthly journal
Availability	General
Cost	£220
Comments	–
Address	NTC Publications Ltd, Farm Road, Henley-on-Thames RG9 1EJ
Tel. / e-mail	01491 411000 email@admap.co.uk
Fax / Web site	01491 571188

9	
	ADMAP
Title	**Advertising Business Indicators**
Coverage	Summary data on economic trends plus general information on advertising and media trends.
Frequency	Monthly in a monthly journal
Availability	General
Cost	£220
Comments	–
Address	NTC Publications Ltd, Farm Road, Henley-on-Thames RG9 1EJ
Tel. / e-mail	01491 411000 email@admap.co.uk
Fax / Web site	01491 571188

10	ADVERTISING ASSOCIATION
Title	**Advertising Statistics Yearbook**
Coverage	General trends in advertising and the annual Advertising Association survey. Statistics by type of advertising, e.g. cinema, direct mail, poster, newspapers, magazines, directories, radio, TV. Also statistics on prices, expenditure by product sector, top advertisers, agencies, complaints, attitudes, and international trends. Data for earlier years and based on various sources.
Frequency	Annual
Availability	General
Cost	£95 (plus £1.50 p+p)
Comments	Some statistics are freely available on the Association's web site.
Address	NTC Publications Ltd, Farm Road, Henley-on-Thames RG9 1EJ
Tel. / e-mail	01491 411000 email@admap.co.uk
Fax / Web site	01491 571188

11	ADVERTISING ASSOCIATION
Title	**Long Term UK Advertising Expenditure Forecast**
Coverage	Tables and commentary on advertising expenditure expectations for the next ten years.
Frequency	Annual
Availability	General
Cost	£950, £495 for members of the Advertising Association
Comments	The fourth edition was published in 1998. Some statistics are freely available on the Association's web site.
Address	NTC Publications Ltd, Farm Road, Henley-on-Thames RG9 1EJ
Tel. / e-mail	01491 411000 email@admap.co.uk
Fax / Web site	01491 571188 www.adassoc.org.uk

12	**ADVERTISING ASSOCIATION**
Title	**Quarterly Survey of Advertising Expenditure**
Coverage	Summary tables on advertising trends by main media followed by specific sections on the total press, national newspapers, regional newspapers, consumer magazines, business and professional magazines, and all magazines. A final section looks at trends in specific industry sectors.
Frequency	Quarterly
Availability	General
Cost	£595, £395 for members of the Advertising Association
Comments	Some statistics are freely available on the Association's web site.
Address	NTC Publications Ltd, Farm Road, Henley-on-Thames RG9 1EJ
Tel. / e-mail	01491 411000 email@admap.co.uk
Fax / Web site	01491 571188 www.adassoc.org.uk

13	**ADVERTISING ASSOCIATION**
Title	**The Advertising Forecast**
Coverage	Forecasts for the main media categories - TV, radio, newspapers, colour supplements, magazines, classifieds, display advertising and posters. Also forecasts of expenditure in the main product sectors, e.g. retail, industrial, financial, government, services, durables, and consumables. Historical data is also included.
Frequency	Quarterly
Availability	General
Cost	£825, £495 for members
Comments	Some statistics are freely available on the Association's web site.
Address	NTC Publications Ltd, Farm Road, Henley-on-Thames RG9 1EJ
Tel. / e-mail	01491 411000 email@admap.co.uk
Fax / Web site	01491 571188 www.adassoc.org.uk

14	**ADVERTISING STANDARDS AUTHORITY**
Title	**ASA Annual Report**
Coverage	Gives a summary of complaints received by media and by type. Based on complaints received by the ASA.
Frequency	Annual
Availability	General
Cost	On request
Comments	–
Address	2 Torrington Place, London WC1E 7HW
Tel. / e-mail	0171 580 5555
Fax / Web site	0171 631 3051

15

AGB

Title	**AGB Superpanel**
Coverage	A consumer panel comprising approximately 8,500 homes regularly surveyed by AGB. Data on consumer spending and purchases of various goods and services.
Frequency	Continuous
Availability	General
Cost	On request
Comments	Various other consumer panels also carried out by AGB.
Address	AGB House, West Gate, London W5 1UA
Tel. / e-mail	0181 967 0007 kerry.thompson@tnagb.com
Fax / Web site	0181 967 4060 www.tnagb.com

16

AGRICULTURAL ENGINEERS' ASSOCIATION

Title	**Trade Statistics**
Coverage	Import and export data for agricultural products and machinery based on Central Government trade statistics.
Frequency	Quarterly
Availability	Members
Cost	On request
Comments	–
Address	Samuelson House, Orton Centre, Peterborough PE2 0LT
Tel. / e-mail	01733 371381
Fax / Web site	01733 370664

17

ALAN JONES & ASSOCIATES

Title	**Company Car Survey Report**
Coverage	A survey of the UK company car market based on research by the company.
Frequency	Annual
Availability	General
Cost	£165
Comments	–
Address	Apex House, Wonaston Road, Monmouth NPT 4YE
Tel. / e-mail	01600 716916 apexhouse@easynet.co.uk
Fax / Web site	01600 715521

18	ALAN JONES & ASSOCIATES
Title	**Maternity & Childcare Policy Survey Report**
Coverage	A survey of UK trends regarding maternity and childcare trends, based on original research by the company.
Frequency	Twice yearly
Availability	General
Cost	£140
Comments	–
Address	Apex House, Wonaston Road, Monmouth NPT 4YE
Tel. / e-mail	01600 716916 apexhouse@easynet.co.uk
Fax / Web site	01600 715521

19	ALAN JONES & ASSOCIATES
Title	**Shift and Overtime Survey Report**
Coverage	A survey of UK trends in shift and overtime work based on original research by the company.
Frequency	Twice yearly
Availability	General
Cost	£140
Comments	–
Address	Apex House, Wonaston Road, Monmouth NPT 4YE
Tel. / e-mail	01600 716916 apexhouse@easynet.co.uk
Fax / Web site	01600 715521

20	ALUMINIUM FEDERATION LTD
Title	**Aluminium Federation Annual Report**
Coverage	Contains some basic statistics covering production, overseas trade etc.
Frequency	Annual
Availability	General
Cost	Free
Comments	More detailed statistics available to members. The web site has a good set of summary statistics.
Address	Broadway House, Calthorpe Road, Five Ways, Birmingham B15 1TN
Tel. / e-mail	0121 456 1103 alfed@alfed.org.uk
Fax / Web site	0121 456 2274 www.alfed.org.uk

21	AP INFORMATION SERVICES
Title	**Directory of Management Consultants in the UK**
Coverage	Contains a 'Statistical Information and Fee Rate Survey' section providing a range of statistics on average daily fees, staff, turnover per annum, areas of specialisation.
Frequency	Annual
Availability	General
Cost	On request
Comments	–
Address	Roman House, 296 Golders Green Road, London NW11 9PZ
Tel. / e-mail	0181 458 0189 mail@ap-info.co.uk
Fax / Web site	0181 455 6381

22	APPAREL KNITTING AND TEXTILES ALLIANCE
Title	**Trends in Textile and Clothing Trade**
Coverage	Detailed import and export statistics for textiles and clothing based on Central Government trade data.
Frequency	Quarterly
Availability	General
Cost	£85, free to members
Comments	–
Address	5 Portland Place, London W1N 3AA
Tel. / e-mail	0171 636 7788
Fax / Web site	0171 636 7515

23	APPLIED MARKET INFORMATION LTD
Title	**199- UK Plastic Industry Handbook**
Coverage	An analysis of trends in the polymer industry and key polymer markets with statistics on production, consumption, capacity, and end user markets.
Frequency	Annual
Availability	General
Cost	£130
Comments	–
Address	45-47 Stokes Croft, Bristol BS1 3QP
Tel. / e-mail	0117 9249442
Fax / Web site	0117 9241598

24	ARCHITECTS' JOURNAL
Title	**Industry Forecast**
Coverage	Commentary and statistics on likely trends in the architecture sector in the coming 12 months.
Frequency	Annual
Availability	General
Cost	£75, £1.80 per issue
Comments	–
Address	EMAP Construct, 151 Rosebery Avenue, London EC1R 4QX
Tel. / e-mail	0171 505 6600
Fax / Web site	0171 505 6701

25	ARCHITECTS' JOURNAL
Title	**Workload Survey**
Coverage	Workload trends for the latest quarter compared to the previous quarter and the corresponding quarter in the previous year. Includes data on the value of new commissions, staffing levels, and sector trends. Based on a survey by the journal.
Frequency	Quarterly in a weekly journal
Availability	General
Cost	£75, £1.80 per issue
Comments	–
Address	EMAP Construct, 151 Rosebery Avenue, London EC1R 4QX
Tel. / e-mail	0171 505 6600
Fax / Web site	0171 505 6701

26	ASD 1A
Title	**Second Tier Pension Provision 1995/96**
Coverage	Analyses members of Contracted-Out Pension Schemes, Appropriate Personal Pension Schemes and those belonging to the State Earnings Related Pension Scheme.
Frequency	Annual
Availability	General
Cost	£15
Comments	–
Address	DSS HQ, Room B2715, Longbenton, Benton Park Road, Newcastle upon Tyne NE98 1YX
Tel. / e-mail	0191 225 7094 fergusod@asd1lbtn.dss-asd.gov.uk
Fax / Web site	0191 225 7671

27	ASHGATE PUBLISHING LTD
Title	**British and European Social Attitudes: How Britain Differs**
Coverage	A survey of social values and attitudes in the UK in the 1980s and 1990s, based on interviews with approximately 3,000 people. Supported by detailed analysis.
Frequency	Annual
Availability	General
Cost	£25
Comments	–
Address	Gower House, Croft Road, Aldershot GU11 3HR
Tel. / e-mail	01252 331551 info@ashgatepub.co.uk
Fax / Web site	01252 317446 www.ashgatepub.co.uk

28	ASSOCIATION FOR PAYMENT CLEARING SERVICES (APACS)
Title	**Clearing Statistics**
Coverage	Statistics on the turnover of inter-bank clearings through the clearing house and automated clearings. Based on figures collected by APACS from its members.
Frequency	Monthly
Availability	General
Cost	Free
Comments	An annual release provides cumulative data for the year. The web site has a range of statistics.
Address	Mercury House, Triton Court, 14 Finsbury Square, London EC2A 1BR
Tel. / e-mail	0171 628 7080
Fax / Web site	0171 256 5527 www.apacs.org.uk

29	ASSOCIATION FOR PAYMENT CLEARING SERVICES (APACS)
Title	**Yearbook of Payment Statistics**
Coverage	Statistics on the turnover of inter-bank clearings, automated clearings, inter-branch clearings, Scottish clearings, and London currency dealings. Based on figures collected by APACS from its members.
Frequency	Annual
Availability	General
Cost	£30
Comments	The web site has a range of statistics.
Address	Mercury House, Triton Court, 14 Finsbury Square, London EC2A 1BR
Tel. / e-mail	0171 628 7080
Fax / Web site	0171 256 5527 www.apacs.org.uk

30

Title	
Coverage	
Frequency	
Availability	
Cost	
Comments	
Address	
Tel. / e-mail	
Fax / Web site	

ASSOCIATION OF BRITISH INSURERS

AGM Statistics

A press release and leaflet giving key industry statistics, and including the first provisional figures on the industry's performance in the preceding year. Issued in June.

Annual

General

Free

Press releases with statistics, and market summaries freely available on the web site. Online ordering facilities.

51 Gresham Street, London EC2V 7HQ

0171 600 3333   info@abi.org.uk

0171 696 8999   www.abi.org.uk

31

ASSOCIATION OF BRITISH INSURERS

Analysis of Motor DTI Returns

Annual report of figures for premiums and claims for private cars and commercial vehicles.

Annual

General

£15

Issued October. Press releases with statistics, and market summaries freely available on the web site. Online ordering facilities.

51 Gresham Street, London EC2V 7HQ

0171 216 7493   info@abi.org.uk

0171 696 8996   www.abi.org.uk

32

ASSOCIATION OF BRITISH INSURERS

Family Spending

Using figures from the Office for National Statistics (ONS), the report shows average expenditure on different types of insurance per households, along with percentage of households with expenditure. Also broken down by type of tenure, region, occupation, and age.

Annual

General

£15 per issue, annual subscription to all the association's titles - £250

Press releases with statistics, and market summaries freely available on the web site. Online ordering facilities.

51 Gresham Street, London EC2V 7HQ

0171 600 3333   info@abi.org.uk

0171 696 8999   www.abi.org.uk

33	ASSOCIATION OF BRITISH INSURERS
Title	**General Insurance Statistics: Sources of Premium Income**
Coverage	A brief report showing the percentage of general business premiums received through different distribution channels. Figures split between commercial and personal lines. Based on the association's own survey and produced in October.
Frequency	Annual
Availability	General
Cost	£15 per issue, annual subscription to all the association's titles - £250
Comments	Press releases with statistics, and market summaries freely available on the web site. Online ordering facilities.
Address	51 Gresham Street, London EC2V 7HQ
Tel. / e-mail	0171 600 3333 info@abi.org.uk
Fax / Web site	0171 696 8999 www.abi.org.uk

34	ASSOCIATION OF BRITISH INSURERS
Title	**Indices of Prices Affecting Motor Insurance**
Coverage	Prices affecting motor insurance. Separate indices for new and used car prices, garage charge-out rates and replacement part prices.
Frequency	Twice yearly
Availability	General
Cost	£15 each
Comments	Issued February and August. Press releases with statistics, and market summaries available on the web site. Online ordering facilities.
Address	51 Gresham Street, London EC2V 7HQ
Tel. / e-mail	0171 216 7493 info@abi.org.uk
Fax / Web site	0171 696 8996 www.abi.org.uk

35	ASSOCIATION OF BRITISH INSURERS
Title	**Insurance Earnings Overseas**
Coverage	Figures showing the contribution of insurance to overall balance of payments results. Based on official data and published in November.
Frequency	Annual
Availability	General
Cost	£15 per issue, annual subscription to all the association's titles - £250
Comments	Press releases with statistics, and market summaries freely available on the web site. Online ordering facilities.
Address	51 Gresham Street, London EC2V 7HQ
Tel. / e-mail	0171 600 3333 info@abi.org.uk
Fax / Web site	0171 696 8999 www.abi.org.uk

36	ASSOCIATION OF BRITISH INSURERS
Title	**Insurance Review**
Coverage	Provides a review of the developments of the key industry statistics over the preceding five years. With 30 statistical tables, commentary, and graphs. Produced annually in September.
Frequency	Annual
Availability	General
Cost	Free
Comments	Press releases with statistics, and market summaries freely available on the web site. Online ordering facilities.
Address	51 Gresham Street, London EC2V 7HQ
Tel. / e-mail	0171 600 3333 info@abi.org.uk
Fax / Web site	0171 696 8999 www.abi.org.uk

	ASSOCIATION OF BRITISH INSURERS
37	
Title	**Insurance Statistics Yearbook**
Coverage	Detailed figures on all classes of long-term and general insurance and most statistics cover a 10 year period. For long-term business, the information includes sources of new business, long-term business revenue accounts, and investment of funds. For general business, the data given includes revenue account figures by class and for UK and overseas business. Based on the association's own survey and usually published in October.
Frequency	Annual
Availability	General
Cost	£50. Annual subscription to all the association's titles - £250
Comments	Press releases with statistics, and market summaries freely available on the web site. Online ordering facilities.
Address	51 Gresham Street, London EC2V 7HQ
Tel. / e-mail	0171 600 3333 info@abi.org.uk
Fax / Web site	0171 696 8999 www.abi.org.uk

	ASSOCIATION OF BRITISH INSURERS
38	
Title	**Insurance Trends**
Coverage	Includes articles on current trends and issues plus 27 statistical tables based mainly on the association's own surveys. Produced in January, April, July, and October.
Frequency	Quarterly
Availability	General
Cost	£25 per copy, or £80 per year, annual subscription to all the association's titles - £250
Comments	Press releases with statistics, and market summaries freely available on the web site. Online ordering facilities.
Address	51 Gresham Street, London EC2V 7HQ
Tel. / e-mail	0171 600 3333 info@abi.org.uk
Fax / Web site	0171 696 8999 www.abi.org.uk

ASSOCIATION OF BRITISH INSURERS

Title	**Long-term Insurance: New Business Results**
Coverage	Detailed figures on new life and pensions business written during the quarter. Brief comments on major influences. Split between whole life, endowment, temporary life policies, personal pensions, and sponsored business. Figures given for last eight quarters and five years for annual figures. Based on the association's own survey.
Frequency	Quarterly
Availability	General
Cost	£15 per issue, annual subscription to all the association's titles - £250
Comments	Press releases with statistics, and market summaries freely available on the web site. Online ordering facilities.
Address	51 Gresham Street, London EC2V 7HQ
Tel. / e-mail	0171 600 3333 info@abi.org.uk
Fax / Web site	0171 696 8999 www.abi.org.uk

ASSOCIATION OF BRITISH INSURERS

Title	**Quarterly General Business Claims**
Coverage	Figures on claims paid split between fire, theft, and weather damage claims for both commercial and domestic business. Figures for business interruption and domestic subsidence are also included. Based on the association's own survey and published in February, May, August, and November.
Frequency	Quarterly
Availability	General
Cost	£15 per issue, annual subscription to all the association's titles - £250
Comments	Press releases with statistics, and market summaries freely available on the web site. Online ordering facilities.
Address	51 Gresham Street, London EC2V 7HQ
Tel. / e-mail	0171 600 3333 info@abi.org.uk
Fax / Web site	0171 696 8999 www.abi.org.uk

41 ASSOCIATION OF BRITISH INSURERS

Title	**Sources of New Premium Income**
Coverage	A brief report showing the percentage of new premium income for long-term business sold through various distribution channels. Based on the association's own survey and published in March, June, September, and December.
Frequency	Quarterly
Availability	General
Cost	£15 per issue, annual subscription to all the association's titles - £250
Comments	Press releases with statistics, and market summaries freely available on the web site. Online ordering facilities.
Address	51 Gresham Street, London EC2V 7HQ
Tel. / e-mail	0171 600 3333 info@abi.org.uk
Fax / Web site	0171 696 8999 www.abi.org.uk

42 ASSOCIATION OF CATERING EQUIPMENT MANUFACTURERS AND IMPORTERS (CESA)

Title	**UK Catering Equipment Market**
Coverage	Based on returns from member companies, and estimates of sales by non-members, the association produces statistics for sales, imports, and exports broken down by type of catering equipment.
Frequency	Annual
Availability	Usually only available to members but some summary data may be made available to bona-fide researchers.
Cost	Free
Comments	–
Address	Carlyle House, 235 Vauxhall Bridge Road, London SW1V 1EJ
Tel. / e-mail	0171 233 7724 enquiries@cesa.org.uk
Fax / Web site	0171 828 0667 www.cesa.org.uk

43 ASSOCIATION OF CONTACT LENS MANUFACTURERS' LIMITED

Title	**Annual Statistics**
Coverage	Annual statistics relating to the production of contact lenses and contact lens solutions. Based on a survey of members' sales by the association.
Frequency	Annual
Availability	–
Cost	–
Comments	ACLM Product Manual.
Address	PO Box 735, Devizes, Wiltshire SN10 3TQ
Tel. / e-mail	01380 860418
Fax / Web site	01380 860121 www.aclm.org.uk

44 ASSOCIATION OF FRANCHISED DISTRIBUTORS OF ELECTRONIC COMPONENTS

Title	**AFDEC Statistical Forecasts**
Coverage	Forecasts of market trends for electronic components based on research by the association.
Frequency	Regular
Availability	General
Cost	On request
Comments	–
Address	Owles Hall, Owles Lane, Buntingford SG9 9PL
Tel. / e-mail	01763 271209 afdec@owles.demon.co.uk
Fax / Web site	01763 273255

45 ASSOCIATION OF INSURERS AND RISK MANAGERS

Title	**Status and Salaries Report**
Coverage	A twice-yearly survey covering salary and trends in working conditions for insurers and risk managers. Based on a survey by the association.
Frequency	Twice yearly
Availability	General
Cost	£25, free to members
Comments	Also publishes various research reports.
Address	6 Lloyds Avenue, London EC3N 3AX
Tel. / e-mail	0171 480 7610 enquiries@airmic.co.uk
Fax / Web site	0171 702 3752 www.airmic.co.uk

46 ASSOCIATION OF MANUFACTURERS OF DOMESTIC ELECTRICAL APPLIANCES (AMDEA)

Title	**AMDEA Quarterly Statistics**
Coverage	Deliveries and imports of various electrical appliances covering over 25 product headings. Similar data to that contained in the AMDEA Statistical Yearbook (see other AMDEA entry) with statistics for the latest quarter and summary data for the earlier quarter. Based primarily on AMDEA data supported by some official statistics.
Frequency	Quarterly
Availability	General
Cost	£750, combined subscription with AMDEA Statistical Yearbook
Comments	–
Address	Rapier House, 40-46 Lambs Conduit Street, London WC1N 3NW
Tel. / e-mail	0171 405 0666 info@amdea.org.uk
Fax / Web site	0171 405 6609

47 ASSOCIATION OF MANUFACTURERS OF DOMESTIC ELECTRICAL APPLIANCES (AMDEA)

Title **AMDEA Statistical Yearbook**

Coverage Deliveries by UK manufacturers and imports by country of origin for various appliances including fridges, freezers, dryers, washing machines, cookers, vacuum cleaners, heaters, electric blankets etc. Additional data on prices and employment. Based primarily on AMDEA data supported by some official statistics.

Frequency Annual

Availability General

Cost £600, or £750 combined subscription with AMDEA Quarterly Statistics (see other AMDEA entry)

Comments –

Address Rapier House, 40-46 Lambs Conduit Street, London WC1N 3NW

Tel. / e-mail 0171 405 0666   info@amdea.org.uk

Fax / Web site 0171 405 6609

48 ASSOCIATION OF MARKET SURVEY ORGANISATIONS (AMSO)

Title **Research Industry Annual Turnover Data**

Coverage Total turnover of AMSO members analysed by client type, data collection type, and research technique. Also details of overseas earnings. Based on a survey of members with a large amount of supporting text.

Frequency Annual

Availability General

Cost Free

Comments In 1998, AMSO merged with the Association of British Market Research Companies to form the British Market Research Association (BMRA). 1998 figures were the last published under the AMSO banner. Address and web site below refer to BMRA - see other entry.

Address 16 Creighton Avenue, London N10 1NU

Tel. / e-mail 0181 374 4095   admin@bmra.org.uk

Fax / Web site 0181 883 9953   www.bmra.org.uk

49	ASSOCIATION OF UNIT TRUSTS AND INVESTMENT TRUSTS
Title	**Equity Income Chart Pack**
Coverage	Quarterly summary of average UK equity income.
Frequency	Quarterly
Availability	General
Cost	Free
Comments	Previously called the Unit Trust Association. The web site has press releases with statistics.
Address	65 Kingsway, London WC2B 6TD
Tel. / e-mail	0171 831 0898 autif@investmentfunds.org.uk
Fax / Web site	0171 831 9975 www.investmentfunds.org.uk

50	ASSOCIATION OF UNIT TRUSTS AND INVESTMENT TRUSTS
Title	**FACETS - Financial Awareness and Consumer Education Tracking Study**
Coverage	A press release outlining the regular findings of a market research survey of consumer financial trends and issues.
Frequency	Monthly
Availability	General
Cost	Free
Comments	Previously called the Unit Trust Association. The web site has press releases with statistics.
Address	65 Kingsway, London WC2B 6TD
Tel. / e-mail	0171 831 0898 autif@investmentfunds.org.uk
Fax / Web site	0171 831 9975 www.investmentfunds.org.uk

51	ASSOCIATION OF UNIT TRUSTS AND INVESTMENT TRUSTS
Title	**Unit Trust and PEP Sales**
Coverage	Sales of unit trusts and PEPs in the previous month, comparisons with earlier months, and cumulative data. Based on the association's own survey and accompanied by a commentary.
Frequency	Monthly
Availability	General
Cost	Free
Comments	Previously called the Unit Trust Association. The web site has press releases with statistics.
Address	65 Kingsway, London WC2B 6TD
Tel. / e-mail	0171 831 0898 autif@investmentfunds.org.uk
Fax / Web site	0171 831 9975 www.investmentfunds.org.uk

52	AUDIENCE SELECTION
Title	**Key Directors Omnibus**
Coverage	200 managing directors and 200 finance directors from the top 10% of UK companies are interviewed each quarter. Results cover purchasing trends, brand awareness, advertising awareness, readership trends etc.
Frequency	Quarterly
Availability	General
Cost	Varies according to amount and nature of data required
Comments	Results available on disc. Other packages and special analysis available.
Address	14-17 St John's Square, London EC1M 4HE
Tel. / e-mail	0171 608 3618 info@audsel.com
Fax / Web site	0171 608 3286 www.audsel.com

53	AUDIENCE SELECTION
Title	**Phonebus**
Coverage	A general omnibus survey carried out every weekend with a sample size of around 1,000. Questions can be agreed up to the Friday and results are available on the Monday.
Frequency	Weekly
Availability	General
Cost	Varies according to amount and nature of data required
Comments	Results available on disc. Other packages and special analysis available.
Address	14-17 St John's Square, London EC1M 4HE
Tel. / e-mail	0171 608 3618 info@audsel.com
Fax / Web site	0171 608 3286 www.audsel.com

54	AUDIT BUREAU OF CIRCULATIONS LTD (ABC)
Title	**ABC Circulation Review**
Coverage	A well-established report on audited certified net sales, circulation, and distribution data for over 2,000 publications. Covers journals, magazines, and newspapers. Based on a survey by the company.
Frequency	Twice yearly
Availability	Members
Cost	Free
Comments	The data is held on a computerised database and various packages and searches are available.
Address	Black Prince Yard, 207-209 High Street, Berkhamstead HP4 1AD
Tel. / e-mail	01442 870800 rayh@abc.org.uk
Fax / Web site	01422 877407 www.abc.org.uk

AUTOMATIC VENDING ASSOCIATION OF GREAT BRITAIN (AVAB)

Title	**AVAB Census**
Coverage	In 1994, the association carried out its first detailed census of the beverage and snack foods vending sector. The survey, now produced annually, has details of machines in use, types of machines, products vended.
Frequency	Regular
Availability	General
Cost	£375 to non-members
Comments	Summary data on the web site.
Address	1 Villiers Court, Upper Mulgrave Road, Cheam SM2 7AJ
Tel. / e-mail	0181 661 1112
Fax / Web site	0181 661 2224 www.avab.org.uk

BAA PLC

Title	**BAA Airport Traffic Data**
Coverage	Based on an ongoing survey of passenger, freight and aircraft movements at BAA airports, this regular publication has statistics on UK traffic.
Frequency	Regular
Availability	General
Cost	Varies according to the amount of data required
Comments	–
Address	Jubilee House, Furlong Way, North Terminal, Gatwick Airport RH6 0JN
Tel. / e-mail	01293 595070
Fax / Web site	01293 595200

BAA PLC

Title	**BAA Monthly Traffic Summary**
Coverage	Based on traffic counts of freight, passengers and aircraft at BAA airports, this monthly report is a traffic summary for the UK.
Frequency	Monthly
Availability	General
Cost	On application
Comments	–
Address	Jubilee House, Furlong Way, North Terminal, Gatwick Airport RH6 0JN
Tel. / e-mail	01293 595070
Fax / Web site	01293 595200

58	
Title	## BAA PLC **Patterns of Traffic**
Coverage	Based on traffic counts at BAA airports, an annual report on passenger movements in the United Kingdom.
Frequency	Annual
Availability	General
Cost	£10
Comments	More detailed statistics available to members who participate in the survey.
Address	Jubilee House, Furlong Way, North Terminal, Gatwick Airport RH6 0JN
Tel. / e-mail	01293 595070
Fax / Web site	01293 595200

59	
Title	## BANK OF ENGLAND **Bank of England Quarterly Bulletin**
Coverage	Articles, comment and a statistical annex covering UK and international banking, money stock, official market operations, government finance, reserves and official borrowing, exchange rates, interest rates and national financial accounts. Mainly the bank's own figures.
Frequency	Quarterly
Availability	General
Cost	£40, combined subscription with Inflation Report, or £10 per issue
Comments	–
Address	Monetary and Financial Statistics Division, Threadneedle Street, London EC2R 8AH
Tel. / e-mail	0171 601 4030 mapublications@bankofengland.co.uk
Fax / Web site	0171 601 5196 www.bankofengland.co.uk

60	
Title	## BANK OF ENGLAND **Bank of England Statistical Release**
Coverage	Summary statistics on monetary and financial trends based largely on the bank's own figures.
Frequency	Monthly
Availability	General
Cost	On request
Comments	Usually published in the first week of the month.
Address	Monetary and Financial Statistics Division, Threadneedle Street, London EC2R 8AH
Tel. / e-mail	0171 601 4030 mapublications@bankofengland.co.uk
Fax / Web site	0171 601 5196 www.bankofengland.co.uk

<table>
<tr><td>**61**</td><td colspan="2">BANK OF ENGLAND</td></tr>
<tr><td>*Title*</td><td colspan="2">**Inflation Report**</td></tr>
<tr><td>*Coverage*</td><td colspan="2">A review of current price trends in the economy and the outlook for prices in the short term.</td></tr>
<tr><td>*Frequency*</td><td colspan="2">Monthly</td></tr>
<tr><td>*Availability*</td><td colspan="2">General</td></tr>
<tr><td>*Cost*</td><td colspan="2">£12, or £40 with a combined subscription to Bank of England Quarterly Bulletin</td></tr>
<tr><td>*Comments*</td><td colspan="2">−</td></tr>
<tr><td>*Address*</td><td colspan="2">Monetary and Financial Statistics Division, Threadneedle Street, London EC2R 8AH</td></tr>
<tr><td>*Tel. / e-mail*</td><td>0171 601 4030</td><td>mapublications@bankofengland.co.uk</td></tr>
<tr><td>*Fax / Web site*</td><td>0171 601 5196</td><td>www.bankofengland.co.uk</td></tr>
</table>

<table>
<tr><td>**62**</td><td colspan="2">BANK RELATIONSHIP CONSULTANCY</td></tr>
<tr><td>*Title*</td><td colspan="2">**Corporate Banking Survey**</td></tr>
<tr><td>*Coverage*</td><td colspan="2">The corporate banking survey examines the bank supply of corporate credit and compares this with the demand for credit from the UK's top 400 companies. Based on original research.</td></tr>
<tr><td>*Frequency*</td><td colspan="2">Annual</td></tr>
<tr><td>*Availability*</td><td colspan="2">General</td></tr>
<tr><td>*Cost*</td><td colspan="2">£550</td></tr>
<tr><td>*Comments*</td><td colspan="2">−</td></tr>
<tr><td>*Address*</td><td colspan="2">17 St Helens Place, London EC3A 6DE</td></tr>
<tr><td>*Tel. / e-mail*</td><td colspan="2">0171 256 5657</td></tr>
<tr><td>*Fax / Web site*</td><td colspan="2">0171 256 5658</td></tr>
</table>

<table>
<tr><td>**63**</td><td colspan="2">BAR ASSOCIATION FOR COMMERCE, FINANCE AND INDUSTRY</td></tr>
<tr><td>*Title*</td><td colspan="2">**Remuneration Survey**</td></tr>
<tr><td>*Coverage*</td><td colspan="2">A survey of members' salaries in all sectors of industry divided into various legal categories. Analysis by age and job and information on fringe benefits.</td></tr>
<tr><td>*Frequency*</td><td colspan="2">Every 2 or 3 years</td></tr>
<tr><td>*Availability*</td><td colspan="2">General</td></tr>
<tr><td>*Cost*</td><td colspan="2">On application</td></tr>
<tr><td>*Comments*</td><td colspan="2">−</td></tr>
<tr><td>*Address*</td><td colspan="2">Po Box 3663, Bracknell RG12 2FH</td></tr>
<tr><td>*Tel. / e-mail*</td><td colspan="2">01344 868752</td></tr>
<tr><td>*Fax / Web site*</td><td colspan="2">01344 868752</td></tr>
</table>

64	**BARCLAYS BANK**
Title	**Annual Importers Survey**
Coverage	A survey covering importing and re-exporting in the UK market. Highlights the impact that the downturn in the global economy is having on importers.
Frequency	Annual
Availability	General
Cost	On application
Comments	–
Address	6th Floor St Swithin's House, 11-12 St Swithins Lane, London EC4N 8AS
Tel. / e-mail	0171 621 5408 susanchappell@barclays.co.uk
Fax / Web site	0171 621 5409 www.economics.intranet.co.uk

65	**BARCLAYS BANK**
Title	**Barclays Economic Review**
Coverage	A general commentary on the UK and international economy and a statistical appendix with data on exchange rates, interest rates, money market. Text covers 50% of the report.
Frequency	Quarterly
Availability	General
Cost	Free
Comments	Also publishes various short pamphlets on specific UK markets and sectors.
Address	1 Wimborne Road, Poole BH15 2BB
Tel. / e-mail	01202 671212
Fax / Web site	01202 402303 www.economics.intranet.co.uk

66	**BARCLAYS BANK**
Title	**Small Business Bulletin**
Coverage	Analysis and data on forthcoming trends in the small business sector and developments over the previous few months.
Frequency	Regular
Availability	General
Cost	On request
Comments	Also publishes various short pamphlets on specific UK markets and sectors.
Address	1 Wimborne Road, Poole BH15 2BB
Tel. / e-mail	01202 671212
Fax / Web site	01202 402303 www.economics.intranet.co.uk

67	BARCLAYS BANK
Title	**UK Construction Survey**
Coverage	Commentary, graphs, and statistical tables covering trends in the UK construction industry. Based on various official and non-official sources.
Frequency	Regular
Availability	General
Cost	Free
Comments	Also publishes various short pamphlets on specific UK markets and sectors.
Address	1 Wimborne Road, Poole BH15 2BB
Tel. / e-mail	01202 671212
Fax / Web site	01202 402303 www.economics.intranet.co.uk

68	BARCLAYS DE ZOETE WEDD SECURITIES LTD
Title	**BZW Equity-Gilt Study: Investment in the London Market Since 1918**
Coverage	Comparison of returns on equity and fixed interest investment, adjusted for inflation, for any period since 1918. Also investment history since 1918 and the impact of taxation on investment returns. A large amount of text supports the data which is based mainly on BZW's information.
Frequency	Annual
Availability	Primarily clients but available to others if stocks available
Cost	£100
Comments	–
Address	4th Floor, Ebgate House, 2 Swan Lane, London EC4B 3TS
Tel. / e-mail	0171 623 2323
Fax / Web site	0171 956 4615

69	BDO HOSPITALITY CONSULTING
Title	**UK Hotel Industry**
Coverage	Part of a worldwide survey of hotels comparing London, provincial England, and Scotland. Covers room occupancy, analysis of guests, revenue, expenses, and costs. Includes comparisons with the previous year.
Frequency	Annual
Availability	General
Cost	£120
Comments	Various other international surveys produced plus detailed occupancy surveys in the UK.
Address	88 Baker Street, London W1M 1DL
Tel. / e-mail	0171 486 5191
Fax / Web site	0171 487 3686 www.bdo.co.uk/hc

70	
Title	**BEAUFORT RESEARCH LTD**
	Welsh Omnibus Survey
Coverage	A quarterly survey of a sample of 1,000 adults resident in Wales. Data on opinions, attitudes, advertising and product recall and awareness, purchase and usage, image and perception. Analysis available by sex, age, gender, social class, region, Welsh speaking.
Frequency	Quarterly
Availability	General
Cost	On application
Comments	Also carries out a regular omnibus survey of Welsh speakers.
Address	2 Museum Place, Cardiff CF1 3BG
Tel. / e-mail	01222 378565 beaufortr@aol.com
Fax / Web site	01222 382872

71	
Title	**BIRDS EYE WALL'S LTD**
	Pocket Money Monitor
Coverage	A commissioned research survey of pocket money given to 5 to 16 year-olds in the UK. Covers average weekly pocket money by age, region, and sex plus earnings from jobs and friends and relatives.
Frequency	Annual
Availability	General
Cost	Free
Comments	–
Address	Station Avenue, Walton-on-Thames KT12 1NT
Tel. / e-mail	01932 228888
Fax / Web site	01932 244109

72	
Title	**BISCUIT, CAKE, CHOCOLATE & CONFECTIONERY ALLIANCE (BCCCA)**
	Four-Weekly Summaries Services
Coverage	Monthly data on the deliveries of products with individual reports on biscuits, chocolate confectionery, and sugar confectionery. Detailed breakdowns in each report by type of product. Based on returns from members.
Frequency	Monthly
Availability	General
Cost	Free to members, prices for others on request
Comments	–
Address	37-41 Bedford Row, London WC1R 4JH
Tel. / e-mail	0171 404 9111 office@bccca.org.uk
Fax / Web site	0171 404 9110 www.bccca.org.uk

	BISCUIT, CAKE, CHOCOLATE & CONFECTIONERY ALLIANCE (BCCCA)
73	
Title	**Statistical Yearbook**
Coverage	Statistics on the deliveries to the home and export markets of biscuits, cakes, and confectionery. Historical trends and data on specific product areas. Based largely on surveys of members with supporting data from other sources.
Frequency	Annual
Availability	General
Cost	Free to members, £350 to others
Comments	–
Address	37-41 Bedford Row, London WC1R 4JH
Tel. / e-mail	0171 404 9111 office@bccca.org.uk
Fax / Web site	0171 404 9110 www.bccca.org.uk

	BOOK MARKETING LTD
74	
Title	**Books and the Consumer**
Coverage	Based on research using a panel of 7,000 households, a report on the book market covering buying, book types purchased, reading habits, prices, retailing of books, postal buying of books, library usage.
Frequency	Annual
Availability	A summary report from the research is available to anyone. Full survey results and tabulations are only available to survey subscribers
Cost	On application
Comments	–
Address	7a Bedford Square, London WC1B 3RA
Tel. / e-mail	0171 580 7282 bookmark@londonweb.net
Fax / Web site	0171 580 7236 www.londonweb.net/users/bookmark

	BOOKSELLER
75	
Title	**Book Prices/Publishers' Output/Libraries**
Coverage	Various surveys appear throughout the year including surveys of book prices, number of titles published, public and academic library expenditure, salary surveys.
Frequency	Regular in a weekly journal
Availability	General
Cost	£135 annual subscription
Comments	–
Address	Bookseller Publications, 12 Dyott Street, London WC1A 1DF
Tel. / e-mail	0171 420 6000
Fax / Web site	0171 420 6103 www.thebookseller.com

BOOKSELLER PUBLICATIONS

76	
Title	**1999 Book Sales Yearbook**
Coverage	Comprehensive analysis of actual sales data in the UK's general retail market.
Frequency	Annual
Availability	General
Cost	£250
Comments	–
Address	12 Dyott Street, FREEPOST WC4593, London WC1A 1BR
Tel. / e-mail	0171 420 6080
Fax / Web site	0171 420 6177 www.thebookseller.com

BOOKTRACK

77	
Title	**Booktrack**
Coverage	A continuous survey of retail sales of books based on a panel of over 4600 retail outlets.
Frequency	Continuous
Availability	On request
Cost	On request
Comments	–
Address	Woolmead House, West Bear Lane, Farnham GU9 7LG
Tel. / e-mail	01252 742555 booktrack-info@teleord.co.uk
Fax / Web site	01252 742556 www.the bookseller.com/booktrak.htm

BORTHWICK FLAVOURS LTD

78	
Title	**Flavours Reports**
Coverage	A series of reports on the flavoured food and drink market with reports on adult food and drink and children's food and drink markets. The reports include data on flavourings, market factors, changing lifestyles, manufacturers, retailers, and future prospects.
Frequency	Regular
Availability	General
Cost	On request
Comments	–
Address	Deningham Road, Wellingborough NN8 2QJ
Tel. / e-mail	01933 440022
Fax / Web site	01933 440053

79	BREWERS' AND LICENSED RETAILERS' ASSOCIATION
Title	**BLRA Statistical Handbook**
Coverage	Production and consumption of beer and other alcoholic drinks, brewing materials, prices, incomes, duties, licensing data, structure of the industry, and drunkenness. Based largely on Central Government data with additional data from the association and other sources. A small amount of supporting text.
Frequency	Annual
Availability	General
Cost	£39.50
Comments	The association was previously known as the Brewers Society. Beer and Pub Facts pages on the web site have production, consumption data. Also publishes an annual report with some statistics.
Address	42 Portman Square, London W1H 0BB
Tel. / e-mail	0171 486 4831 mailbox@blra.co.uk
Fax / Web site	0171 935 3991 www.blra.co.uk

80	BREWING AND DISTILLING INTERNATIONAL
Title	**Crop Commentary**
Coverage	Details of the UK barley crop and hop output based on BDI's European Malting Barley Survey.
Frequency	Regular in a weekly journal
Availability	General
Cost	£48 annual subscription
Comments	UK beer production figures and surveys of specific areas of the brewing trade are also included in the journal at regular intervals.
Address	52 Glenhouse Road, Eltham, London SE9 1JQ
Tel. / e-mail	0181 859 4300
Fax / Web site	0181 859 5813

81 BRICK DEVELOPMENT ASSOCIATION

Title **Brick Usage and Deliveries**

Coverage Analysis of brick deliveries by member firms into the various construction sectors. Based on a survey of the association's members and the association claims to have 95% of the industry as members.

Frequency Quarterly

Availability Members

Cost Free

Comments –

Address Woodside House, Winkfield, Windsor   SL4 2DX

Tel. / e-mail 01344 885651   brick@brick.org.uk

Fax / Web site 01344 890129   www.brick.org.uk

82 BRITISH ADHESIVES AND SEALANTS ASSOCIATION

Title **Sales of Sealants**

Coverage Sales in value terms of various types of sealant plus value and volume sales split by chemical type. Based on a survey of members.

Frequency Twice yearly

Availability Members

Cost Free

Comments –

Address 33 Fellowes Way, Stevenage SG2 8BW

Tel. / e-mail 01438 358514

Fax / Web site

83 BRITISH AEROSOL MANUFACTURERS' ASSOCIATION

Title **BAMA Annual Report**

Coverage Gives details of aerosol filling statistics by various product categories. Based on a survey of members.

Frequency Annual

Availability General

Cost Free

Comments –

Address King's Building, Smith Square, London   SW1P 3JJ

Tel. / e-mail 0171 828 5111

Fax / Web site 0171 834 4469

84 BRITISH AGRICULTURAL AND GARDEN MACHINERY ASSOCIATION

Title	**Market Guide**
Coverage	A guide to the used tractors and farm machinery market based on a survey by the association.
Frequency	Regular
Availability	General
Cost	£114, £90 to members
Comments	–
Address	14-16 Church Street, Rickmansworth WD3 1RQ
Tel. / e-mail	01923 720241 info@bagma.com
Fax / Web site	01923 896063 www.bagma.com

85 BRITISH AGROCHEMICALS ASSOCIATION

Title	**BAA Annual Review and Handbook**
Coverage	Contains a section on industry sales and pesticide usage in the UK plus data on the world agrochemicals market. Sales data is based on a survey of members with a time series covering the last seven years. Sales data broken down into herbicides, insecticides, fungicides, and others.
Frequency	Annual
Availability	General
Cost	Free
Comments	–
Address	4 Lincoln Court, Lincoln Road, Peterborough PE1 2RP
Tel. / e-mail	01733 349225
Fax / Web site	01733 62523 www.baa.org.uk

86 BRITISH ALCAN CONSUMER PRODUCTS LTD

Title	**Wraps Market Household and Catering Review**
Coverage	Graphs and commentary on aluminium foil, bin liners, greaseproof paper, plastic wraps, cooking bags, food and freezer bags. Based primarily on Nielsen data.
Frequency	Regular
Availability	General
Cost	Free
Comments	–
Address	Raans Road, Amersham HP6 6JY
Tel. / e-mail	01753 887373
Fax / Web site	01753 889667

87

	BRITISH APPAREL AND TEXTILE CONFEDERATION
Title	**Industry Statistical Overview**
Coverage	Statistics covering production, consumption, overseas trade, employment etc.
Frequency	Annual
Availability	General
Cost	£35
Comments	Latest published volume - 1997.
Address	5 Portland Place, London W1N 3AA
Tel. / e-mail	0171 636 7788 batc@dial.pipex.com
Fax / Web site	0171 636 7515 www.batc.co.uk

88

	BRITISH APPAREL AND TEXTILE CONFEDERATION
Title	**Quarterly Export Data - All Textiles and Made-up Items**
Coverage	Export statistics by product category.
Frequency	Quarterly
Availability	General
Cost	£50 annual subscription
Comments	–
Address	5 Portland Place, London W1N 3AA
Tel. / e-mail	0171 636 7788 batc@dial.pipex.com
Fax / Web site	0171 636 7515 www.batc.co.uk

89

	BRITISH APPAREL AND TEXTILE CONFEDERATION
Title	**Quarterly Import Data - All Textiles and Made-up Items**
Coverage	Import statistics by product category.
Frequency	Quarterly
Availability	General
Cost	£70 annual subscription
Comments	–
Address	5 Portland Place, London W1N 3AA
Tel. / e-mail	0171 636 7788 batc@dial.pipex.com
Fax / Web site	0171 636 7515 www.batc.co.uk

90	BRITISH APPAREL AND TEXTILE CONFEDERATION
Title	**Quarterly Production Data - Cotton and Allied Textiles**
Coverage	Production trends for cotton and textiles.
Frequency	Quarterly
Availability	General
Cost	£70 annual subscription
Comments	–
Address	5 Portland Place, London W1N 3AA
Tel. / e-mail	0171 636 7788 batc@dial.pipex.com
Fax / Web site	0171 636 7515 www.batc.co.uk

91	BRITISH APPAREL AND TEXTILE CONFEDERATION
Title	**Quarterly Statistical Review - Cotton & Allied Textiles**
Coverage	Statistics on production, imports, exports, and apparent consumption particularly for cotton and allied fibres. Based on a mixture of official and non-official sources.
Frequency	Quarterly
Availability	General
Cost	£135 annual subscription
Comments	–
Address	5 Portland Place, London W1N 3AA
Tel. / e-mail	0171 636 7788 batc@dial.pipex.com
Fax / Web site	0171 636 7515 www.batc.co.uk

92	BRITISH APPAREL AND TEXTILE CONFEDERATION
Title	**Trendata**
Coverage	Statistics covering production, exports, imports, balance of trade, consumer expenditure, employment for the UK apparel and textile industry. Based on both official and non-official sources.
Frequency	Quarterly
Availability	General
Cost	£95 per annum (members), £195 for non-members
Comments	Available in loose-leaf format.
Address	5 Portland Place, London W1N 3AA
Tel. / e-mail	0171 636 7788 batc@dial.pipex.com
Fax / Web site	0171 636 7515 www.batc.co.uk

93	BRITISH BANKERS' ASSOCIATION
Title	**Abstract of Banking Statistics**
Coverage	Detailed statistics on the banks and banking with sections on bank groups, clearing statistics, credit card statistics, branches, and financial data. Based on various sources, including data from the association. Many tables have ten-year statistical series.
Frequency	Annual
Availability	General
Cost	On request
Comments	Some basic data and online ordering facilities on the web site.
Address	10 Lombard Street, London EC3V 9AP
Tel. / e-mail	0171 623 4001
Fax / Web site	0171 283 7037 www.bba.org.uk

94	BRITISH BANKERS' ASSOCIATION
Title	**Major British Banking Groups' Mortgage Lending**
Coverage	Trends in mortgage advances by UK banks with figures for the latest month and cumulative data. Based on returns from members.
Frequency	Monthly
Availability	General
Cost	On request
Comments	Some basic data and online ordering facilities on the web site.
Address	10 Lombard Street, London EC3V 9AP
Tel. / e-mail	0171 623 4001
Fax / Web site	0171 283 7037 www.bba.org.uk

95	BRITISH BANKERS' ASSOCIATION
Title	**Monthly Statement**
Coverage	General statistics covering the activities of the major UK banks. Based largely on data from members.
Frequency	Monthly
Availability	General
Cost	On request
Comments	Some basic data and online ordering facilities on the web site.
Address	10 Lombard Street, London EC3V 9AP
Tel. / e-mail	0171 623 4001
Fax / Web site	0171 283 7037 www.bba.org.uk

96	**BRITISH BANKERS' ASSOCIATION**
Title	**Sterling Lending**
Coverage	Trends in sterling lending with data for the latest available month and cumulative statistics. Based on data supplied by members.
Frequency	Monthly
Availability	General
Cost	On request
Comments	Some basic data and online ordering facilities on the web site.
Address	10 Lombard Street, London EC3V 9AP
Tel. / e-mail	0171 623 4001
Fax / Web site	0171 283 7037 www.bba.org.uk

97	**BRITISH CARPET MANUFACTURERS' ASSOCIATION**
Title	**Annual Report**
Coverage	A statistical section concentrates on carpet imports and exports. Based mainly on Central Government data.
Frequency	Annual
Availability	General
Cost	Free
Comments	–
Address	PO Box 1155, Kidderminster DY11 6NP
Tel. / e-mail	01562 747351 bcma@clara.net
Fax / Web site	01562 747359

98	**BRITISH CERAMIC CONFEDERATION**
Title	**Annual Production and Trade Statistics by Sub-Sector**
Coverage	Summary of the total production and sales of the ceramic industry, plus overseas trade data. Based largely on government statistics.
Frequency	Annual
Availability	Usually only available to members
Cost	Free
Comments	–
Address	Federation House, Station Road, Stoke-on-Trent ST4 2SA
Tel. / e-mail	01782 744631 bcc@ceramfed.co.uk
Fax / Web site	01782 744102

99   BRITISH CERAMIC CONFEDERATION

Title	**Quarterly Trade Statistics**
Coverage	Details of the imports and exports of ceramic products broken down into various industry sub-sectors. Based on government statistics.
Frequency	Quarterly
Availability	Usually only available to members
Cost	Free
Comments	–
Address	Federation House, Station Road, Stoke-on-Trent ST4 2SA
Tel. / e-mail	01782 744631 bcc@ceramfed.co.uk
Fax / Web site	01782 744102

100   BRITISH CHAMBERS OF COMMERCE

Title	**Quarterly Economic Survey**
Coverage	A quarterly review of business and economic conditions based on returns from a sample of members of a selection of the major regional chambers.
Frequency	Quarterly
Availability	General
Cost	£200 per annum, £60 each
Comments	Summary analysis of the latest survey on the web site.
Address	22 Carlisle Place, London SW1P 1JA
Tel. / e-mail	0171 565 2000 info@britishchambers.org.uk
Fax / Web site	0171 565 2049 www.britishchambers.org.uk

101   BRITISH CHICKEN INFORMATION SERVICE

Title	**199- Market Review**
Coverage	Commentary and statistics covering trends in the UK chicken market with data on value and volume sales by types of chicken, prices, retail distribution, and the future outlook. Based on data collected by the British Chicken Information Service.
Frequency	Annual
Availability	General
Cost	On request
Comments	–
Address	126-128 Cromwell Road, London SW7 4ET
Tel. / e-mail	0171 373 7757
Fax / Web site	0171 373 3926

102 BRITISH CLOTHING INDUSTRY ASSOCIATION

Title   **Report of Activities**

Coverage   Includes a facts and figures section with data on output, trade, production, consumer expenditure, top markets, and EU production.

Frequency   Annual

Availability   General

Cost   On request

Comments   –

Address   5 Portland Place, London W1N 3AA

Tel. / e-mail   0171 636 7788   bcia@dial.pipex.com

Fax / Web site   0171 636 7515

103 BRITISH EDUCATIONAL SUPPLIERS' ASSOCIATION

Title   **UK School Survey**

Coverage   Includes data for expenditure by schools on supplies and equipment.

Frequency   Annual

Availability   General

Cost   On request

Comments   –

Address   20 Beaufort Court, Admirals Way, London   E14 9XL

Tel. / e-mail   0171 537 4997   besa@besanet.org.uk

Fax / Web site   0171 537 4846   www.besanet.org.uk

104 BRITISH EGG INFORMATION SERVICE

Title   **BEIS Facts and Figures**

Coverage   Data on value and volume of sales, laying flocks, trade, consumption, regional breakdown of sales, egg production systems.

Frequency   Regular

Availability   General

Cost   On request

Comments   –

Address   126-128 Cromwell Road, London SW7 4ET

Tel. / e-mail   0171 370 7411

Fax / Web site   0171 373 3926

105 BRITISH EGG PRODUCTS ASSOCIATION

Title	**Breaking and Production**
Coverage	Includes data on egg production and breakages.
Frequency	Ten issues per annum
Availability	General
Cost	On request
Comments	–
Address	Suite 101, Albany House, 324-326 Regent Street, London W1R 5AA
Tel. / e-mail	0171 580 7172 british.egg.industry@farmline.com
Fax / Web site	0171 580 7082 www.britegg.co.uk

106 BRITISH EGG PRODUCTS ASSOCIATION

Title	**Import and Export Statistics**
Coverage	Overseas trade statistics for eggs and egg products based on data obtained from Central Government sources.
Frequency	10 issues per year
Availability	General
Cost	On request
Comments	–
Address	Suite 101, Albany House, 324-326 Regent Street, London W1R 5AA
Tel. / e-mail	0171 580 7172 british.egg.industry@farmline.com
Fax / Web site	0171 580 7082 www.britegg.co.uk

107 BRITISH ENERGY ASSOCIATION

Title	**British Annual Energy Review**
Coverage	A review of trends in the British energy industry, broken down by sector and based on a combination of sources.
Frequency	Annual
Availability	General
Cost	On request
Comments	–
Address	34 St James's Street, London SW1A 1HD
Tel. / e-mail	0171 930 1211
Fax / Web site	0171 925 0452

108	BRITISH FLUID POWER ASSOCIATION
Title	**Annual Salary Survey**
Coverage	Based on a survey of members, it includes data on remuneration, company cars, working hours, holiday entitlements.
Frequency	Annual
Availability	Members
Cost	On application
Comments	–
Address	Cheriton House, Cromwell Business Park, Banbury Road, Chipping Norton OX7 5SR
Tel. / e-mail	01608 644114 bfpa@bfpa.demon.co.uk
Fax / Web site	01608 643738 www.bfpa.co.uk

109	BRITISH FLUID POWER ASSOCIATION
Title	**BFPA Annual Hydraulic Equipment Survey**
Coverage	A survey of a sample of member companies providing information on market trends and characteristics. The survey is supplemented by some official statistics and international data.
Frequency	Annual
Availability	Members
Cost	On application
Comments	–
Address	Cheriton House, Cromwell Business Park, Banbury Road, Chipping Norton OX7 5SR
Tel. / e-mail	01608 644114 bfpa@bfpa.demon.co.uk
Fax / Web site	01608 643738 www.bfpa.co.uk

110	BRITISH FLUID POWER ASSOCIATION
Title	**BFPA Hose and Fittings Survey**
Coverage	A survey of a sample of member and non-member companies (the only BFPA survey to cover non-members), with information on market trends. Supplemented by some official statistics and international data.
Frequency	Annual
Availability	Members
Cost	On application
Comments	–
Address	Cheriton House, Cromwell Business Park, Banbury Road, Chipping Norton OX7 5SR
Tel. / e-mail	01608 644114 bfpa@bfpa.demon.co.uk
Fax / Web site	01608 643738 www.bfpa.co.uk

111	BRITISH FLUID POWER ASSOCIATION
Title	**BFPA Pneumatic Control Equipment Survey**
Coverage	A survey of a sample of member companies providing information on market trends. Also includes some official statistics and international data.
Frequency	Annual
Availability	Members
Cost	On application
Comments	–
Address	Cheriton House, Cromwell Business Park, Banbury Road, Chipping Norton OX7 5SR
Tel. / e-mail	01608 644114 bfpa@bfpa.demon.co.uk
Fax / Web site	01608 643738 www.bfpa.co.uk

112	BRITISH FLUID POWER ASSOCIATION
Title	**Distributor Annual Survey**
Coverage	A survey of distributors providing information on sales, market trends, end users, and companies. Also includes salary structure data and some official statistics.
Frequency	Annual
Availability	Members
Cost	On application
Comments	Established in 1994 to replace the Distributor Profiles.
Address	Cheriton House, Cromwell Business Park, Banbury Road, Chipping Norton OX7 5SR
Tel. / e-mail	01608 644114 bfpa@bfpa.demon.co.uk
Fax / Web site	01608 643738 www.bfpa.co.uk

113	BRITISH FLUID POWER ASSOCIATION
Title	**Hydraulic Equipment Monthly UK Orders and Sales Index**
Coverage	Orders and sales trends based on returns from member companies.
Frequency	Monthly
Availability	Members
Cost	On application
Comments	–
Address	Cheriton House, Cromwell Business Park, Banbury Road, Chipping Norton OX7 5SR
Tel. / e-mail	01608 644114 bfpa@bfpa.demon.co.uk
Fax / Web site	01608 643738 www.bfpa.co.uk

114

BRITISH FLUID POWER ASSOCIATION

Title	**Hydraulic Equipment/Pneumatic Control Equipment: Short Term Trends Survey**
Coverage	Commentary and statistics on short-term trends based on returns from member companies.
Frequency	Quarterly
Availability	Members
Cost	On application
Comments	–
Address	Cheriton House, Cromwell Business Park, Banbury Road, Chipping Norton OX7 5SR
Tel. / e-mail	01608 644114 bfpa@bfpa.demon.co.uk
Fax / Web site	01608 643738 www.bfpa.co.uk

115

BRITISH FLUID POWER ASSOCIATION

Title	**Pneumatic Control Equipment Monthly UK Orders and Sales Index**
Coverage	Orders and sales trends based on returns from member companies.
Frequency	Monthly
Availability	Members
Cost	On application
Comments	–
Address	Cheriton House, Cromwell Business Park, Banbury Road, Chipping Norton OX7 5SR
Tel. / e-mail	01608 644114 bfpa@bfpa.demon.co.uk
Fax / Web site	01608 643738 www.bfpa.co.uk

116

BRITISH FLUID POWER ASSOCIATION

Title	**Statistics Newsletter**
Coverage	Summary data and news on the industry plus details of new statistical developments relevant to the industry.
Frequency	Regular
Availability	Members
Cost	On application
Comments	–
Address	Cheriton House, Cromwell Business Park, Banbury Road, Chipping Norton OX7 5SR
Tel. / e-mail	01608 644114 bfpa@bfpa.demon.co.uk
Fax / Web site	01608 643738 www.bfpa.co.uk

117	BRITISH FOOTWEAR ASSOCIATION
Title	**Footwear Industry Statistical Review**
Coverage	Statistics on the industry structure, materials, production, profitability, employment and earnings, prices, supplies to the home market, expenditure, retailing, imports and exports. Based mainly on Central Government sources.
Frequency	Annual
Availability	General
Cost	£50
Comments	–
Address	5 Portland Place, London W1N 3AA
Tel. / e-mail	0171 580 8687 bfa@easynet.co.uk
Fax / Web site	0171 580 8687 www.shoeworld.co.uk

118	BRITISH FOOTWEAR ASSOCIATION
Title	**Monthly Statistics**
Coverage	Short-term economic indicators for the industry with a brief commentary. Data covers deliveries, employment, prices, retail sales, imports, exports.
Frequency	Monthly
Availability	General
Cost	£110 with quarterly publication
Comments	–
Address	5 Portland Place, London W1N 3AA
Tel. / e-mail	0171 580 8687 bfa@easynet.co.uk
Fax / Web site	0171 580 8687 www.shoeworld.co.uk

119	BRITISH FOOTWEAR ASSOCIATION
Title	**Quarterly Statistics**
Coverage	Detailed production, imports and exports, and consumption data for specific sectors of the footwear industry. Based mainly on Central Government data.
Frequency	Quarterly
Availability	General
Cost	£110 with the monthly publication
Comments	–
Address	5 Portland Place, London W1N 3AA
Tel. / e-mail	0171 580 8687 bfa@easynet.co.uk
Fax / Web site	0171 580 8687 www.shoeworld.co.uk

120	BRITISH FRANCHISE ASSOCIATION
Title	**NATWEST/BFA Franchise Survey**
Coverage	Statistics and commentary on the number of franchisees, types, sectors, sales, employment with the latest year's data compared to the previous year. Based on original research by the association. Commentary supports the text.
Frequency	Annual
Availability	General
Cost	£77.50
Comments	Produced in association with the National Westminster Bank.
Address	Thames View, Newtown Road, Henley-on-Thames RG9 1HG
Tel. / e-mail	01491 578050 mailroom@british-franchise.org.uk
Fax / Web site	01491 573517 www.british-franchise.org.uk

121	BRITISH FROZEN FOOD FEDERATION
Title	**Monthly Bulletin**
Coverage	Includes statistics on the UK frozen food market with data on consumption, expenditure, and markets for specific frozen foods. Based on various sources.
Frequency	Regular
Availability	General
Cost	£40
Comments	The federation also publishes a yearbook with statistics but this has not appeared in every year. An industry overview on the web site.
Address	55 High Street, Grantham, Lincolnshire NG31 6NE
Tel. / e-mail	01476 590194
Fax / Web site	01476 590152 www.bfff.co.uk

122	BRITISH GLASS MANUFACTURERS' CONFEDERATION
Title	**Recycling Statistics**
Coverage	Statistics on the recycling of glass bottles and other glass products based on data collected by the confederation.
Frequency	Regular
Availability	General
Cost	On request
Comments	The web site includes some statistics.
Address	Northumberland Road, Sheffield S10 2UA
Tel. / e-mail	0114 268 6201 sales@britglass.co.uk
Fax / Web site	0114 268 1073 www.britglass.co.uk

123	BRITISH HARDWARE AND HOUSEWARES MANUFACTURERS' ASSOCIATION
Title	**Business Trends Survey**
Coverage	Based on a survey of members with data on sales, stocks, margins, and business expectations.
Frequency	Quarterly
Availability	General
Cost	£50, £25 members, £5 participants
Comments	Produced in association with 'DIY Week' and summary data from the survey is included in the journal.
Address	Brooke House, 4 The Lakes, Bedford Road, Northampton NN4 7YD
Tel. / e-mail	01604 622023
Fax / Web site	01604 631252

124	BRITISH HOSPITALITY ASSOCIATION
Title	**British Hospitality: Trends and Statistics**
Coverage	Commentary and statistics on tourism and hospitality trends. Based on a combination of government data and other data.
Frequency	Annual
Availability	General
Cost	£195
Comments	–
Address	Queen's House, 55-56 Lincoln's Inn Fields, London WC2A 3BH
Tel. / e-mail	0171 404 7744 bha@bha.org.uk
Fax / Web site	0171 404 7799 www.bha.org.uk

125	BRITISH HOSPITALITY ASSOCIATION
Title	**Commercial Prospects of the UK Hotel Industry**
Coverage	Commentary and statistics on the performance of, and the prospects for, the UK hotel sector.
Frequency	Regular
Availability	General
Cost	£275
Comments	–
Address	Queen's House, 55-56 Lincoln's Inn Fields, London WC2A 3BH
Tel. / e-mail	0171 404 7744 bha@bha.org.uk
Fax / Web site	0171 404 7799 www.bha.org.uk

126	**BRITISH HOSPITALITY ASSOCIATION**
Title	**UK Contract Catering Industry**
Coverage	A detailed annual review of the UK contract catering industry with commentary and statistics on the number of businesses, turnover, costs, number of meals served, summary data on the international contract catering industry, and future trends. The report is based on a survey by the association.
Frequency	Annual
Availability	General
Cost	£95
Comments	Leaflets summarising the research are available free.
Address	Queen's House, 55-56 Lincoln's Inn Fields, London WC2A 3BH
Tel. / e-mail	0171 404 7744 bha@bha.org.uk
Fax / Web site	0171 404 7799 www.bha.org.uk

127	**BRITISH IRON AND STEEL PRODUCERS' ASSOCIATION**
Title	**BISPA Annual Report**
Coverage	A review, with statistics, of the UK steel market and UK trade based on a combination of official and non-official sources. Includes details of the key consuming sectors, producer deliveries, and some forecasts.
Frequency	Annual
Availability	General
Cost	Free
Comments	–
Address	5 Cromwell Road, London SW7 2HX
Tel. / e-mail	0171 581 0231
Fax / Web site	0171 589 4009

128	**BRITISH IRON AND STEEL PRODUCERS' ASSOCIATION**
Title	**Key Statistics Leaflet**
Coverage	Basic data on steel consumption, production, deliveries, raw materials, and productivity. Statistics based on industry sources and trade data.
Frequency	Twice yearly
Availability	General
Cost	Free
Comments	–
Address	5 Cromwell Road, London SW7 2HX
Tel. / e-mail	0171 581 0231
Fax / Web site	0171 589 4009

129

BRITISH IRON AND STEEL PRODUCERS' ASSOCIATION

Title	**SI News**
Coverage	Regular bulletin with data from the UK Steel Information Service on various sectors of the steel industry. Statistics based on industry sources and trade data.
Frequency	Quarterly
Availability	General
Cost	Free
Comments	–
Address	5 Cromwell Road, London SW7 2HX
Tel. / e-mail	0171 581 0231
Fax / Web site	0171 589 4009

130

BRITISH MARINE INDUSTRIES FEDERATION

Title	**British Marine Industry Annual Statistics**
Coverage	Annual trends in the boating industry and market based on original research.
Frequency	Annual
Availability	General
Cost	£50 members, £100 non members
Comments	–
Address	Meadlake Place, Thorpe Lea Road, Egham TW20 8HE
Tel. / e-mail	01784 473377 bmif@bmif.co.uk
Fax / Web site	01784 439678 www.bmif.co.uk

131

BRITISH MARINE INDUSTRIES FEDERATION

Title	**National Survey of Boating and Watersports Participation**
Coverage	A review of the percentage of the population participating, expenditure, equipment and services, training, craft ownership by type, frequency of visits to water, attitudes to watersports, and consumer profiles. Based largely on original research.
Frequency	Every 3 or 4 years
Availability	General
Cost	£100 members, £195 non members
Comments	The latest issue was published in 1999.
Address	Meadlake Place, Thorpe Lea Road, Egham TW20 8HE
Tel. / e-mail	01784 473377 bmif@bmif.co.uk
Fax / Web site	01784 439678 www.bmif.co.uk

BRITISH MARKET RESEARCH ASSOCIATION (BMRA)

Title **BMRA Annual Statistics**

Coverage The BMRA publishes a league table of its member companies by turnover, plus industry-wide data on turnover by type of client (ie, sector), turnover by research method, turnover by survey type. Based on a survey of members.

Frequency Annual

Availability General

Cost On request

Comments The BMRA was formed in 1998 through a merger of the Association of Market Survey Organisations (AMSO) and the Association of British Market Research Companies (ABMRC).

Address 16 Creighton Avenue, London N10 1NU

Tel. / e-mail 0181 374 4095   admin@bmra.org.uk

Fax / Web site 0181 883 9953   www.bmra.org.uk

BRITISH MARKET RESEARCH BUREAU (BMRB) INTERNATIONAL

Title **Access Face-to-Face/Access by Telephone**

Coverage The first is a weekly omnibus survey of 2,000 adults above the age of 14 with face-to-face interviews carried out in the home. The telephone survey is carried out every weekend and uses a sample of 1,000 adults.

Frequency Weekly

Availability General

Cost On application

Comments –

Address Hadley House, 79-81 Uxbridge Road, Ealing   W5 5SU

Tel. / e-mail 0181 566 5000   mailbox@bmrb.co.uk

Fax / Web site 0181 579 7280   www.bmrb.co.uk

134	BRITISH MARKET RESEARCH BUREAU (BMRB) INTERNATIONAL
Title	**Premier: The Upmarket TGI**
Coverage	TGI data specifically for consumers in the AB social grades with data covering holidays, leisure, sports, travel, clothing, personal possessions, cosmetics, gifts, household goods, home and car, drinks, and food.
Frequency	Annual
Availability	General
Cost	Varies according to the range and nature of the information required. Standard results published in 8 volumes.
Comments	Also available online.
Address	Hadley House, 79-81 Uxbridge Road, Ealing W5 5SU
Tel. / e-mail	0181 566 5000 mailbox@bmrb.co.uk
Fax / Web site	0181 579 7280 www.bmrb.co.uk

135	BRITISH MARKET RESEARCH BUREAU (BMRB) INTERNATIONAL
Title	**Target Group Index (TGI)**
Coverage	A national product and media survey based on information from 24,000 adults. The results are published in 34 volumes: volumes 1 and 2 give general demographic information while volumes 3 to 34 cover individual consumer product areas. Detailed consumer profiles and penetration data for each product. A separate volume also provides a general description of the survey.
Frequency	Annual
Availability	General
Cost	£4,250 per volume
Comments	Specific prices available for reports on individual brands or specific consumer fields. Also available online.
Address	Hadley House, 79-81 Uxbridge Road, Ealing W5 5SU
Tel. / e-mail	0181 566 5000 mailbox@bmrb.co.uk
Fax / Web site	0181 579 7280 www.bmrb.co.uk

136 BRITISH MARKET RESEARCH BUREAU (BMRB) INTERNATIONAL

Title	**Youth TGI**
Coverage	TGI data specifically for children and youths aged between 7 and 19. Includes data on purchases and consumption of key products.
Frequency	Annual
Availability	General
Cost	Varies according to the range and nature of the information required. Standard results published in 2 volumes.
Comments	Also available online.
Address	Hadley House, 79-81 Uxbridge Road, Ealing W5 5SU
Tel. / e-mail	0181 566 5000 mailbox@bmrb.co.uk
Fax / Web site	0181 579 9809 www.bmrb.co.uk

137 BRITISH MEDIA RESEARCH COMMITTEE

Title	**British Business Survey**
Coverage	A survey, sponsored by the media owners, examining readership patterns of business managers and executives. Includes data on readership by key demographic group, by occupation, by industry, and by decision making involvement. Further information on the use of services and profiles of British business.
Frequency	Annual
Availability	General
Cost	£1,000, £350 for sponsoring organisations
Comments	Produced for the Business Media Research Committee by IPSOS-RSL Ltd at the address below. The survey is also available in electronic form from Donovan Data Systems, HRS, IMS (UK) Ltd, Telmar Communication Ltd, and BMRB (see other entries).
Address	Kings House, Kymberley Road, Harrow HA1 1PT
Tel. / e-mail	0181 861 8099 information@ipsos-rsl.com
Fax / Web site	0181 863 6647 www.ipsos.rslmedia.co.uk

138	BRITISH METALS FEDERATION
Title	**Annual Report**
Coverage	Commentary and statistics on trends in the industry with sections on production, scrap consumption, stocks, exports, imports, and prices. Based on a number of sources.
Frequency	Annual
Availability	General
Cost	On request
Comments	–
Address	16 High Street, Brampton, Huntingdon PE18 8TU
Tel. / e-mail	01480 455249 admin@britmetfed.org.uk
Fax / Web site	01480 453680 www.britmetfed.org.uk

139	BRITISH METALS FEDERATION
Title	**Annual Report**
Coverage	Includes statistics on scrap consumption, scrap stocks, exports, imports, and scrap prices. Based on a combination of the federation's own data and official statistics.
Frequency	Annual
Availability	General
Cost	Free
Comments	–
Address	16 High Street, Brampton, Huntingdon PE18 8TU
Tel. / e-mail	01480 455249 admin@britmetfed.org.uk
Fax / Web site	01480 453680 www.britmetfed.org.uk

140	BRITISH OFFICE SYSTEMS AND STATIONERY FEDERATION (BOSS)
Title	**Growth of Manufacturers' Turnover**
Coverage	The BOSS Federation survey of manufacturers' turnover gives quarterly data, and comparable data for previous quarters, for three sectors: furniture, machines, office products. The survey is based on returns from companies representing approximately one third of the total market.
Frequency	Quarterly
Availability	Detailed results only available to members. A summary of the results with sector statistics is issued as a press release to the trade press.
Cost	Free
Comments	–
Address	6 Wimpole Street, London W1M 8AS
Tel. / e-mail	0171 637 7692
Fax / Web site	0171 436 3137

141	BRITISH PHONOGRAPHIC INDUSTRY (BPI)
Title	**BPI Statistical Handbook**
Coverage	Includes statistics on the production of CDs, tapes and records plus imports and exports, deliveries, sales, prices, advertising expenditure, hardware ownership, video trends, piracy, and leisure market trends.
Frequency	Annual
Availability	General
Cost	£30
Comments	Quarterly statistics freely available on the web site.
Address	25 Savile Row, London W1X 1AA
Tel. / e-mail	0171 287 4422 kaylee.coxell@bpi.co.uk
Fax / Web site	0171 287 2252 www.bpi.co.uk

142	BRITISH PHONOGRAPHIC INDUSTRY (BPI)
Title	**Market Information Sheets**
Coverage	Pamphlets with summary data and commentary on trends in the audio software market. Produced at regular intervals throughout the year.
Frequency	Regular
Availability	General
Cost	£100 annual subscription
Comments	Quarterly statistics freely available on the web site.
Address	25 Savile Row, London W1X 1AA
Tel. / e-mail	0171 287 4422 kaylee.coxell@bpi.co.uk
Fax / Web site	0171 287 2252 www.bpi.co.uk

143	BRITISH PLASTICS FEDERATION
Title	**BPF Business Trends Survey**
Coverage	A survey of companies in three areas: materials supplies, processing, and machinery manufacturers. Data on sales, orders, stocks, exports, investment, profits, prices, and capacity utilisation. Includes an opinion survey outlining likely future trends and a commentary supports the text.
Frequency	Twice yearly
Availability	General
Cost	Free to members, £50 non members
Comments	–
Address	6 Bath Place, Rivington Street, London EC2A 3JE
Tel. / e-mail	0171 457 5000 imcilwee@bpf.co.uk
Fax / Web site	0171 235 8045 www.bpf.co.uk

144	**BRITISH PLASTICS FEDERATION**
Title	**BPF Statistics Handbook**
Coverage	Statistics on the UK consumption of plastic materials, material consumption by major end-use, imports, exports, and plastics in packaging, building, and the automotive sectors. Based on BPF and other data with some supporting text. Published in two volumes: 1 - The Bulk Polymers; 2 - The Semi-Commodity Engineering Plastics.
Frequency	Annual
Availability	General
Cost	£350 per volume
Comments	–
Address	6 Bath Place, Rivington Street, London EC2A 3JE
Tel. / e-mail	0171 457 5000 imcilwee@bpf.co.uk
Fax / Web site	0171 235 8045 www.bpf.co.uk

145	**BRITISH PRINTING INDUSTRIES' FEDERATION**
Title	**Directions**
Coverage	A report on the economic state of the printing industry with statistics covering the last 30 months.
Frequency	Quarterly
Availability	General
Cost	£25
Comments	Facts and figures pages freely available on the web site.
Address	11 Bedford Row, London WC1R 4DX
Tel. / e-mail	0171 915 8300 info@bpif.org.uk
Fax / Web site	0171 405 7784 www.bpif.org.uk

146	**BRITISH PRINTING INDUSTRIES' FEDERATION**
Title	**Facts and Figures about the Printing Industry**
Coverage	Basic data on sales, overseas trade, costs, prices, profits, redundancies etc. Based on a mixture of official and non-official sources.
Frequency	Every few years
Availability	General
Cost	Free
Comments	Facts and figures pages freely available on the web site.
Address	11 Bedford Row, London WC1R 4DX
Tel. / e-mail	0171 915 8300 info@bpif.org.uk
Fax / Web site	0171 405 7784 www.bpif.org.uk

147

BRITISH RADIO AND ELECTRONIC EQUIPMENT MANUFACTURERS' ASSOCIATION (BREEMA)

Title	**Annual Report**
Coverage	The annual report contains some statistics on deliveries of consumer electronic products and a report on the statistical activities of the association.
Frequency	Annual
Availability	General
Cost	Free
Comments	–
Address	Landseer House, 19 Charing Cross Road, London WC2H 0ES
Tel. / e-mail	0171 930 3206
Fax / Web site	0171 839 4613

148

BRITISH RETAIL CONSORTIUM

Title	**Retail Crime Costs Survey**
Coverage	Based on a survey of approximately 53,000 outlets, the report analyses retail crime and includes data on the total cost, crime by retailers, type of crime.
Frequency	Annual
Availability	General
Cost	£25
Comments	–
Address	5 Grafton Street, London W1X 3LB
Tel. / e-mail	0171 647 1500
Fax / Web site	0171 647 1599

149

BRITISH RETAIL CONSORTIUM

Title	**Retail Sales Press Release**
Coverage	Volume and value of UK retail sales based mainly on government statistics supported by data from some non-official sources.
Frequency	Monthly
Availability	Usually only available to members and the press
Cost	Free
Comments	–
Address	5 Grafton Street, London W1X 3LB
Tel. / e-mail	0171 647 1500
Fax / Web site	0171 647 1599

	BRITISH ROAD FEDERATION
150	
Title	**Basic Road Statistics**
Coverage	Data on roads and road transport including data on traffic, energy, taxation, public expenditure, accidents, and some international comparisons. Mainly based on Central Government sources.
Frequency	Annual
Availability	General
Cost	£22
Comments	–
Address	194-202 Old Kent Road, London SE1 5TY
Tel. / e-mail	0171 703 9769
Fax / Web site	0171 701 0029 www.britishroadfederation.co.uk

	BRITISH ROBOT AND AUTOMATION ASSOCIATION
151	
Title	**Robot Facts**
Coverage	Annual report on UK robot installations within a given year.
Frequency	Annual
Availability	General
Cost	Free to members, £50 to non-members
Comments	Also publishes a yearbook.
Address	Aston Science Park, Love Lane, Birmingham B7 4BJ
Tel. / e-mail	0121 628 1745 bra@globalnet.co.uk
Fax / Web site	0121 628 1746 www.bra-automation.co.uk

	BRITISH SECONDARY METALS ASSOCIATION
152	
Title	**Member Survey**
Coverage	A survey of member companies by employment size, number of sites, investment, turnover.
Frequency	Regular
Availability	Primarily members but requests from non-members considered
Cost	Free
Comments	–
Address	Sandford Court, 21 Sandford Street, Lichfield WS13 6QA
Tel. / e-mail	01543 255450
Fax / Web site	01543 255325

153

Title	**BRITISH SECURITY INDUSTRY ASSOCIATION (BSIA)** **CCTV Market Survey**
Coverage	An analysis of the UK closed-circuit television security market based on turnover figures from relevant BSIA member companies and some independent market research.
Frequency	Annual
Availability	Usually only members but some data may be made available to others on request
Cost	Free
Comments	Also publishes surveys of the manned guarding market.
Address	Security House, Barbourne Road, Worcester WR1 1RS
Tel. / e-mail	01905 21464 info@bsia.co.uk
Fax / Web site	01905 613625 www.bsia.co.uk

154

Title	**BRITISH SECURITY INDUSTRY ASSOCIATION (BSIA)** **Wage Survey**
Coverage	A wage survey covering security guards, alarm installations, and central station connections. Based on a survey by the association.
Frequency	Twice yearly
Availability	Usually members only but some data may be made available to others on request
Cost	Free
Comments	–
Address	Security House, Barbourne Road, Worcester WR1 1RS
Tel. / e-mail	01905 21464 info@bsia.co.uk
Fax / Web site	01905 613625 www.bsia.co.uk

155

Title	**BRITISH SOFT DRINKS ASSOCIATION LTD** **Bottled Water - The Facts**
Coverage	Basic data on the bottled water market based largely on original research.
Frequency	Regular
Availability	General
Cost	Free
Comments	–
Address	20-22 Stukely Street, London WC2B 5LR
Tel. / e-mail	0171 430 0356
Fax / Web site	0171 831 6014

156	**BRITISH SOFT DRINKS ASSOCIATION LTD**
Title	**Factsheets**
Coverage	Information sheets containing statistics on various aspects of the industry, e.g. sales, consumption, packaging etc. Each factsheet contains a large amount of text supported by statistics mainly collected by the association.
Frequency	Regular
Availability	General
Cost	Free
Comments	–
Address	20-22 Stukely Street, London WC2B 5LR
Tel. / e-mail	0171 430 0356
Fax / Web site	0171 831 6014

157	**BRITISH TOURIST AUTHORITY**
Title	**Britain: Tourism Facts and Figures**
Coverage	Tourism facts on volume and value, regional distribution, economic contribution, forecasts, origin of visitors, most visited attractions, purpose and seasonality and trends.
Frequency	Regular
Availability	General
Cost	£0.50
Comments	The regional tourist boards also publish statistics.
Address	Research Department, Thames Tower, Black's Road, Hammersmith, London W6 9EL
Tel. / e-mail	0181 846 9000
Fax / Web site	0181 563 0302 www.visitbritain.com

158	**BRITISH TOURIST AUTHORITY**
Title	**British on Holiday**
Coverage	A summary of the BTA annual survey of British residents' holiday-taking.
Frequency	Annual
Availability	General
Cost	£22.50
Comments	Published as a special report in 'Tourism Intelligence Quarterly' (see other entry) but also available separately. The regional tourist boards also publish statistics.
Address	Department D, Thames Tower, Black's Road, Hammersmith, London W6 9EL
Tel. / e-mail	0181 846 9000
Fax / Web site	0181 563 0302 www.visitbritain.com

159	BRITISH TOURIST AUTHORITY
Title	**BTA Annual Report**
Coverage	Includes summary statistics on tourism in the UK with a general review of the short-term outlook for tourism.
Frequency	Annual
Availability	General
Cost	£15
Comments	The regional tourist boards also publish statistics.
Address	Department D, Thames Tower, Black's Road, Hammersmith, London W6 9EL
Tel. / e-mail	0181 846 9000
Fax / Web site	0181 563 0302 www.visitbritain.com

160	BRITISH TOURIST AUTHORITY
Title	**Digest of Tourist Statistics**
Coverage	Includes extracts and summaries from various travel and tourism surveys including the International Passenger Survey, the UK tourism survey of the residents of Britain, the British National Travel Survey, and many other BTA/ETB and other tourist boards' research results.
Frequency	Annual
Availability	General
Cost	£75
Comments	The regional tourist boards also publish statistics.
Address	Research Department, Thames Tower, Black's Road, Hammersmith, London W6 9EL
Tel. / e-mail	0181 846 9000
Fax / Web site	0181 563 0302 www.visitbritain.com

161	BRITISH TOURIST AUTHORITY
Title	**Overseas Visitor Survey**
Coverage	A survey of overseas visitors to the UK based on the BTA's Overseas Visitor Survey. Some survey questions are asked each year while special topics are also covered in some years.
Frequency	Annual
Availability	General
Cost	£65
Comments	The regional tourist boards also publish statistics.
Address	Department D, Thames Tower, Black's Road, Hammersmith, London W6 9EL
Tel. / e-mail	0181 846 9000
Fax / Web site	0181 563 0302 www.visitbritain.com

162	BRITISH TOURIST AUTHORITY
Title	**The British on Holiday**
Coverage	Summary of British holiday-making statistics.
Frequency	Regular
Availability	General
Cost	£25
Comments	–
Address	Research Deparment, Thames Tower, Black's Road, London W6 9EL
Tel. / e-mail	0181 846 9000
Fax / Web site	0181 563 0302 www.visitbritain.com

163	BRITISH TOURIST AUTHORITY
Title	**The Student Information Pack**
Coverage	Research pack of tourism statistics aimed at students. Includes national and regional facts.
Frequency	Regular
Availability	General
Cost	£10
Comments	–
Address	Research Department, Thames Tower, Black's Road, London W6 9EL
Tel. / e-mail	0181 846 9000
Fax / Web site	0181 563 0302 www.visitbritain.com

164	BRITISH TOURIST AUTHORITY
Title	**Tourism Intelligence Quarterly**
Coverage	Summary and interpretation of up-to-date trends in tourism.
Frequency	Quarterly
Availability	General
Cost	£95 subscription
Comments	–
Address	Research Department, Thames Tower, Black's Road, London W6 9EL
Tel. / e-mail	0181 846 9000
Fax / Web site	0181 563 0302 www.visitbritain.com

165	**BRITISH TOURIST AUTHORITY**
Title	**Visits to Tourist Attractions**
Coverage	Gives details of attendances at tourist attractions in the UK, seasonal opening, ownership, and information on free admission. Attractions include: historic houses, gardens, museums and art galleries, wildlife attractions, country parks, steam railways, and workplaces.
Frequency	Annual
Availability	General
Cost	£19.50
Comments	The regional tourist boards also publish statistics.
Address	Research Department, Thames Tower, Black's Road, Hammersmith, London W6 9EL
Tel. / e-mail	0181 846 9000
Fax / Web site	0181 563 0302 www.visitbritain.com

166	**BRITISH TOY AND HOBBY ASSOCIATION**
Title	**BTHA Handbook**
Coverage	Includes a section with statistics on the sales and imports and exports of specific types of toys and hobbies. Based on a combination of industry supplied data and Central Government statistics.
Frequency	Annual
Availability	General
Cost	£9.50
Comments	Also publishes a monthly 'Briefing'.
Address	80 Camberwell Road, London SE5 0EG
Tel. / e-mail	0171 701 7271
Fax / Web site	0171 708 2437

167	**BRITISH VEHICLE RENTAL AND LEASING ASSOCIATION**
Title	**BVRLA Statistical Review**
Coverage	Data on the size of the chauffeur drive/private hire, rental, and leasing fleets operated by members of the BVRLA. Usually published around 6 months after the completion of the survey. A large amount of commentary supports the text.
Frequency	Annual
Availability	General
Cost	£100, free to members
Comments	–
Address	River Lodge, Badminton Court, Amersham HP7 0DD
Tel. / e-mail	01494 434747 bvrlamail@bvrla.co.uk
Fax / Web site	01494 434499 www.bvrla.co.uk

168 BRITISH VEHICLE RENTAL AND LEASING ASSOCIATION

Title **Residual Value Survey**

Coverage Trends in the residual value of fleets operated by members and based on a survey of members.

Frequency Quarterly

Availability Members

Cost Free

Comments –

Address River Lodge, Badminton Court, Amersham   HP7 0DD

Tel. / e-mail 01494 434747   bvrlamail@bvrla.co.uk

Fax / Web site 01494 434499   www.bvrla.co.uk

169 BRITISH VENTURE CAPITAL ASSOCIATION

Title **Report on Investment Activity**

Coverage Investment trends and activities of member companies over the previous year. Commentary and statistics based on the association's own survey.

Frequency Annual

Availability General

Cost £30

Comments –

Address Essex House, 12-13 Essex Street, London   WC2R 3AA

Tel. / e-mail 0171 240 3846   bvca@bvca.co.uk

Fax / Web site 0171 240 3849   www.bvca.co.uk

170 BRITISH VIDEO ASSOCIATION

Title **British Video Association Yearbook**

Coverage Commentary, statistical tables and charts covering sales and rental of video tapes. The sales section includes data on distribution channels, sales by video type, sales by month, region, price group, retailer shares, number of tapes bought, best sellers, and a demographic breakdown. The rental section has data on the market value, seasonality, rentals by video type, source of rentals, frequency of rentals, viewing, and a demographic breakdown. A final section gives statistics on hardware, cinema admissions, employment, and lists BVA members. Many tables give historical data.

Frequency Annual

Availability General

Cost £35

Comments First published in 1994. Some statistics on the web site.

Address 167 Great Portland Street, London W1N 5FD

Tel. / e-mail 0171 436 0041   general@bva.org.uk

Fax / Web site 0171 436 0043   www.bva.org.uk

171	**BRITISH WOODPULP ASSOCIATION**
Title	**Annual Report**
Coverage	Includes a statistical section with data on imports of pulp by grade and country of origin, production and consumption of paper and board.
Frequency	Annual
Availability	Members and some others on request
Cost	Free to members, a small charge to others
Comments	–
Address	9 Glenair Avenue, Lower Parkstone, Poole BH14 5AD
Tel. / e-mail	01202 738732
Fax / Web site	01202 738747

172	**BRITISH WOODPULP ASSOCIATION**
Title	**Digest of Woodpulp Import Statistics**
Coverage	Tonnage imports of wood pulp for paper making and other purposes based on data supplied by HM Customs and Excise.
Frequency	Monthly
Availability	Members and some others on request
Cost	Free to members, annual subscription to others
Comments	–
Address	9 Glenair Avenue, Lower Parkstone, Poole BH14 5AD
Tel. / e-mail	01202 738732
Fax / Web site	01202 738747

173	**BRITISH WOOL MARKETING BOARD**
Title	**Annual Report and Accounts**
Coverage	Mainly details of the board and its finances, but also contains statistics on wool production by type of wool produced. Based on the board's own figures.
Frequency	Annual
Availability	Primarily members and wool producers but other requests considered
Cost	Free
Comments	–
Address	Oak Mills, Station Road, Bradford BD14 6JD
Tel. / e-mail	01274 882091 bwmb@compuserve.com
Fax / Web site	01274 818277 www.britishwool.org.uk

174 BRITISH WOOL MARKETING BOARD

Title	**Basic Data**
Coverage	Summary information on the sheep population, wool production, prices, registered producers, and the production of mutton and lamb. Based on a board survey.
Frequency	Annual
Availability	Primarily members and wool producers but other requests considered
Cost	Free
Comments	–
Address	Oak Mills, Station Road, Bradford BD14 6JD
Tel. / e-mail	01274 882091 bwmb@compuserve.com
Fax / Web site	01274 818277 www.britishwool.org.uk

175 BRITISH WOOL MARKETING BOARD

Title	**Price Schedule**
Coverage	Data on prices sent automatically to producers.
Frequency	Annual
Availability	Primarily members and wool producers but other requests considered
Cost	Free
Comments	–
Address	Oak Mills, Station Road, Bradford BD14 6JD
Tel. / e-mail	01274 882091 bwmb@compuserve.com
Fax / Web site	01274 818277 www.britishwool.org.uk

176 BRITVIC SOFT DRINKS LTD

Title	**Britvic Soft Drinks Report**
Coverage	Graphs, tables, and commentary on trends in the soft drinks market with data on market values, brands, and consumer behaviour. Based on commissioned research.
Frequency	Annual
Availability	General
Cost	On request
Comments	–
Address	Britvic House, Broomfield Road, Chelmsford CM1 1TU
Tel. / e-mail	01245 261871
Fax / Web site	01245 267147

177

BROADCASTERS AUDIENCE RESEARCH BOARD (BARB)

Title	**BARB Weekly Audience Report**
Coverage	Television viewing figures produced from a sample survey of 11,000 respondents using electronic TV meters.
Frequency	Weekly
Availability	General
Cost	On request
Comments	Detailed figures for clients but also general data published in a weekly press release. Weekly and monthly summaries plus a TV Facts page on the web site. Other types of analysis available on request.
Address	Glenthorne House, Hammersmith Grove, London W6 0ND
Tel. / e-mail	0181 741 9110
Fax / Web site	0181 741 1943 www.barb.co.uk

178

BUILDER GROUP PLC

Title	**Building Economist**
Coverage	A regular newsletter with a Data File section containing statistics on housebuilding, new orders, contracting, prices, and features on specific market sectors. Based on a combination of official and non-official data.
Frequency	Monthly
Availability	General
Cost	£150
Comments	–
Address	Exchange Tower, 2 Harbour Exchange Square, London E14 9GE
Tel. / e-mail	0171 560 4000 106173.632@compuserve.com
Fax / Web site	0171 560 4009

179

BUILDERS MERCHANTS' FEDERATION

Title	**BMF Sales Indicators**
Coverage	Indexed comparison of turnovers of builders merchants by region and commodity classification. Both adjusted and unadjusted figures are produced. Based on BMF's survey.
Frequency	Monthly
Availability	General
Cost	£85 annual subscription - members, £115 annual subscription - non-members
Comments	–
Address	15 Soho Square, London W1V 5FB
Tel. / e-mail	0171 439 1753 info@bmf.org.uk
Fax / Web site	0171 734 2766

180	BUILDING
Title	**Construction Monitor**
Coverage	Includes statistics on building output, employment, and construction materials costs with different series published in different months. Also has news items and new legislation relating to the industry.
Frequency	Monthly in a weekly journal
Availability	General
Cost	£110, £2.20 per issue
Comments	Published by Building for the Department of the Environment.
Address	Exchange Tower, 2 Harbour Exchange Square, London E14 9GE
Tel. / e-mail	0171 560 4000
Fax / Web site	0171 560 4009

181	BUILDING
Title	**Cost Update**
Coverage	Details of unit rates, material prices, and labour costs.
Frequency	Quarterly in a weekly journal
Availability	General
Cost	£110, £2.20 per issue
Comments	–
Address	Exchange Tower, 2 Harbour Exchange Square, London E14 9GE
Tel. / e-mail	0171 560 4000
Fax / Web site	0171 560 4009

182	BUILDING
Title	**Employment Survey**
Coverage	A survey caried out by Gallup examining trends in temporary and permanent employment broken down into two sectors, consultants and contractors.
Frequency	Regular in a weekly journal
Availability	General
Cost	£110, £2.20 per issue
Comments	The first survey was published in 'Building' on 27 October 1995 and further surveys are planned.
Address	Exchange Tower, 2 Harbour Exchange Square, London E14 9GE
Tel. / e-mail	0171 560 4000
Fax / Web site	0171 560 4009

183	
Title	BUILDING **Indicators**
Coverage	Graphs and commentary on general trends in the building industry, based largely on Central Government data.
Frequency	Monthly in a weekly journal
Availability	General
Cost	£110, £2.20 per issue
Comments	–
Address	Exchange Tower, 2 Harbour Exchange Square, London E14 9GE
Tel. / e-mail	0171 560 4000
Fax / Web site	0171 560 4009

184	
Title	BUILDING **Procurement Lead Times**
Coverage	Average procurement lead times for specific types of work and for specialist contractors.
Frequency	6 times per year in a weekly journal
Availability	General
Cost	£110, £2.20 per issue
Comments	–
Address	Exchange Tower, 2 Harbour Exchange Square, London E14 9GE
Tel. / e-mail	0171 560 4000
Fax / Web site	0171 560 4009

185	
Title	BUILDING **Share Watch**
Coverage	General changes in share prices for the building sector plus specific details of the week's main gainers and losers.
Frequency	Weekly in a weekly journal
Availability	General
Cost	£110, £2.20 per issue
Comments	–
Address	Exchange Tower, 2 Harbour Exchange Square, London E14 9GE
Tel. / e-mail	0171 560 4000
Fax / Web site	0171 560 4009

186	BUILDING
Title	**Tender Cost Forecast**
Coverage	Tender prices for various types of work, and broken down by region. Tender prices are compared with general price trends and forecasts are given for the coming year.
Frequency	Quarterly
Availability	General
Cost	£110, £2.20 per issue
Comments	–
Address	Exchange Tower, 2 Harbour Exchange Square, London E14 9GE
Tel. / e-mail	0171 560 4000
Fax / Web site	0171 560 4009

187	BUILDING COST INFORMATION SERVICE
Title	**BCIS Main Bulletin Service**
Coverage	An annual subscription service covering tenders, labour, and materials and based on information supplied by members of BCIS.
Frequency	Monthly
Availability	General
Cost	£495, £370 to members
Comments	–
Address	12 Great George Street, Parliament Square, London SW1P 3AD
Tel. / e-mail	0171 222 7000
Fax / Web site	0171 222 9430

188	BUILDING COST INFORMATION SERVICE
Title	**BCIS Quarterly Review of Building Prices**
Coverage	Prices by type of building and by region based on a survey of subscribers to BCIS.
Frequency	Quarterly
Availability	General
Cost	£222, or £70 for a single issue
Comments	–
Address	12 Great George Street, Parliament Square, London SW1P 3AD
Tel. / e-mail	0171 222 7000
Fax / Web site	0171 222 9430

BUILDING COST INFORMATION SERVICE

189	
Title	**Indices and Forecasts**
Coverage	Data on housebuilding costs by area and condition and type of building. Based on original research by BCIS.
Frequency	Quarterly
Availability	General
Cost	£222, or £70 for a single issue
Comments	–
Address	12 Great George Street, Parliament Square, London SW1P 3AD
Tel. / e-mail	0171 222 7000
Fax / Web site	0171 222 9430

BUILDING COST INFORMATION SERVICE

190	
Title	**RICS Workload Statistics**
Coverage	A regular survey of architects' workload based on a sample survey of RICS members. Includes an opinion survey covering the short-term outlook for the sector.
Frequency	Quarterly
Availability	General
Cost	£50
Comments	–
Address	12 Great George Street, Parliament Square, London SW1P 3AD
Tel. / e-mail	0171 222 7000
Fax / Web site	0171 222 9430

BUILDING COST INFORMATION SERVICE

191	
Title	**Surveys of Tender Prices**
Coverage	Price indices for various building materials based on information supplied by BCIS members.
Frequency	Quarterly
Availability	General
Cost	£222, or £70 for a single issue
Comments	–
Address	12 Great George Street, Parliament Square, London SW1P 3AD
Tel. / e-mail	0171 222 7000
Fax / Web site	0171 222 9430

192	BUILDING EMPLOYERS' CONFEDERATION
Title	**BEC State of Trade Enquiry Report**
Coverage	Prospects for the building workload, capacity of operations, tender prices and the availability of labour and materials. Based on survey of members with the confederation stating that members account for 75% of all building work. Some commentary supports the survey results.
Frequency	Quarterly
Availability	General
Cost	£50, or £15 per issue
Comments	Subscriptions are handled by CIP Ltd, Federation House, 2309 Coventry Road, Birmingham B26 3PL, telephone 0121 742 0824.
Address	82 New Cavendish Street, London W1M 8AD
Tel. / e-mail	0171 580 5588
Fax / Web site	0171 631 3872

193	BUILDING SERVICES RESEARCH AND INFORMATION ASSOCIATION (BSRIA)
Title	**BSRIA Statistics Bulletin**
Coverage	A bulletin with brief market reviews of the key building services and construction sectors. Also includes special features and forecasts of construction trends. Based on a mixture of Central Government sources, BSRIA's research, and other sources.
Frequency	Quarterly
Availability	General
Cost	£155
Comments	Also publishes various market reports and operates an inquiry service.
Address	Old Bracknell Lane West, Bracknell RG12 4AH
Tel. / e-mail	01344 426511
Fax / Web site	01344 487575

	BUILDING SOCIETIES ASSOCIATION
194	
Title	**Building Society Yearbook**
Coverage	Key statistics on housing finance and building societies with data on loans, assets, mortgages, commitments etc. Based largely on data collected by the association.
Frequency	Annual
Availability	General
Cost	£50
Comments	The annual report is available on the web site and this has some basic statistics. Also publishes some titles jointly with the Council of Mortgage Lenders based at the same address (see separate entry).
Address	3 Savile Row, London W1X 1AF
Tel. / e-mail	0171 437 0655
Fax / Web site	0171 734 6416 www.bsa.org.uk

	BUSINESS AND TRADE STATISTICS LTD
195	
Title	**External Trade Statistics**
Coverage	Detailed statistics, from 1979 onwards, on product imports and exports, analysed by trading partners, port of entry and exit. Business and Trade Statistics is an official agent of HM Customs and Excise.
Frequency	Monthly
Availability	General
Cost	Depends on the amount and type of data required
Comments	Available in various machine readable formats.
Address	Lancaster House, More Lane, Esher KT10 8AP
Tel. / e-mail	01372 63121 BTS@dial.pipex.com
Fax / Web site	01372 69847

	BUSINESS GEOGRAPHICS LTD
196	
Title	**Censys 95**
Coverage	A geodemographic service offering geodemographic profiles, lifestyle profiles, area profiles and geographical information systems. Based on an analysis of 1991 census data plus electoral roll data and market research sources including Target Group Index, BARB, NRS, and RAJAR.
Frequency	Continuous
Availability	General
Cost	On request
Comments	Locate is claimed to be the first web-based source of Census data.
Address	8-10 Dryden Street, London WC2E 9BP
Tel. / e-mail	0171 520 5800 info@geoweb.co.uk
Fax / Web site	0171 520 5801 www.geoweb.co.uk

197 BYRANT & MAY

Title	**Byrant & May Report**
Coverage	A report covering the UK market for lights (ie, matches and lighters), plus tobacco and smokers' sundries. Commentary supported by market size based on research commissioned by the company.
Frequency	Annual
Availability	General
Cost	Free
Comments	Previously titled the 'Lights Report' but name changed to reflect changing market.
Address	Sword House, Totteridge Road, High Wycombe HP13 6EJ
Tel. / e-mail	01494 556174
Fax / Web site	

198 C B HILLIER PARKER

Title	**Average Yields**
Coverage	Average property yields for shops, offices, and industrial property with comparative data for gilt and equity yields. Includes a regional breakdown. Based on the company's own survey.
Frequency	Quarterly
Availability	General
Cost	£15
Comments	–
Address	77 Grosvenor Street, London W1A 2BT
Tel. / e-mail	0171 629 7666
Fax / Web site	0171 409 3016 www.cbhillierparker.com

199 C B HILLIER PARKER

Title	**Central London Investment Market**
Coverage	Property investment overview and trends in central London by property type.
Frequency	Quarterly
Availability	General
Cost	£15
Comments	–
Address	77 Grosvenor Street, London W1A 2BT
Tel. / e-mail	0171 629 7666
Fax / Web site	0171 409 3016 www.cbhillierparker.com

200	C B HILLIER PARKER
Title	**Central London Office Market**
Coverage	An overview of trends in the central London office market.
Frequency	Quarterly
Availability	General
Cost	£15
Comments	–
Address	77 Grosvenor Street, London W1A 2BT
Tel. / e-mail	0171 629 7666
Fax / Web site	0171 409 3016 www.cbhillierparker.com

201	C B HILLIER PARKER
Title	**HP Rent Index**
Coverage	Statistics on the general rents for shops, offices, and industrial premises with data over a 5-year period, and a regional breakdown. Based on the company's own survey.
Frequency	Quarterly
Availability	General
Cost	£15
Comments	–
Address	77 Grosvenor Street, London W1A 2BT
Tel. / e-mail	0171 629 7666
Fax / Web site	0171 409 3016 www.cbhillierparker.com

202	C B HILLIER PARKER
Title	**Property Investment**
Coverage	Investment trends for property in various sectors.
Frequency	Twice yearly
Availability	General
Cost	£15
Comments	–
Address	77 Grosvenor Street, London W1A 2BT
Tel. / e-mail	0171 629 7666
Fax / Web site	0171 409 3016 www.cbhillierparker.com

203	**C B HILLIER PARKER**
Title	**Retail Warehouse Parks in the Pipeline**
Coverage	Details of specific warehouse parks and aggregate data on numbers and floorspace. Based on the company's own data.
Frequency	Twice yearly
Availability	General
Cost	£15
Comments	–
Address	77 Grosvenor Street, London W1A 2BT
Tel. / e-mail	0171 629 7666
Fax / Web site	0171 409 3016 www.cbhillierparker.com

204	**C B HILLIER PARKER**
Title	**Shopping Centres in the Pipeline**
Coverage	Details of specific shopping centres, aggregate data and projected floorspace. Based on the company's own survey.
Frequency	Twice yearly
Availability	General
Cost	£15
Comments	–
Address	77 Grosvenor Street, London W1A 2BT
Tel. / e-mail	0171 629 7666
Fax / Web site	0171 409 3016 www.cbhillierparker.com

205	**C B HILLIER PARKER**
Title	**Shopping Centres Investment Activity**
Coverage	Investment trends in the shop property sector. Based on a survey by the company.
Frequency	Annual
Availability	General
Cost	£15
Comments	–
Address	77 Grosvenor Street, London W1A 2BT
Tel. / e-mail	0171 629 7666
Fax / Web site	0171 409 3016 www.cbhillierparker.com

C CZARNIKOW SUGAR LTD

206	
Title	**The UK Sugar Market**
Coverage	A brief review of the UK sugar market with commentary and statistics covering production, imports, consumption, and companies.
Frequency	Regular
Availability	General
Cost	Free
Comments	–
Address	24 Chiswell Street, London EC1Y 4SG
Tel. / e-mail	0171 972 6600
Fax / Web site	0171 972 6699

CACI INFORMATION SERVICES

207	
Title	**Acorn Profiles/PIN Neighbourhood Classifications**
Coverage	Various demographic and area profiles based on an analysis of 1991 census data plus postcode address files and electoral roll data. Also uses Target Group Index (TGI) and Financial Research Survey (FRS) data as well as some other market research sources.
Frequency	Continuous
Availability	General
Cost	On application, and depending on range and nature of information required
Comments	–
Address	CACI House, Kensington Village, Avonmore Road, London W14 8TS
Tel. / e-mail	0171 602 6000
Fax / Web site	0171 603 5862

CAMBRIDGE ECONOMETRICS

208	
Title	**Industry and the British Economy**
Coverage	A detailed forecast of the British economy and industry with forecasts up to ten years ahead. Detailed analysis of over 40 industrial sectors and 19 service sectors.
Frequency	Twice yearly
Availability	General
Cost	£1,750
Comments	–
Address	Covent Garden, Cambridge CB1 2HS
Tel. / e-mail	01223 460760 info@camecon.com
Fax / Web site	01223 464378 www.camecon.co.uk

CAMBRIDGE ECONOMETRICS

209	
Title	**Regional Economic Prospects**
Coverage	Detailed analysis and forecasts on economic trends in the UK regions. Long-term forecasts and commentary.
Frequency	Twice yearly
Availability	General
Cost	£1,750
Comments	–
Address	Covent Garden, Cambridge CB1 2HS
Tel. / e-mail	01223 460760 info@camecon.com
Fax / Web site	01223 464378 www.camecon.co.uk

CAN MAKERS

210	
Title	**Can Makers Report**
Coverage	Details of the beverage can industry and market, broken down by soft drinks and beer. The 1995 report includes a consumer attitudes survey and a profitability analysis. Market data covers the latest five years and there is also some data on European trends. Based mainly on a mixture of non-official sources including trade association, market research and Gallup data. Detailed commentary supports the tables.
Frequency	Twice yearly
Availability	General
Cost	Free
Comments	Also publishes regular press releases and bulletins with statistics.
Address	1 Chelsea Manor Gardens, London SW3 5PN
Tel. / e-mail	0171 351 2400 canmakers@gciuk.com
Fax / Web site	0171 352 6244 www.canmakers.co.uk

CAPSCAN LTD

211	
Title	**Cenario**
Coverage	A CD-ROM providing access to the 1991 Census small area statistics. The Cenario software provides a range of analytical functions including mapping, graphics, customer profiles, postcode sector ranking etc.
Frequency	Annual
Availability	General
Cost	Minimum entry level - £3,000
Comments	–
Address	Tranley House, Tranley Mews, Fleet Road, London NW3 2QW
Tel. / e-mail	0171 267 7055 sales@capscan.co.uk
Fax / Web site	0171 267 2745 www.capscan.com

212

CARPET AND FLOORCOVERINGS REVIEW

Title **Business Trends**

Coverage A quarterly survey of trends in the carpet industry based on returns from carpet suppliers and retailers. Includes data on sales by carpet type.

Frequency Quarterly in a monthly journal

Availability General

Cost £70

Comments Also publishes regular surveys on wholesaling, retailing, and specific carpet and floorcoverings markets.

Address Miller Freeman Publications Ltd, Sovereign Way, Tonbridge TN9 1RW

Tel. / e-mail 01732 377021

Fax / Web site 01732 361534

213

CARRICK JAMES MARKET RESEARCH

Title **All Ages Omnibus**

Coverage Based on a sample size of 3,000, this regular survey asks questions of adults and children from the age of seven upwards.

Frequency Monthly

Availability General

Cost Varies according to the range of questions/information required

Comments –

Address 6 Homer Street, London W1H 1HN

Tel. / e-mail 0171 724 3836   cjmr@easynet.co.uk

Fax / Web site 0171 224 8257

214

CARRICK JAMES MARKET RESEARCH

Title **Child and Teenage Omnibus**

Coverage Continuous survey of children from the age of five upwards and teenagers up to the age of 19. Various questions relating to spending, behaviour, opinions, awareness etc.

Frequency Monthly

Availability General

Cost Varies according to the range of questions/information required

Comments Also carries out a regular 'European Child Omnibus'.

Address 6 Homer Street, London W1H 1HN

Tel. / e-mail 0171 724 3836   cjmr@easynet.co.uk

Fax / Web site 0171 224 8257

215	**CARRICK JAMES MARKET RESEARCH**
Title	**Parent Omnibus**
Coverage	Based on a survey of 1,000 parents of children aged between 0 and 14. Parents of 5 to 14 year olds are surveyed every two months while parents of 0 to 14 year olds are surveyed quarterly.
Frequency	6 times per year
Availability	General
Cost	Varies according to the range of questions/information required
Comments	–
Address	6 Homer Street, London W1H 1HN
Tel. / e-mail	0171 724 3836 cjmr@easynet.co.uk
Fax / Web site	0171 224 8257

216	**CARRICK JAMES MARKET RESEARCH**
Title	**Youth Omnibus**
Coverage	Based on a sample of 1,200 young people aged between 11 and 24. Questions cover behaviour, spending, product and advertising awareness etc.
Frequency	6 times per year
Availability	General
Cost	Varies according to the range of questions/information required
Comments	–
Address	6 Homer Street, London W1H 1HN
Tel. / e-mail	0171 724 3836 cjmr@easynet.co.uk
Fax / Web site	0171 224 8257

217	**CATERER & HOTELKEEPER**
Title	**Industry Trends**
Coverage	Various statistics on the catering and hotel trades including hotel occupancy rates, turnover figures for various catering sectors, share prices. The data available varies from week to week depending on the sources used.
Frequency	Weekly in a weekly journal
Availability	General
Cost	£89, £1.70 per issue
Comments	The journal also has occasional features on hotel and catering sectors.
Address	Reed Business Publishing Ltd, Quadrant House, The Quadrant, Sutton SM2 5AS
Tel. / e-mail	0181 652 3500 chotserv@rbp.co.uk
Fax / Web site	0181 652 8973 www.rbp.co.uk

CATERER & HOTELKEEPER

Title	**Market Prices**
Coverage	Based on a survey of 18 specialist catering suppliers, prices are given for various fresh foods. Food categories covered are meat, poultry, game, fresh fish, fruit, vegetables, and salad.
Frequency	Weekly in a weekly journal
Availability	General
Cost	£89, £1.70 per issue
Comments	The journal also has occasional features on catering and hotel sectors.
Address	Reed Business Publishing Ltd, Quadrant House, The Quadrant, Sutton SM2 5AS
Tel. / e-mail	0181 652 3500 chotserv@rbp.co.uk
Fax / Web site	0181 652 8973 www.rbp.co.uk

CCN SYSTEMS LTD

Title	**Mosaic/Chorus**
Coverage	Geodemographic services based on various sources including census and lifestyle data, electoral roll data, postcode address files, Target Group Index (TGI) and Financial Research Survey (FRS).
Frequency	Continuous
Availability	General
Cost	On application, depending on the range and nature of the information required
Comments	–
Address	Abbey House, Abbeyfield Road, Nottingham NG7 2SW
Tel. / e-mail	0115 986 0801
Fax / Web site	0115 961 0888 www.experian.com

CDMS MARKETING SERVICES

Title	**Super Profiles**
Coverage	A geodemographic service based on a range of sources including the 1991 Census, postcode address files, the electoral roll, Target Group Index (TGI), and specialist files from the Littlewoods organisation.
Frequency	Continuous
Availability	General
Cost	On application, depending on the range and nature of the information required
Comments	–
Address	Kershaw Avenue, Crosby, Liverpool L23 0XA
Tel. / e-mail	0151 949 1900
Fax / Web site	0151 920 1288

221	**CEMENT ADMIXTURES ASSOCIATION**
Title	**Statistical Return**
Coverage	Sales by weight and value for a variety of admixtures based on a survey of members.
Frequency	Regular
Availability	Members
Cost	Free
Comments	–
Address	36a Tilehouse Green Lane, Knowle B93 9EY
Tel. / e-mail	01564 776362
Fax / Web site	01564 776362

222	**CENTRE FOR THE STUDY OF REGULATED INDUSTRIES**
Title	**The Uk Electricity Industry: Charges**
Coverage	The first edition of this publication appeared in 1995 following the privatisation of the electricity industry. Based on returns from the companies and CRI research.
Frequency	Annual
Availability	General
Cost	£25
Comments	–
Address	Chancery House, 53-64 Chancery Lane, London WC2A 1QS
Tel. / e-mail	0171 242 7364 cri@dircon.co.uk
Fax / Web site	0171 831 0815

223	**CENTRE FOR THE STUDY OF REGULATED INDUSTRIES**
Title	**The UK Electricity Industry: Financial and Operating Review**
Coverage	Financial and operating data on the UK electricity industry.
Frequency	Annual
Availability	General
Cost	£40
Comments	–
Address	Chancery House, 53-64 Chancery Lane, London WC2A 1QS
Tel. / e-mail	0171 242 7364 cri@dircon.co.uk
Fax / Web site	0171 831 0815

CENTRE FOR THE STUDY OF REGULATED INDUSTRIES

Title	**The UK Regulated Industries: Financial Facts**
Coverage	The first edition of this publication appeared in 1994 and gives financial data on the newly privatised utilities. Based mainly on financial data supplied by the companies themselves.
Frequency	Annual
Availability	General
Cost	£25
Comments	–
Address	Chancery House, 53-64 Chancery Lane, London WC2A 1QS
Tel. / e-mail	0171 242 7364 cri@dircon.co.uk
Fax / Web site	0171 831 0815

CENTRE FOR THE STUDY OF REGULATED INDUSTRIES

Title	**The UK Water Industry: Charges for Water Services**
Coverage	The first edition of this publication appeared in 1994 and gives details of water charges. Based on data supplied by the companies and some CIPFA analysis.
Frequency	Annual
Availability	General
Cost	£25
Comments	–
Address	Chancery House, 53-64 Chancery Lane, London WC2A 1QS
Tel. / e-mail	0171 242 7364 cri@dircon.co.uk
Fax / Web site	0171 831 0815

CENTRE FOR THE STUDY OF REGULATED INDUSTRIES

Title	**UK Airports Industry: Airport Statistics**
Coverage	Operating and financial statistics on UK airports with aggregate data and statistics on specific airports. Based on data collected by CIPFA and the centre.
Frequency	Annual
Availability	General
Cost	£40
Comments	First published in 1996 to replace Airport Statistics previously published by the Chartered Institute of Public Finance and Accountancy (CIPFA). CRI is a research centre of the Chartered Institute of Public Finance and Accountancy (see other entry).
Address	Chancery House, 53-64 Chancery Lane, London WC2A 1QS
Tel. / e-mail	0171 242 7364 cri@dircon.co.uk
Fax / Web site	0171 831 0815

227	CHALVINGTON PRESS
Title	**The Business Book of the Electrical Retail Market in Great Britain**
Coverage	A general overview of the consumer electrical market is followed by specific sections on consumer electronics by product type, domestic appliances, and small appliances. Each section has details of market size, segments, brands, manufacturers, and distribution trends. Each market has statistics for the last five years. Based on various sources including research by the compiler.
Frequency	Annual
Availability	General
Cost	Free to members, £95 to non-members
Comments	First published in 1990.
Address	Plestor House, Farnham Road, West Liss GU33 6JQ
Tel. / e-mail	01730 894059 iercirculation@chalvington.co.uk
Fax / Web site	01730 895298

228	CHAMBER OF SHIPPING
Title	**Annual Review**
Coverage	Some statistics on fleet, trade, and other market trends.
Frequency	Annual
Availability	General
Cost	On application
Comments	–
Address	12 Carthusian Street, London EC1M 6EZ
Tel. / e-mail	0171 417 8400 postmaster@british-shipping.org
Fax / Web site	0171 600 1534 www.british-shipping.org

229	CHARITIES AID FOUNDATION
Title	**Dimensions of the Voluntary Sector**
Coverage	Commentary and statistics on the 'givers' and 'receivers' with tables giving historical figures. Based largely on the foundation's own data with a detailed supporting text.
Frequency	Annual
Availability	General
Cost	£35
Comments	Previously titled 'Charity Trends'.
Address	Kings Hill, West Malling ME19 47A
Tel. / e-mail	01732 520125
Fax / Web site	01732 520001 www.charitynet.org

230	CHARITY RECRUITMENT
Title	**Annual Voluntary Sector Salary Survey**
Coverage	Salaries for various job categories and grades in large and small charities. Based on a survey by the company.
Frequency	Annual
Availability	General
Cost	£170 plus VAT, £120 plus VAT for charities with less than 30 staff
Comments	–
Address	40 Rosebery Avenue, London EC1R 4RX
Tel. / e-mail	0171 833 0770 cr@charityrec.sarce.co.uk
Fax / Web site	0171 833 0188 www.charec.co.uk
231	CHARTERED INSTITUTE OF MANAGEMENT ACCOUNTANTS
Title	**CIMA Survey**
Coverage	Quarterly survey which asks the financial directors of Britain's companies how they perceive their own company's future and what their view is of the economy as a whole.
Frequency	Quarterly
Availability	General
Cost	Free
Comments	–
Address	63 Portland Place, London W1N 4AB
Tel. / e-mail	0171 637 2311
Fax / Web site	0171 631 5309 www.cima.org.uk
232	CHARTERED INSTITUTE OF MARKETING
Title	**State of the Market Report**
Coverage	A review of economic and business trends and the effect of these trends on the marketing sector.
Frequency	Quarterly
Availability	Primarily members
Cost	Free
Comments	Some basic data on the web site.
Address	Moor Hall, Cookham, Maidenhead SL6 9QH
Tel. / e-mail	01628 427500 marketing@cim.co.uk
Fax / Web site	01628 427499 www.cim.co.uk

233

CHARTERED INSTITUTE OF PUBLIC FINANCE AND ACCOUNTANCY (CIPFA)

Title	**Administration of Justice - Combined Actuals and Estimates**
Coverage	Expenditure and income figures for both magistrates' and coroners' courts per thousand population. Based on returns received by CIPFA.
Frequency	Annual
Availability	General
Cost	£55
Comments	–
Address	3 Robert Street, London WC2N 6BH
Tel. / e-mail	0171 543 5600 webco-ordinator@cipfa.org
Fax / Web site	0171 543 5700 www.cipfa.sift.co.uk

234

CHARTERED INSTITUTE OF PUBLIC FINANCE AND ACCOUNTANCY (CIPFA)

Title	**Airports - Actuals**
Coverage	An analysis of the revenue accounts and balance sheets of local authority airports plus a range of non-financial information. Based on data supplied to CIPFA by local authorities.
Frequency	Annual
Availability	General
Cost	£55
Comments	First published in 1996 to replace Airport Statistics published by the Chartered Institute of Public Finance and Accountancy (CIPFA). CRI is a research centre of the Chartered Institute of Public Finance and Accountancy (see other entry).
Address	3 Robert Street, London WC2N 6BH
Tel. / e-mail	0171 543 5600 webco-ordinator@cipfa.org
Fax / Web site	0171 543 5700 www.cipfa.sift.co.uk

235

CHARTERED INSTITUTE OF PUBLIC FINANCE AND ACCOUNTANCY (CIPFA)

Title	**Archives - Estimates**
Coverage	Statistics on the organisation and financing of archives based on returns from local authorities collected by CIPFA.
Frequency	Annual
Availability	General
Cost	£55
Comments	–
Address	3 Robert Street, London WC2N 6BH
Tel. / e-mail	0171 543 5600 webco-ordinator@cipfa.org
Fax / Web site	0171 543 5700 www.cipfa.sift.co.uk

236

	CHARTERED INSTITUTE OF PUBLIC FINANCE AND ACCOUNTANCY (CIPFA)
Title	**Capital Expenditure and Treasury Management**
Coverage	An analysis of capital payments and debt statistics for individual local authorities in England, Wales, Scotland, and Northern Ireland. Based on data collected by CIPFA.
Frequency	Annual
Availability	General
Cost	£105
Comments	–
Address	3 Robert Street, London WC2N 6BH
Tel. / e-mail	0171 543 5600 webco-ordinator@cipfa.org
Fax / Web site	0171 543 5700 www.cipfa.sift.co.uk

237

	CHARTERED INSTITUTE OF PUBLIC FINANCE AND ACCOUNTANCY (CIPFA)
Title	**Cemetries - Actuals**
Coverage	Expenditure, income, fees, and non-financial data on cemetries in local authority areas. Based on data collected by CIPFA.
Frequency	Annual
Availability	General
Cost	£55
Comments	–
Address	3 Robert Street, London WC2N 6BH
Tel. / e-mail	0171 543 5600 webco-ordinator@cipfa.org
Fax / Web site	0171 543 5700 www.cipfa.sift.co.uk

238

	CHARTERED INSTITUTE OF PUBLIC FINANCE AND ACCOUNTANCY (CIPFA)
Title	**Council Tax Demands and Precepts - Estimates**
Coverage	Statistics on the level of demands and revenues from council tax based on returns from local authorities collected by CIPFA.
Frequency	Annual
Availability	General
Cost	£55
Comments	–
Address	3 Robert Street, London WC2N 6BH
Tel. / e-mail	0171 543 5600 webco-ordinator@cipfa.org
Fax / Web site	0171 543 5700 www.cipfa.sift.co.uk

239	CHARTERED INSTITUTE OF PUBLIC FINANCE AND ACCOUNTANCY (CIPFA)
Title	**County Farms and Rural Estates - Actuals**
Coverage	Financial and other data on county farms and rural estates by local authority area. Based on data collected by CIPFA.
Frequency	Annual
Availability	General
Cost	£55
Comments	–
Address	3 Robert Street, London WC2N 6BH
Tel. / e-mail	0171 543 5600 webco-ordinator@cipfa.org
Fax / Web site	0171 543 5700 www.cipfa.sift.co.uk

240	CHARTERED INSTITUTE OF PUBLIC FINANCE AND ACCOUNTANCY (CIPFA)
Title	**Crematoria - Actuals**
Coverage	Expenditure, income, fees and non-financial data on crematoria by local authority area. Based on data collected by CIPFA.
Frequency	Annual
Availability	General
Cost	£55
Comments	–
Address	3 Robert Street, London WC2N 6BH
Tel. / e-mail	0171 543 5600 webco-ordinator@cipfa.org
Fax / Web site	0171 543 5700 www.cipfa.sift.co.uk

241	CHARTERED INSTITUTE OF PUBLIC FINANCE AND ACCOUNTANCY (CIPFA)
Title	**Direct Service Organisations - Actuals**
Coverage	Financial, organisational, and related data on direct service organisations in local authorities. Based on returns to CIPFA from local authorities.
Frequency	Annual
Availability	General
Cost	£105
Comments	–
Address	3 Robert Street, London WC2N 6BH
Tel. / e-mail	0171 543 5600 webco-ordinator@cipfa.org
Fax / Web site	0171 543 5700 www.cipfa.sift.co.uk

242	CHARTERED INSTITUTE OF PUBLIC FINANCE AND ACCOUNTANCY (CIPFA)
Title	**Education (Including Unit Costs) - Actuals**
Coverage	Non-financial data on pupil, school, and teacher numbers and financial data split by types of school and local authority area. The publication now also includes education unit costs, previously published in a separate volume. These costs cover institutional costs, pupil and student support costs, capital costs, salary costs, recurrent expenditure, and university costs. Based largely on Central Government data.
Frequency	Annual
Availability	General
Cost	£80
Comments	–
Address	3 Robert Street, London WC2N 6BH
Tel. / e-mail	0171 543 5600 webco-ordinator@cipfa.org
Fax / Web site	0171 543 5700 www.cipfa.sift.co.uk

243	CHARTERED INSTITUTE OF PUBLIC FINANCE AND ACCOUNTANCY (CIPFA)
Title	**Education - Estimates**
Coverage	Financial and non-financial estimates for education authorities.
Frequency	Annual
Availability	General
Cost	£80
Comments	–
Address	3 Robert Street, London WC2N 6BH
Tel. / e-mail	0171 543 5600 webco-ordinator@cipfa.org
Fax / Web site	0171 543 5700 www.cipfa.sift.co.uk

244	CHARTERED INSTITUTE OF PUBLIC FINANCE AND ACCOUNTANCY (CIPFA)
Title	**Environmental Health - Actuals**
Coverage	Financial and other data relating to environmental health in specific local authorities. Based on data collected by CIPFA.
Frequency	Annual
Availability	General
Cost	£80
Comments	–
Address	3 Robert Street, London WC2N 6BH
Tel. / e-mail	0171 543 5600 webco-ordinator@cipfa.org
Fax / Web site	0171 543 5700 www.cipfa.sift.co.uk

245	CHARTERED INSTITUTE OF PUBLIC FINANCE AND ACCOUNTANCY (CIPFA)
Title	**Finance and General - Estimates**
Coverage	Summary information on local authority income and expenditure with data for each local authority in England and Wales. Based on estimates collected by CIPFA with additional data on estimated income and expenditure per head of the population.
Frequency	Annual
Availability	General
Cost	£105
Comments	–
Address	3 Robert Street, London WC2N 6BH
Tel. / e-mail	0171 543 5600 webco-ordinator@cipfa.org
Fax / Web site	0171 543 5700 www.cipfa.sift.co.uk

246	CHARTERED INSTITUTE OF PUBLIC FINANCE AND ACCOUNTANCY (CIPFA)
Title	**Fire - Combined Actuals and Estimates**
Coverage	Summary data on fire service income and expenditure and similar figures for each local authority and per thousand population. Also statistics on fire stations, training, manpower, applications, return of calls, inspections. Based on returns from local authorities received by CIPFA.
Frequency	Annual
Availability	General
Cost	£80
Comments	–
Address	3 Robert Street, London WC2N 6BH
Tel. / e-mail	0171 543 5600 webco-ordinator@cipfa.org
Fax / Web site	0171 543 5700 www.cipfa.sift.co.uk

247	CHARTERED INSTITUTE OF PUBLIC FINANCE AND ACCOUNTANCY (CIPFA)
Title	**Highways and Transportation - Combined Actuals and Estimates**
Coverage	Data on highways and transportation expenditure by county councils in England and Wales. Based on returns received by CIPFA.
Frequency	Annual
Availability	General
Cost	£80
Comments	–
Address	3 Robert Street, London WC2N 6BH
Tel. / e-mail	0171 543 5600 webco-ordinator@cipfa.org
Fax / Web site	0171 543 5700 www.cipfa.sift.co.uk

248	CHARTERED INSTITUTE OF PUBLIC FINANCE AND ACCOUNTANCY (CIPFA)
Title	**Homelessness - Actuals**
Coverage	A financial survey of the operations of the Housing (Homeless Persons) Act with data for individual local authorities. Based on data collected by CIPFA.
Frequency	Annual
Availability	General
Cost	£55
Comments	–
Address	3 Robert Street, London WC2N 6BH
Tel. / e-mail	0171 543 5600 webco-ordinator@cipfa.org
Fax / Web site	0171 543 5700 www.cipfa.sift.co.uk

249	CHARTERED INSTITUTE OF PUBLIC FINANCE AND ACCOUNTANCY (CIPFA)
Title	**Housing Rent Arrears and Benefits - Actuals**
Coverage	An analysis of rent arrears and benefits by local authority area. Based on returns to CIPFA from local authorities.
Frequency	Annual
Availability	General
Cost	£80
Comments	–
Address	3 Robert Street, London WC2N 6BH
Tel. / e-mail	0171 543 5600 webco-ordinator@cipfa.org
Fax / Web site	0171 543 5700 www.cipfa.sift.co.uk

250	CHARTERED INSTITUTE OF PUBLIC FINANCE AND ACCOUNTANCY (CIPFA)
Title	**Housing Rents - Actuals**
Coverage	An analysis of the housing stock by age and type, average weekly rents and rebates, and allowances. Data for individual local authorities and summary tables for individual planning regions. Based on returns to CIPFA from local authorities.
Frequency	Annual
Availability	General
Cost	£80
Comments	–
Address	3 Robert Street, London WC2N 6BH
Tel. / e-mail	0171 543 5600 webco-ordinator@cipfa.org
Fax / Web site	0171 543 5700 www.cipfa.sift.co.uk

251	CHARTERED INSTITUTE OF PUBLIC FINANCE AND ACCOUNTANCY (CIPFA)
Title	**Housing Revenue Account - Combined Actuals and Estimates**
Coverage	Figures for Housing Revenue Account income in total and for each housing authority in England and Wales. Based on a combination of Central Government statistics and CIPFA data.
Frequency	Annual
Availability	General
Cost	£80
Comments	–
Address	3 Robert Street, London WC2N 6BH
Tel. / e-mail	0171 543 5600 webco-ordinator@cipfa.org
Fax / Web site	0171 543 5700 www.cipfa.sift.co.uk

252	CHARTERED INSTITUTE OF PUBLIC FINANCE AND ACCOUNTANCY (CIPFA)
Title	**Leisure and Recreation - Estimates**
Coverage	Estimated expenditure and income on sports and recreation, cultural and other related facilities by local authory area. Based on data collected by CIPFA from local authorities.
Frequency	Annual
Availability	General
Cost	£80
Comments	–
Address	3 Robert Street, London WC2N 6BH
Tel. / e-mail	0171 543 5600 webco-ordinator@cipfa.org
Fax / Web site	0171 543 5700 www.cipfa.sift.co.uk

253	CHARTERED INSTITUTE OF PUBLIC FINANCE AND ACCOUNTANCY (CIPFA)
Title	**Leisure Charges - Actuals**
Coverage	Sample survey of charges for leisure centre facilities, swimming pools and outdoor sports. Based on a sample of 150 local authorities.
Frequency	Annual
Availability	General
Cost	£55
Comments	–
Address	3 Robert Street, London WC2N 6BH
Tel. / e-mail	0171 543 5600 webco-ordinator@cipfa.org
Fax / Web site	0171 543 5700 www.cipfa.sift.co.uk

254	CHARTERED INSTITUTE OF PUBLIC FINANCE AND ACCOUNTANCY (CIPFA)
Title	**Local Government Comparative Statistics**
Coverage	Summary statistical indicators covering the range of local authority services. Based on a combination of data collected by CIPFA and other non-official sources.
Frequency	Annual
Availability	General
Cost	£105
Comments	–
Address	3 Robert Street, London WC2N 6BH
Tel. / e-mail	0171 543 5600 webco-ordinator@cipfa.org
Fax / Web site	0171 543 5700 www.cipfa.sift.co.uk

255	CHARTERED INSTITUTE OF PUBLIC FINANCE AND ACCOUNTANCY (CIPFA)
Title	**Personal Social Services - Actuals**
Coverage	An analysis of residential, day, and community care provision giving gross and net expenditure and the number of clients by local authority area. Based on data collected by CIPFA.
Frequency	Annual
Availability	General
Cost	£80
Comments	–
Address	3 Robert Street, London WC2N 6BH
Tel. / e-mail	0171 543 5600 webco-ordinator@cipfa.org
Fax / Web site	0171 543 5700 www.cipfa.sift.co.uk

256

CHARTERED INSTITUTE OF PUBLIC FINANCE AND ACCOUNTANCY (CIPFA)

Title   **Personal Social Services - Estimates**

Coverage   Data on revenue, income, and expenditure plus some non-financial data.

Frequency   Annual

Availability   General

Cost   £80

Comments   –

Address   3 Robert Street, London WC2N 6BH

Tel. / e-mail   0171 543 5600   webco-ordinator@cipfa.org

Fax / Web site   0171 543 5700   www.cipfa.sift.co.uk

257

CHARTERED INSTITUTE OF PUBLIC FINANCE AND ACCOUNTANCY (CIPFA)

Title   **Planning and Development - Combined Actuals and Estimates**

Coverage   Capital and revenue expenditure on the planning and development functions in summary and by individual local authority. Based on data collected by CIPFA.

Frequency   Annual

Availability   General

Cost   £80

Comments   –

Address   3 Robert Street, London WC2N 6BH

Tel. / e-mail   0171 543 5600   webco-ordinator@cipfa.org

Fax / Web site   0171 543 5700   www.cipfa.sift.co.uk

258

CHARTERED INSTITUTE OF PUBLIC FINANCE AND ACCOUNTANCY (CIPFA)

Title   **Police - Actuals**

Coverage   Figures are given for income, expenditure and manpower in total and by individual police force and regional crime squad. Based on data collected by CIPFA.

Frequency   Annual

Availability   General

Cost   £80

Comments   –

Address   3 Robert Street, London WC2N 6BH

Tel. / e-mail   0171 543 5600   webco-ordinator@cipfa.org

Fax / Web site   0171 543 5700   www.cipfa.sift.co.uk

259	CHARTERED INSTITUTE OF PUBLIC FINANCE AND ACCOUNTANCY (CIPFA)
Title	**Police - Estimates**
Coverage	Financial and non-financial data on police service operations.
Frequency	Annual
Availability	General
Cost	£80
Comments	–
Address	3 Robert Street, London WC2N 6BH
Tel. / e-mail	0171 543 5600 webco-ordinator@cipfa.org
Fax / Web site	0171 543 5700 www.cipfa.sift.co.uk

260	CHARTERED INSTITUTE OF PUBLIC FINANCE AND ACCOUNTANCY (CIPFA)
Title	**Probation - Combined Actuals and Estimates**
Coverage	Expenditure and income in the probation service per thousand population aged 15-29 and manpower for the service in England and Wales. Based on data collected by CIPFA.
Frequency	Annual
Availability	General
Cost	£55
Comments	–
Address	3 Robert Street, London WC2N 6BH
Tel. / e-mail	0171 543 5600 webco-ordinator@cipfa.org
Fax / Web site	0171 543 5700 www.cipfa.sift.co.uk

261	CHARTERED INSTITUTE OF PUBLIC FINANCE AND ACCOUNTANCY (CIPFA)
Title	**Public Libraries - Actuals**
Coverage	Final out-turn figures for income and expenditure, manpower, agency services, books, and other stocks and service points are given in total and for each library service in Great Britain and Northern Ireland.
Frequency	Annual
Availability	General
Cost	£80
Comments	–
Address	3 Robert Street, London WC2N 6BH
Tel. / e-mail	0171 543 5600 webco-ordinator@cipfa.org
Fax / Web site	0171 543 5700 www.cipfa.sift.co.uk

262	CHARTERED INSTITUTE OF PUBLIC FINANCE AND ACCOUNTANCY (CIPFA)
Title	**Public Libraries - Estimates**
Coverage	Financial and non-financial estimates of public library operations.
Frequency	Annual
Availability	General
Cost	£55
Comments	–
Address	3 Robert Street, London WC2N 6BH
Tel. / e-mail	0171 543 5600 webco-ordinator@cipfa.org
Fax / Web site	0171 543 5700 www.cipfa.sift.co.uk

263	CHARTERED INSTITUTE OF PUBLIC FINANCE AND ACCOUNTANCY (CIPFA)
Title	**Revenue Collection - Actuals**
Coverage	Revenue collection statistics broken down by local authority area and based on returns to CIPFA from local authorities.
Frequency	Annual
Availability	General
Cost	£80
Comments	–
Address	3 Robert Street, London WC2N 6BH
Tel. / e-mail	0171 543 5600 webco-ordinator@cipfa.org
Fax / Web site	0171 543 5700 www.cipfa.sift.co.uk

264	CHARTERED INSTITUTE OF PUBLIC FINANCE AND ACCOUNTANCY (CIPFA)
Title	**Superannuation Fund Investment Statistics**
Coverage	A ten-year historical record of superannuation statistics with the first issue, published in 1995, covering the years 1985 to 1995. Based on data supplied by local authorities.
Frequency	Annual
Availability	General
Cost	£180
Comments	–
Address	3 Robert Street, London WC2N 6BH
Tel. / e-mail	0171 543 5600 webco-ordinator@cipfa.org
Fax / Web site	0171 543 5700 www.cipfa.sift.co.uk

265

CHARTERED INSTITUTE OF PUBLIC FINANCE AND
ACCOUNTANCY (CIPFA)

Title **Trading Standards - Actuals and Estimates**

Coverage Financial and non-financial data on trading standards
departments with data for individual local authorities. Based
on data collected by CIPFA.

Frequency Annual

Availability General

Cost £55

Comments –

Address 3 Robert Street, London WC2N 6BH

Tel. / e-mail 0171 543 5600   webco-ordinator@cipfa.org

Fax / Web site 0171 543 5700   www.cipfa.sift.co.uk

266

CHARTERED INSTITUTE OF PUBLIC FINANCE AND
ACCOUNTANCY (CIPFA)

Title **Waste Collection - Actuals**

Coverage Data on waste collection including income and expenditure,
staff numbers, charges, quantities collected, and methods and
frequency of collection. Aggregate data and data by local
authority area. Based on data collected by CIPFA.

Frequency Annual

Availability General

Cost £80

Comments –

Address 3 Robert Street, London WC2N 6BH

Tel. / e-mail 0171 543 5600   webco-ordinator@cipfa.org

Fax / Web site 0171 543 5700   www.cipfa.sift.co.uk

267

CHARTERED INSTITUTE OF PUBLIC FINANCE AND
ACCOUNTANCY (CIPFA)

Title **Waste Collection and Disposal - Actuals**

Coverage Data on revenue income and expenditure, capital expenditure
and financing, treatment methods, waste arising and reclaimed
waste by tonnage, vehicle disposals, manpower, and unit costs.
Summary data and by local authority area. Based on data
collected by CIPFA.

Frequency Annual

Availability General

Cost £105

Comments –

Address 3 Robert Street, London WC2N 6BH

Tel. / e-mail 0171 543 5600   webco-ordinator@cipfa.org

Fax / Web site 0171 543 5700   www.cipfa.sift.co.uk

268	**CHARTERHOUSE PLC**
Title	**UK Economica**
Coverage	A review of UK economic trends with short-term forecasts. Forecasts produced by the company with existing data from Central Government sources.
Frequency	Quarterly
Availability	General
Cost	On request
Comments	–
Address	1 Paternoster Row, London EC4M 7DH
Tel. / e-mail	0171 248 4000
Fax / Web site	0171 246 2033

269	**CHEMICAL INDUSTRIES ASSOCIATION**
Title	**Economics Bulletin**
Coverage	Monitors, analyses and forecasts the economic performance of the UK chemical industry. A main table of chemical industry basic economic indicators is also included. Based on official and non-official sources.
Frequency	3 issues per year
Availability	General
Cost	Free to members, £75 non-members
Comments	–
Address	Kings Building, Smith Square, London SW1P 3JJ
Tel. / e-mail	0171 834 3399 publications@cia.org.uk
Fax / Web site	0171 834 4469

270	**CHEMICAL INDUSTRIES ASSOCIATION**
Title	**Investment Intentions Survey**
Coverage	A survey of CIA member company investment intentions covering actual capital expenditure in the previous year together with investment intentions for the coming three years. Total figures plus a breakdown by region, chemicals sector, and purpose of investment.
Frequency	Annual
Availability	General
Cost	£20 to members, £55 non-members
Comments	The results are announced at an annual Investment Intentions Conference. The association also publishes international statistics.
Address	Kings Building, Smith Square, London SW1P 3JJ
Tel. / e-mail	0171 834 3399 publications@cia.org.uk
Fax / Web site	0171 834 4469

CHEMICAL INDUSTRIES ASSOCIATION

271	
Title	**UK Chemical Industry Facts**
Coverage	Leaflet with basic statistics on the UK chemical industry with historical data over a ten-year period.
Frequency	Annual
Availability	General
Cost	Free (single copy)
Comments	Published in July each year. Also available on 35mm slides and overhead transparencies. The association also publishes international statistics.
Address	Kings Building, Smith Square, London SW1P 3JJ
Tel. / e-mail	0171 834 3399 publications@cia.org.uk
Fax / Web site	0171 834 4469

CHEMIST AND DRUGGIST

272	
Title	**Chemist & Druggist Price List**
Coverage	Trade and retail prices for various products sold by chemists. Based on the journal's own survey with prices usually one month old.
Frequency	Weekly
Availability	General
Cost	£127 per annum
Comments	The journal also has regular features on specific markets and specific products sold via chemists.
Address	Miller Freeman UK Ltd, Miller Freeman House, Sovereign Way, Tonbridge TN9 1RW
Tel. / e-mail	01732 364422
Fax / Web site	01732 361534 www.pharmacy.com

CHESTERTON RESEARCH

273	
Title	**City Centre Office Markets**
Coverage	A review of rents, rates, vacancies, occupancies in the major cities based on data collected by the company.
Frequency	Regular
Availability	General
Cost	£55
Comments	–
Address	54 Brook Street, London W1A 2BU
Tel. / e-mail	0171 499 0404
Fax / Web site	0171 629 7804

274	**CHILDREN'S RESEARCH UNIT**
Title	**Juvenile Perspectives**
Coverage	An annual survey of 7 to 15 year-olds in the UK and other European countries. Based on a sample of around 8,000, and the survey is conducted by the company.
Frequency	Annual
Availability	General
Cost	On request
Comments	–
Address	220 Queenstown Road, London SW8 4LP
Tel. / e-mail	0171 622 0286 glen@yorg.com
Fax / Web site	0171 720 0537 www.yorg.com

275	**CINEMA ADVERTISING ASSOCIATION**
Title	**CAA Admissions Monitor**
Coverage	A monthly measure of the attendances at all UK cinemas accepting advertising. Based on the association's own research.
Frequency	Monthly
Availability	General
Cost	Free
Comments	The data is also available online and on disc. Conducted by Entertainment Data International for the CAA.
Address	12 Golden Square, London W1R 3AF
Tel. / e-mail	0171 534 6363
Fax / Web site	0171 534 6464

276	**CINEMA ADVERTISING ASSOCIATION**
Title	**Caviar - Cinema and Video Industry Audience Research**
Coverage	Provides audience data for cinema and pre-recorded videos from the age of 7 upwards by film, genre, certificate. Based on a survey of almost 3,000 people in various randomly selected sampling points around the country.
Frequency	Annual
Availability	General
Cost	£7,150
Comments	The data is also available online, and on disc.
Address	12 Golden Square, London W1R 3AF
Tel. / e-mail	0171 534 6363
Fax / Web site	0171 534 6464

<table>
<tr><td>277</td><td colspan="2">CIVIL AVIATION AUTHORITY</td></tr>
<tr><td>Title</td><td colspan="2">Annual Punctuality Statistics</td></tr>
<tr><td>Coverage</td><td colspan="2">Punctuality statistics by airline and destination are available, for four London airports, plus Manchester and Birmingham. Comparisons with the previous year are given.</td></tr>
<tr><td>Frequency</td><td colspan="2">Annual</td></tr>
<tr><td>Availability</td><td colspan="2">General</td></tr>
<tr><td>Cost</td><td colspan="2">£42 for the detailed report, £10.50 for the summary report</td></tr>
<tr><td>Comments</td><td colspan="2">–</td></tr>
<tr><td>Address</td><td colspan="2">Greville House, 37 Gratton Road, Cheltenham   GL50 2BN</td></tr>
<tr><td>Tel. / e-mail</td><td colspan="2">01242 35151</td></tr>
<tr><td>Fax / Web site</td><td colspan="2">01242 584139</td></tr>
</table>

<table>
<tr><td>278</td><td colspan="2">CIVIL AVIATION AUTHORITY</td></tr>
<tr><td>Title</td><td colspan="2">Punctuality Statistics</td></tr>
<tr><td>Coverage</td><td colspan="2">Punctuality statistics by airline and destination are available, for four London airports, plus Manchester and Birmingham. Comparisons are made with the month in the previous year.</td></tr>
<tr><td>Frequency</td><td colspan="2">Monthly</td></tr>
<tr><td>Availability</td><td colspan="2">General</td></tr>
<tr><td>Cost</td><td colspan="2">£310 for the detailed reports, £64 for summary reports</td></tr>
<tr><td>Comments</td><td colspan="2">–</td></tr>
<tr><td>Address</td><td colspan="2">Greville House, 37 Gratton Road, Cheltenham   GL50 2BN</td></tr>
<tr><td>Tel. / e-mail</td><td colspan="2">01242 35151</td></tr>
<tr><td>Fax / Web site</td><td colspan="2">01242 584139</td></tr>
</table>

<table>
<tr><td>279</td><td colspan="2">CIVIL AVIATION AUTHORITY</td></tr>
<tr><td>Title</td><td colspan="2">UK Airlines</td></tr>
<tr><td>Coverage</td><td colspan="2">Operating and traffic statistics for UK airlines by domestic and international services, and by types of operation, based on the CAA's own data. Statistics usually cover the previous month.</td></tr>
<tr><td>Frequency</td><td colspan="2">Monthly</td></tr>
<tr><td>Availability</td><td colspan="2">General</td></tr>
<tr><td>Cost</td><td colspan="2">£59</td></tr>
<tr><td>Comments</td><td colspan="2">CAA statistics also available on magnetic discs in Word for Windows format or on Excel spreadsheets. Disc subscription - £118 per annum, £11.80 for individual discs.</td></tr>
<tr><td>Address</td><td colspan="2">Greville House, 37 Gratton Road, Cheltenham   GL50 2BN</td></tr>
<tr><td>Tel. / e-mail</td><td colspan="2">01242 35151</td></tr>
<tr><td>Fax / Web site</td><td colspan="2">01242 584139</td></tr>
</table>

280

CIVIL AVIATION AUTHORITY

UK Airports

Title	UK Airports
Coverage	Monthly statements of movements, passengers, and cargo at UK airports, based on data collected by the CAA. Statistics usually cover the previous month.
Frequency	Monthly
Availability	General
Cost	£59
Comments	CAA statistics also available on magnetic disc in Word for Windows format or on Excel spreadsheeets. Disc subscription - £118 per annum, £11.80 for individual discs.
Address	Greville House, 37 Gratton Road, Cheltenham GL50 2BN
Tel. / e-mail	01242 35151
Fax / Web site	01242 584139

281

COCA-COLA & SCHWEPPES BEVERAGES LTD

Bottled Water Market Profile

Title	Bottled Water Market Profile
Coverage	A review of the UK bottled water market with sales data for the total market and by type of water. Also includes data on brands, retailing, new products.
Frequency	Regular
Availability	General
Cost	On request
Comments	–
Address	Charter Place, Uxbridge UB8 1EZ
Tel. / e-mail	01895 231313
Fax / Web site	01895 239092

282

COMBINED ACTUARIAL PERFORMANCE SERVICES

Quarterly Survey of Pooled Pension Funds

Title	Quarterly Survey of Pooled Pension Funds
Coverage	Summarises the returns achieved by different types of pooled pension funds including sector-specific and mixed funds. Based on an analysis of almost 700 funds.
Frequency	Quarterly
Availability	General
Cost	£430, £175 per issue
Comments	–
Address	11 Albion Street, Leeds LS1 5ES
Tel. / e-mail	0113 2460416
Fax / Web site	

283	COMBINED HEAT AND POWER ASSOCIATION
Title	**Market Review**
Coverage	Market trends in the combined heat and power sector with commentary and statistics covering the last few years. Based on research by the association.
Frequency	Annual
Availability	General
Cost	Free
Comments	A copy of the Market Review is available on the web site.
Address	Grosvenor House, 35-37 Grosvenor Gardens, London SW1 0BS
Tel. / e-mail	0171 828 4077 info@chpa.co.uk
Fax / Web site	0171 828 0311 www.energy.rochester.edu/uk/chpa

284	COMPANY CAR
Title	**Databank**
Coverage	Prices of new cars and the standing, running, and operating costs of car fleets.
Frequency	Monthly in a monthly journal
Availability	General
Cost	£66, £8 per issue
Comments	–
Address	DMG Business Media Ltd, Queensway House, 2 Queensway, Redhill RH1 1QS
Tel. / e-mail	01737 768611 companycar@dmg.co.uk
Fax / Web site	01737 760564 www.dmg.co.uk

285	COMPUTER BUSINESS REVIEW
Title	**Trends and Indicators**
Coverage	Basic data on general economic trends and indicators relevant to the computer sector based on information compiled from various sources.
Frequency	Monthly in a monthly journal
Availability	General
Cost	£55
Comments	–
Address	12 Sutton Row, London W1V 5FH
Tel. / e-mail	0171 208 4245 cbred@computerwire.com
Fax / Web site	0171 439 1105 www.computerwire.com

286	COMPUTER ECONOMICS LTD
Title	**Computer Staff Salary Survey**
Coverage	A survey of 50 job descriptions analysed by location, age, experience, areas of responsibility, fringe benefits etc. Based on a survey by the company. A small commentary supports the text.
Frequency	Twice yearly
Availability	General
Cost	On application
Comments	–
Address	Survey House, 51 Portland Road, Kingston-upon-Thames KT1 2SH
Tel. / e-mail	0181 549 8726
Fax / Web site	0181 541 5705 www.celre.co.uk

287	COMPUTING SERVICES AND SOFTWARE ASSOCIATION
Title	**Annual Report**
Coverage	Includes the association's annual survey based on voluntary responses from member companies. Data on business activities, total revenue, revenue by business sector, revenue per employee, employment trends, profits, and future prospects. A detailed commentary supports the text.
Frequency	Annual
Availability	General
Cost	Free
Comments	–
Address	Hanover House, 73-74 High Holborn, London WC1V 6LE
Tel. / e-mail	0171 405 2171 cssa@cssa.co.uk
Fax / Web site	0171 404 4119 www.cssa.co.uk

288	CONFEDERATION OF BRITISH FORGERS
Title	**BFIA Annual Report**
Coverage	Contains some statistics on the economic performance of the forging industry.
Frequency	Annual
Availability	General
Cost	On request
Comments	–
Address	245 Grove Lane, Handsworth, Birmingham B20 2HB
Tel. / e-mail	0121 554 3311
Fax / Web site	0121 523 0761

289

CONFEDERATION OF BRITISH FORGERS

Title	**End of Year Statistics**
Coverage	Annual statistics on the forging industry including market developments, prices, deliveries. Based on the association's own survey.
Frequency	Annual
Availability	General
Cost	£10, free to members
Comments	–
Address	245 Grove Lane, Handsworth, Birmingham B20 2HB
Tel. / e-mail	0121 554 3311
Fax / Web site	0121 523 0761

290

CONFEDERATION OF BRITISH INDUSTRY (CBI)

Title	**CBI Distributive Trades Survey**
Coverage	A survey of trends in over 20 distributive sectors with data on sales volume, orders, stocks, employment, investment, prices, business expenditure etc. Based on a CBI survey.
Frequency	Monthly
Availability	General
Cost	£425, £255 to members
Comments	–
Address	103 New Oxford Street, London WC1A 1DU
Tel. / e-mail	0171 395 8104
Fax / Web site	0171 836 5856 www.cbi.org.uk

291

CONFEDERATION OF BRITISH INDUSTRY (CBI)

Title	**CBI/BSL Regional Trends Survey**
Coverage	A survey of economic and business trends in the UK regions based on a survey of a sample of companies in these regions.
Frequency	Annual
Availability	General
Cost	£300, £170 to members
Comments	Produced in association with Business Strategies Ltd.
Address	103 New Oxford Street, London WC1A 1DU
Tel. / e-mail	0171 395 8104
Fax / Web site	0171 836 5856 www.cbi.org.uk

292

CONFEDERATION OF BRITISH INDUSTRY (CBI)

Title **CBI/Deloitte & Touche Consumer, Business and Professional Services Survey**

Coverage A quarterly survey of the services sector based on results from a sample of service industry companies.

Frequency Quarterly

Availability General

Cost On request

Comments First published in December 1998.

Address 103 New Oxford Street, London WC1A 1DU

Tel. / e-mail 0171 379 7400

Fax / Web site 0171 240 1578 www.cbi.org.uk

293

CONFEDERATION OF BRITISH INDUSTRY (CBI)

Title **CBI/GVA Grimley Property Trends Survey**

Coverage A survey of short-term and long-term property requirements of the private sector.

Frequency Twice yearly

Availability General

Cost On request

Comments –

Address 103 New Oxford Street, London WC1A 1DU

Tel. / e-mail 0171 379 7400

Fax / Web site 0171 240 1578 www.cbi.org.uk

294

CONFEDERATION OF BRITISH INDUSTRY (CBI)

Title **CBI/Pannell Kerr Forster SME Trends Report**

Coverage Quarterly review of trends in the small and medium-sized business sector based on a survey of companies.

Frequency Quarterly

Availability General

Cost £90, £45 members

Comments –

Address 103 New Oxford Street, London WC1A 1DU

Tel. / e-mail 0171 395 8104

Fax / Web site 0171 836 5856 www.cbi.org.uk

295	CONFEDERATION OF BRITISH INDUSTRY (CBI)
Title	**Economic Situation Report**
Coverage	An economic survey plus a forecast up to six months ahead. Also a general survey of industrial and regional trends and some comparative data for other European countries. Based on a combination of CBI data and official statistics.
Frequency	Monthly
Availability	General
Cost	£366, £208 to members
Comments	–
Address	103 New Oxford Street, London WC1A 1DU
Tel. / e-mail	0171 395 8104
Fax / Web site	0171 836 5856 www.cbi.org.uk

296	CONFEDERATION OF BRITISH INDUSTRY (CBI)
Title	**Financial Services Survey**
Coverage	A survey of trends in various financial services sectors with data on income, employment, short-term expectations etc. Based on a CBI survey.
Frequency	Quarterly
Availability	General
Cost	£325, £180 to members
Comments	Published in association with Price Waterhouse Coopers.
Address	103 New Oxford Street, London WC1A 1DU
Tel. / e-mail	0171 395 8104
Fax / Web site	0171 836 5856 www.cbi.org.uk

297	CONFEDERATION OF BRITISH INDUSTRY (CBI)
Title	**Industrial Trends Survey**
Coverage	Trends for over 40 industry groups covering orders, stocks, output, capital expenditure, exports, costs, labour etc for the last four months and the next four months. Based on a CBI survey of around 1,700 companies.
Frequency	Quarterly
Availability	General
Cost	£455, £245 to members, joint subscription with Monthly Trends Enquiry (see below) £665, £400 to members
Comments	–
Address	103 New Oxford Street, London WC1A 1DU
Tel. / e-mail	0171 395 8104
Fax / Web site	0171 836 5856 www.cbi.org.uk

298	CONFEDERATION OF BRITISH INDUSTRY (CBI)
Title	**Monthly Trends Enquiry**
Coverage	Essentially an abbreviated version of the quarterly 'Industrial Trends Survey' with summary statistics on orders, stocks, output, prices etc. A short commentary supports the statistics. Data is based on a survey of companies with responses varying from around 1,300 to over 1,500.
Frequency	Monthly
Availability	General
Cost	£665, £400 to members, a joint subscription with Industrial Trends Survey (see entry above)
Comments	–
Address	103 New Oxford Street, London WC1A 1DU
Tel. / e-mail	0171 395 8104
Fax / Web site	0171 836 5856 www.cbi.org.uk

299	CONSENSUS RESEARCH INTERNATIONAL
Title	**Unit Trust Survey**
Coverage	A survey of the awareness of, and attitudes towards, unit trusts amongst unitholders and intermediaries. Based on a company survey. A commentary supports the data.
Frequency	Quarterly
Availability	General
Cost	On application
Comments	Also produces an annual Stockbroker Survey, based on the ratings of brokers' analysts by company executives.
Address	1-2 Castle Lane, London SW1E 6DR
Tel. / e-mail	0171 592 1700 mail@consensus-research.co.uk
Fax / Web site	0171 738 1271

300	CONSTRUCTION FORECASTING AND RESEARCH LTD
Title	**Construction Forecasts**
Coverage	Short-term construction forecasts, and current trends, covering housing, industrial, commercial, and infrastructure. Value and volume forecasts are included and a detailed analysis of the forecasts accompanies the tables.
Frequency	Quarterly
Availability	General
Cost	£225
Comments	Published on behalf of the Joint Forecasting Committee for the Construction Industries. Statistics on European construction trends and corporate performance in the construction industry also produced.
Address	Princes House, 39 Kingsway, London WC2B 6TP
Tel. / e-mail	0171 379 5339 cfrjgph@aol.com
Fax / Web site	0171 379 5426

301	CONSTRUCTION FORECASTING AND RESEARCH LTD
Title	**Construction Industry Focus**
Coverage	Data on contractors' activity, order books, tender prices, and short-term prospects for employment and tender prices. Based on a combination of official and non-official data.
Frequency	Monthly
Availability	General
Cost	£40 annual subscription
Comments	Statistics on European construction trends and corporate performance in the construction industry also produced.
Address	Princes House, 39 Kingsway, London WC2B 6TP
Tel. / e-mail	0171 379 5339 cfrjgph@aol.com
Fax / Web site	0171 379 5426

302

CONSTRUCTION FORECASTING AND RESEARCH LTD

Title **Process Industries Investment Forecast**

Coverage Forecasts of capital expenditure and expenditure on process plant in the chemical, nuclear fuel reprocessing, oil and gas production, petroleum refining, electricity generation, gas, steel, water and sewerage, and food and drink industries.

Frequency Annual

Availability General

Cost £95

Comments Statistics on European construction trends and corporate performance in the construction industry also produced.

Address Princes House, 39 Kingsway, London   WC2B 6TP

Tel. / e-mail 0171 379 5339   cfrjgph@aol.com

Fax / Web site 0171 379 5426

303

CONSTRUCTION NEWS

Title **Annual Contracts Review**

Coverage An annual review of contracts awarded by type of construction, e.g. residential, commercial, industrial, and by region. Also statistics on work out to tender.

Frequency Annual in a weekly journal

Availability General

Cost £72.50

Comments 'FT'-Actuaries Indices are also included in each issue.

Address EMAP Construct, 151 Roseberry Avenue, London   EC1R 4GB

Tel. / e-mail 0171 505 6600   cned@construct.emap.co.uk

Fax / Web site 0171 505 6610   www.careersinconstruction.co.uk

304

CONSTRUCTION NEWS

Title **Workload Trends**

Coverage Statistics covering new contracts awarded by construction type updating the data in the annual survey noted in the previous entry.

Frequency Monthly in a weekly journal

Availability General

Cost £72.50

Comments 'FT'-Actuaries Indices are also included in each issue.

Address EMAP Construct, 151 Roseberry Avenue, London   EC1R 4GB

Tel. / e-mail 0171 505 6600   cned@construct.emap.co.uk

Fax / Web site 0171 505 6610   www.careersinconstrutction.co.uk

305

Title	**CONSTRUCTION PLANT HIRE ASSOCIATION** **CPA Activity and Hire Rate Studies**
Coverage	Activity percentages and average hire rates for typical machines. Based on a survey of members.
Frequency	Quarterly
Availability	Only available to participating members.
Cost	Free
Comments	–
Address	28 Eccleston Place, London SW1W 9PY
Tel. / e-mail	0171 730 7117 enquiries@c-p-a.co.uk
Fax / Web site	0171 730 7110 www.c-p-a.co.uk

306

Title	**CONSTRUCTION PLANT HIRE ASSOCIATION** **CPA Driver Cost Studies**
Coverage	Details of the costs attached to the employment of drivers under civil engineering or plant hire working rule agreements. Based on a survey by the association.
Frequency	Annual
Availability	General
Cost	Free to members but there may be a small charge to others
Comments	–
Address	28 Eccleston Place, London SW1W 9PY
Tel. / e-mail	0171 730 7117 enquiries@c-p-a.co.uk
Fax / Web site	0171 730 7110 www.c-p-a.co.uk

307

Title	**CONSTRUCTION PLANT HIRE ASSOCIATION** **CPA Machine Cost Studies**
Coverage	Details of the costs to plant hire companies of running typical machines and cost movement indices. Based on data collected by the association.
Frequency	Twice yearly
Availability	General
Cost	Free to members but there may be a small charge to others
Comments	–
Address	28 Eccleston Place, London SW1W 9PY
Tel. / e-mail	0171 730 7117 enquiries@c-p-a.co.uk
Fax / Web site	0171 730 7110 www.c-p-a.co.uk

CONSUMER CREDIT TRADE ASSOCIATION

308	
Title	**Consumer Credit**
Coverage	Commentary and statistics on consumer credit trends with comparisons trends in the previous year.
Frequency	6 issues per year
Availability	General
Cost	£3.50 to members £5.50 to non-members
Comments	–
Address	1st Floor, Tennyson House, 159-163 Great Portland Street, London W1N 5FD
Tel. / e-mail	0171 636 7564 cctassoc.demon.co.uk
Fax / Web site	0171 323 0096

CONSUMER PROFILE RESEARCH LTD

309	
Title	**Decisions**
Coverage	A regular omnibus survey aimed at researching issues relating to advertising, packaging, new product development etc.
Frequency	Regular
Availability	General
Cost	On application
Comments	–
Address	18 High Street, Thame, Oxford OX4 2BZ
Tel. / e-mail	01844 215672
Fax / Web site	01844 261324

CONTEXT

310	
Title	**PC Shipments Report**
Coverage	An analysis of distribution channels and sales trends for personal computers based on a dealer survey by the company.
Frequency	Monthly
Availability	General
Cost	£5,450
Comments	Other regular reports on European computer markets.
Address	177-179 Hammersmith Road, London W6 8BS
Tel. / e-mail	0171 343 8000
Fax / Web site	0171 343 8001 www.context1.com

311	CONTEXT
Title	**Printer Shipments Report**
Coverage	An analysis of distribution channels and sales trends for computer printers based on a dealer survey by the company.
Frequency	Monthly
Availability	General
Cost	£4,950
Comments	Other regular reports on European computer markets.
Address	177-179 Hammersmith Road, London W6 8BS
Tel. / e-mail	0171 343 8000
Fax / Web site	0171 343 8001 www.context1.com

312	CONTEXT
Title	**Software Shipments Report**
Coverage	An analysis of distribution channels and sales trends for computer software based on a dealer survey by the company.
Frequency	Monthly
Availability	General
Cost	£5,450
Comments	Other regular reports on European computer markets.
Address	177-179 Hammersmith Road, London W6 8BS
Tel. / e-mail	0171 343 8000
Fax / Web site	0171 343 8001 www.context1.com

313	CONTINENTAL RESEARCH
Title	**Internet Report**
Coverage	Annual review with statistics on Internet penetration, use.
Frequency	Annual
Availability	General
Cost	£85
Comments	–
Address	132-140 Goswell Road, London EC1V 7DP
Tel. / e-mail	0171 490 5944 mail@continentalresearch.com
Fax / Web site	0171 490 1174 www.continentalresearch.com

314	CONTINENTAL RESEARCH
Title	**Internet Report**
Coverage	Annual review with detailed statistics on Internet penetration, use etc.
Frequency	Annual
Availability	General
Cost	£85
Comments	–
Address	132-140 Goswell Road, London EC1V 7DP
Tel. / e-mail	0171 490 5944 mail@continentalresearch.com
Fax / Web site	0171 490 1174 www.continentalresearch.com

315	CONTINENTAL RESEARCH
Title	**Mobile Phone Report**
Coverage	Annual review with statistics on phone use, penetration.
Frequency	Annual
Availability	General
Cost	£85
Comments	–
Address	132-140 Goswell Road, London EC1V 7DP
Tel. / e-mail	0171 490 5944 mail@continentalresearch.com
Fax / Web site	0171 490 1174 www.continentalresearch.com

316	CONTINENTAL RESEARCH
Title	**Satellite and Cable Monitor**
Coverage	Monthly commentary and statistics on the number of satellite dishes, SMATV, and cable installations in the UK. Also figures on intentions to purchase and viewing levels. Based on original research by the company.
Frequency	Monthly
Availability	General
Cost	£2,200
Comments	–
Address	132-140 Goswell Road, London EC1V 7OP
Tel. / e-mail	0171 490 5944 mail@continentalresearch.com
Fax / Web site	0171 490 1174 www.continentalresearch.com

CONTINENTAL RESEARCH

Title	**STAR Report**
Coverage	A monthly review of audience figures for satellite television and satellite channels. Also includes audience share, reach figures, an analysis by demographic sector, forecasts up to five years ahead, and details of the top 50 programmes. Based on research by the company.
Frequency	Monthly
Availability	General
Cost	£1,200
Comments	–
Address	132-140 Goswell Road, London EC1V 7OP
Tel. / e-mail	0171 490 5944 mail@continentalresearch.com
Fax / Web site	0171 490 1174 www.continentalresearch.com

317

CONTROL RISKS GROUP

Title	**Business Security Outlook**
Coverage	Based on a survey of senior executives in the UK and the USA, the report considers the main security issues for UK and US overseas investors.
Frequency	Annual
Availability	General
Cost	£158
Comments	–
Address	83 Victoria Street, London SW1H 0HW
Tel. / e-mail	0171 222 1552
Fax / Web site	0171 222 2296 www.crg.com

318

COOPERATIVE UNION LTD

Title	**Cooperative Statistics**
Coverage	Retail distribution by individual cooperative societies and other information on cooperative wholesaling, banking, and insurance. Based almost entirely on the organisation's own research.
Frequency	Annual
Availability	General
Cost	On request
Comments	–
Address	Holyoake House, Hanover Street, Manchester M60 0AS
Tel. / e-mail	0161 832 4300
Fax / Web site	0161 831 7684

319

320 CORRUGATED PACKAGING ASSOCIATION

Title	**Annual Production Statistics**
Coverage	Production by weight and area and the sales invoice value of solid and corrugated fibreboard produced in the UK. Based on a survey of members.
Frequency	Annual
Availability	Members
Cost	Free
Comments	At the time of preparing this directory, the statistics produced by the association were under review.
Address	2 Saxon Court, Freeschool Street, Northampton NN1 1ST
Tel. / e-mail	01604 621002 postbox@corrugated.org.uk
Fax / Web site	01604 620636 www.corrugated.org.uk

321 COUNCIL OF MORTGAGE LENDERS

Title	**Compendium of Housing Finance Statistics**
Coverage	Historical statistics covering housing tenure, stock, transactions, prices, mortgages, rates of interest, and building society information.
Frequency	Regular
Availability	General
Cost	On request
Comments	Published jointly with the Building Societies Association. The latest edition was published in 1995 following the previous edition in 1990. Some statistics on the web site.
Address	3 Savile Row, London W1X 1AF
Tel. / e-mail	0171 437 0655
Fax / Web site	0171 734 6416 www.cml.org.uk

322 COUNCIL OF MORTGAGE LENDERS

Title	**Housing Finance**
Coverage	Includes articles and a diary of events plus a statistical section covering trends in housing, building, mortgage lending, prices, transactions, and savings. Also data on specific building societies.
Frequency	Quarterly
Availability	General
Cost	£20 per issue
Comments	Based at the same address as the Building Societies Association and involved in some joint publications (see next entry). Some statistics on the web site.
Address	3 Savile Row, London W1X 1AF
Tel. / e-mail	0171 437 0655
Fax / Web site	0171 734 6416 www.cml.org.uk

323

CREMATION SOCIETY OF GREAT BRITAIN

Title	**Directory of Crematoria**
Coverage	Progress of cremation over the last 100 years. Facts and figures section includes number of crematoria, cremations carried out, fees etc. Based on the Society's own survey.
Frequency	Annual
Availability	General
Cost	£19 with binder, £15 loose-leaf
Comments	–
Address	Brecon House (2nd Floor), 16/16a Albion Place, Maidstone ME14 5DZ
Tel. / e-mail	01622 688292 cremsoc@aol.com
Fax / Web site	01622 686698 www.cremation.org.uk

324

CROOKES HEALTHCARE LTD

Title	**Farley's Market Report**
Coverage	A review of the baby food market with statistics and commentary on various product sectors. Based on commissioned research.
Frequency	Regular
Availability	General
Cost	On request
Comments	–
Address	Central Park, Lenton Lane, Nottingham NG7 2LJ
Tel. / e-mail	0115 953 9922
Fax / Web site	0115 968 8722

325

DATASTREAM INTERNATIONAL LTD

Title	**Economic Series Database**
Coverage	Datastream is primarily a provider of company information but it also has a database of economic statistics covering the UK and various other countries.
Frequency	Continuous
Availability	General
Cost	On request
Comments	–
Address	Monmouth House, 58-64 City Road, London EC1Y 2AL
Tel. / e-mail	0171 250 3000
Fax / Web site	0171 253 0171 www.datastream.com

326	**DEL MONTE FOODS INTERNATIONAL**
Title	**Canned Fruit and Juices Report**
Coverage	Commentary and statistics on the canned fruit and juices market with data on market size, brands, consumer trends in specific product sectors. Based on commissioned research.
Frequency	Annual
Availability	General
Cost	On request
Comments	–
Address	Del Monte House, London Road, Staines TW18 4JD
Tel. / e-mail	01784 447400
Fax / Web site	01784 465301

327	**DHL INTERNATIONAL (UK) LTD**
Title	**Quarterly Export Indicator**
Coverage	This publication surveys the level of business confidence amongst the UK's manufacturing export industries and it is based on telephone interviews with approximately 500 directors and managers responsible for exports in British manufacturing. The survey results include export expectations over the next 3 and 12 months, trends in the main factors affecting exports, opinions on the role of the EU and the single European currency, trends in raw material costs.
Frequency	Quarterly
Availability	General
Cost	Free
Comments	The opinion survey is carried out by Gallup on behalf of DHL. Press release relating to latest survey on the web site.
Address	Orbital Park, 178-188 Great South West Road, Hounslow, Middlesex TW4 6JS
Tel. / e-mail	0181 818 8049
Fax / Web site	0181 818 8581 www.dhl.co.uk

DIALOG CORPORATION

328	
Title	**Tradstat**
Coverage	An online database of UK import and export statistics with data on specific products. Based on data supplied by HM Customs and Excise and part of an international database of foreign trade statistics.
Frequency	Regular
Availability	General
Cost	On request
Comments	–
Address	3rd Floor, Palace House, 3 Cathedral Street, London SE1 6EE
Tel. / e-mail	0171 930 5503 contact@dialog.com
Fax / Web site	0171 940 6800 www.dialog.com

DIRECT MAIL INFORMATION SERVICE

329	
Title	**Consumer Direct Mail Trends**
Coverage	Commentary and graphs on the volume of direct mail, mail opened, responses, purchases, awareness. Based on interviews with over 600 interviewees.
Frequency	Every two years
Availability	General
Cost	On request
Comments	Published every two years since 1985.
Address	5 Carlisle Street, London W1V 6JX
Tel. / e-mail	0171 494 0483 jo.howard-brown@virgin.net
Fax / Web site	0171 494 0455 www.dmis.co.uk

DIRECT MARKETING ASSOCIATION

330	
Title	**Direct Marketing Statistics**
Coverage	A compilation of statistics on direct marketing from a variety of non-official sources.
Frequency	Annual
Availability	General
Cost	Free
Comments	The association changed its name from the British Direct Marketing Association in 1992.
Address	1 Oxenden Street, London SW1Y 4EE
Tel. / e-mail	0171 321 2525 dma@dma.org.uk
Fax / Web site	0171 321 0191 www.dma.org.uk

331	DIRECT MARKETING ASSOCIATION
Title	**DMA Census of the UK Direct Marketing Industry**
Coverage	A detailed survey of the industry covering structure, sales, postings etc based largely on original research.
Frequency	Annual
Availability	General
Cost	Free - members, £285 non-members
Comments	–
Address	1 Oxenden Street, London SW1Y 4EE
Tel. / e-mail	0171 321 2525 dma@dma.org.uk
Fax / Web site	0171 321 0191 www.dma.org.uk

332	DIY SUPERSTORE
Title	**Review of the Year and Statistical Analysis**
Coverage	Commentary and statistics on developments in the DIY superstore sector with data on the number of superstores, openings during the year, and market shares.
Frequency	Annual in a monthly journal
Availability	General
Cost	
Comments	Usually appears in the November/December issue of the journal.
Address	Faversham House Group Ltd, Faversham House, 232a Addington Road, South Croydon CR2 8LE
Tel. / e-mail	0181 651 7100
Fax / Web site	0181 651 7117

333	DIY WEEK
Title	**DIY Trak Market Monitor**
Coverage	Statistics on DIY retail sales by product sector and by retail channels based on continuous research carried out by GfK Marketing Services (see other entry).
Frequency	Quarterly in a weekly journal
Availability	General
Cost	£65, £3.80 single issue
Comments	The journal also has regular features and market reports on specific DIY product sectors and DIY retailers, wholesalers.
Address	Miller Freeman Publications, Sovereign Way, Tonbridge TN9 1RW
Tel. / e-mail	01732 364422
Fax / Web site	01732 361534

334 DONOVAN DATA SYSTEMS

Title	**Donovan Database Services**
Coverage	Donovan has access to a number of media and consumer surveys held on computer, including the British Business Survey (see other entry), and other advertising and audience/readership surveys.
Frequency	Continuous
Availability	General
Cost	On request, depending on the nature and range of information required
Comments	–
Address	7 Farm Street, London W1X 7RB
Tel. / e-mail	0171 629 7654
Fax / Web site	0171 493 0239

335 DTZ DEBENHAM THORPE

Title	**Core - Central London Offices Research**
Coverage	Office floorspace and rent trends in the centre of London based on surveys by the company.
Frequency	Quarterly
Availability	General
Cost	On request
Comments	Publishes various other reports on key European cities and one-off reports on property issues, eg business parks, retailing, overseas investment in commercial property.
Address	DTZ Debenham Thorpe, 44 Brook Street, London W1A 4AG
Tel. / e-mail	0171 408 1161
Fax / Web site	0171 491 4593

336 DTZ DEBENHAM THORPE

Title	**Regional Annual Property Reviews**
Coverage	Regional trends in floorspace, rents, and availability. Based on surveys carried out by the company.
Frequency	Annual
Availability	General
Cost	Free
Comments	Publishes various other reports on key European cities and one-off reports on property issues, eg business parks, retailing, overseas investment in commercial property.
Address	44 Brook Street, London W1A 4AG
Tel. / e-mail	0171 408 1161
Fax / Web site	0171 491 4593

337	**DUN AND BRADSTREET LTD**
Title	**Business Failure Statistics**
Coverage	Company liquidations and bankruptcies analysed by sector and region. A commentary supports the data which comes from records maintained by the company.
Frequency	Quarterly
Availability	General
Cost	Free
Comments	–
Address	Holmers Farm Way, High Wycombe HP12 4UL
Tel. / e-mail	01494 423689
Fax / Web site	01494 422332 www.dunandbrad.co.uk

338	**DUN AND BRADSTREET LTD**
Title	**Key Business Ratios**
Coverage	20 key ratios arranged by SIC industry group with data for the latest three years available. Based on the company's own analysis of company financial data.
Frequency	Annual
Availability	General
Cost	
Comments	–
Address	Holmers Farm Way, High Wycombe HP12 4UL
Tel. / e-mail	01494 423689
Fax / Web site	01494 422332 www.dunandbrad.co.uk

339	**DURLACHER**
Title	**Durlacher Quarterly Internet Report**
Coverage	Internet user surveys and profiles, analysis of Internet usage, and web-site growth statistics with the focus on the UK. Based on surveys by the company.
Frequency	Quarterly
Availability	General
Cost	£195
Comments	Produces various other surveys and analysis of Internet developments and Internet companies.
Address	4 Chiswell Street, London EC1Y 4UP
Tel. / e-mail	0171 459 3613 nick@durlacher.com
Fax / Web site	0171 628 4306 www.durlacher.co.uk

340 ECONOMIST PUBLICATIONS LTD

Title	**United Kingdom Quarterly Economic Review**
Coverage	Commentary and statistics on general economic trends and business conditions in the UK. Based mainly on official sources.
Frequency	Quarterly
Availability	General
Cost	On request
Comments	Various other one-off and regular reports published on UK and international markets.
Address	15 Regent Street, London SW1Y 4LR
Tel. / e-mail	0171 830 1000 london@eiu.com
Fax / Web site	0171 499 9767 www.eiu.com

341 ELECTRIC VEHICLE ASSOCIATION OF GREAT BRITAIN

Title	**Yardstick Costs for Battery Electrics**
Coverage	Basic costs for electric vehicles used in warehouses and airports. Based on data collected by the association.
Frequency	Regular
Availability	General
Cost	On request
Comments	Also produces the EVA Manual.
Address	Alexandra House, Harrowden Road, Wellingborough NN8 5BD
Tel. / e-mail	01933 276618
Fax / Web site	01933 276618

342 ELECTRICITY ASSOCIATION

Title	**Electricity Statistics**
Coverage	Statistics on the production, consumption of electricity and electricity capacity.
Frequency	Annual
Availability	General
Cost	On request
Comments	Statistics on the industry are freely available on the web site.
Address	30 Millbank, London SW1P 4RD
Tel. / e-mail	0171 963 5700
Fax / Web site	0171 963 5959 www.electricity.org.uk

343 ELLIS, RICHARD

Title	**London Market Bulletin**
Coverage	Rents, values and property availability in various areas of London, e.g. Docklands, West End, City, Mid-Town etc. Based on data collected by the company.
Frequency	Quarterly
Availability	General
Cost	Free
Comments	Occasional reports on property trends and issues.
Address	Berkeley Square House, London W1X 6AN
Tel. / e-mail	0171 629 6290
Fax / Web site	0171 493 3734

344 ELLIS, RICHARD

Title	**Monthly Index**
Coverage	General commentary and statistics on property values and yields with a monthly index covering the latest 12 months. Based on data collected by the company.
Frequency	Monthly
Availability	General
Cost	Free
Comments	Occasional reports on property trends and issues.
Address	Berkeley Square House, London W1X 6AN
Tel. / e-mail	0171 629 6290
Fax / Web site	0171 493 3734

345 ELSEVIER SCIENCE LTD

Title	**Laxtons' Building Price Book**
Coverage	A listing of 250,000 price elements relevant in the development of small and large building works.
Frequency	Annual
Availability	General
Cost	£87.50
Comments	–
Address	The Boulevard, Langford Lane, Kidlington OX51GD
Tel. / e-mail	01865 843000 office@vtjw.demon.co.uk
Fax / Web site	

346	EMAP MEDIA LTD
Title	**British Rate and Data (BRAD)**
Coverage	Details of all UK media advertising rates, subscription rates, cover prices, circulation trends etc. Also general data on advertising expenditure, number of cinemas.
Frequency	Monthly
Availability	General
Cost	£130 per issue
Comments	–
Address	33-39 Bowling Green Lane, London EC1R 0DA
Tel. / e-mail	0171 505 8275
Fax / Web site	0171 505 8293

347	ENGINEERING EMPLOYERS' FEDERATION
Title	**Business Trends Survey**
Coverage	National and regional statistics on industry and sector trends based on surveys carried out by the regional associations of the federation. Commentary supports the data.
Frequency	Quarterly
Availability	General
Cost	£35
Comments	Produced in association with Alex Lawrie. Some summary statistics on the web site.
Address	Broadway House, Tothill Street, London SW1H 9NQ
Tel. / e-mail	0171 222 7777
Fax / Web site	0171 222 2782 www.eef.org.uk

348	ENGINEERING EMPLOYERS' FEDERATION
Title	**Engineering Economic Trends**
Coverage	Graphs, tables, and commentary on engineering output and sales and imports and exports. Some forecasts are included usually up to one year ahead and a commentary accompanies the data. Based on a combination of official and non-official sources.
Frequency	Twice yearly
Availability	General
Cost	£25
Comments	Some summary statistics on the web site.
Address	Broadway House, Tothill Street, London SW1H 9NQ
Tel. / e-mail	0171 222 7777
Fax / Web site	0171 222 2782 www.eef.org.uk

349	ENGLISH TOURIST BOARD
Title	**English Tourism: Facts and Figures**
Coverage	Summary of most frequently requested information on tourism.
Frequency	Regular
Availability	General
Cost	Free
Comments	–
Address	Research Deparment, Thames Tower, Black's Road, Hammersmith, London W6 9EL
Tel. / e-mail	0181 846 9000
Fax / Web site	0181 563 0302 www.travelengland.com

350	ENGLISH TOURIST BOARD
Title	**Insights: The Tourism Intelligence Marketing Service**
Coverage	Features market profiles, case studies, tourism intelligence and UK statistics.
Frequency	Every 2 months
Availability	General
Cost	£170 members, £195 non-members
Comments	–
Address	Research Deparment, Thames Tower, Black's Road, Hammersmith, London W6 9EL
Tel. / e-mail	0181 846 9000
Fax / Web site	0181 563 0302 www.travelengland.com

351	ENGLISH TOURIST BOARD
Title	**Regional Tourism Facts**
Coverage	Series of ten regional reports.
Frequency	Regular
Availability	General
Cost	£10 per report, £80 set
Comments	–
Address	Research Deparment, Thames Tower, Black's Road, Hammersmith, London W6 9EL
Tel. / e-mail	0181 846 9000
Fax / Web site	0181 563 0302 www.travelengland.com

352

Title **Sightseeing in the UK**

ENGLISH TOURIST BOARD

Coverage Statistics and trends for the UK's tourist attractions. Data on visits and revenues, overseas visitors, child admissions, charges, new attractions, demand relative to capacity, capital expenditure, advertising expenditure, and employment. Also details of the factors influencing sightseeing trends.

Frequency Annual

Availability General

Cost £22.50

Comments The regional tourist boards also publish statistics.

Address Research Department, Thames Tower, Black's Road, Hammersmith, London   W6 9EL

Tel. / e-mail 0181 846 9000

Fax / Web site 0181 563 0302   www.travelengland.com

353

ENGLISH TOURIST BOARD

Title **The Heritage Monitor**

Coverage Includes details of the numbers of historic buildings and conservation areas, admission charges, and visitor trends.

Frequency Annual

Availability General

Cost £17.50

Comments The regional tourist boards also publish statistics.

Address Research Department, Thames Tower, Black's Road, Hammersmith, London   W6 9EL

Tel. / e-mail 0181 846 9000

Fax / Web site 0181 563 0302   www.travelengland.com

354

ENGLISH TOURIST BOARD

Title **The UK Tourist Statistics**

Coverage An annual report based on the United Kingdom Tourism Survey (UKTS). Data includes the volume of UK residents' tourism, characteristics of their trips, and the people taking them. Subjects covered include purpose of trip, destinations, types of transport, accommodation used, categories of tourist spending. Also includes historical data.

Frequency Annual

Availability General

Cost £95

Comments The regional tourist boards also publish statistics.

Address Research Department, Thames Tower, Black's Road, Hammersmith, London   W6 9EL

Tel. / e-mail 0181 846 9000

Fax / Web site 0181 563 0302   www.travelengland.com

355 ENGLISH TOURIST BOARD

Title	**UK Occupancy Survey**
Coverage	Statistics relating to national occupancy levels in serviced accommodation, seasonal variations, regional differences, types of accommodation and length of stay.
Frequency	Regular
Availability	General
Cost	£25
Comments	–
Address	Research Deparment, Thames Tower, Black's Road, Hammersmith, London W6 9EL
Tel. / e-mail	0181 846 9000
Fax / Web site	0181 563 0302 www.travelengland.com

356 ENVIRONMENTAL TRANSPORT ASSOCIATION

Title	**Factsheets**
Coverage	Various factsheets relating to transport and the environment and based on various sources.
Frequency	Regular
Availability	General
Cost	Free
Comments	The association is relatively new, having been established in 1990.
Address	10 Church Street, Weybridge KT13 8RS
Tel. / e-mail	01932 828882 eta@eta.co.uk
Fax / Web site	01932 829015 www.eta.co.uk

357 EQUIFAX EUROPE

Title	**Define**
Coverage	Define is a Census-based geodemographic system including 1991 Census data, financial data from the Equifax database, unemployment statistics, and electoral roll variables.
Frequency	Continuous
Availability	General
Cost	On application, depending on the range and nature of the information required
Comments	–
Address	Sentinel House, 16 Harcourt Street, London W1H 2AE
Tel. / e-mail	0171 724 6116
Fax / Web site	0181 686 7777 www.equifax.com

358	
	ERDMAN LEWIS
Title	**Midsummer Retail Report**
Coverage	Analysis and statistics covering trends in the retailing sector and the retail property market. Based on data collected by the company.
Frequency	Annual
Availability	General
Cost	On request
Comments	Various other property reports and town reports produced.
Address	9 Marylebone Lane, London W1M 5FA
Tel. / e-mail	0171 629 8191
Fax / Web site	0171 487 1904

359	
	ERNST AND YOUNG ITEM CLUB
Title	**UK Economic Prospects**
Coverage	A detailed review of economic trends and prospects with data on all the main economic indicators.
Frequency	Quarterly
Availability	Item Club participants
Cost	£200 per issue
Comments	–
Address	4th Floor, Abbey House, 121 St Aldates, Oxford OX1 1HB
Tel. / e-mail	01865 268913 itemclub@oef.co.uk
Fax / Web site	01865 202533

360	
	ESA MARKET RESEARCH LTD
Title	**ESA Monthly Shopping Basket Report**
Coverage	A regular report analysing price differences between retailers during the current month and price differences over time. Based on a survey of 132 product categories at 85 outlets covering different retailing formats.
Frequency	Monthly
Availability	General
Cost	£195 per month
Comments	–
Address	4 Woodland Court, Soothouse Spring, St Albans AL3 6NR
Tel. / e-mail	01727 847572
Fax / Web site	01727 837337

361	**ESRC DATA ARCHIVE**
Title	**ESRC Data Archive**
Coverage	The archive holds surveys from various official and non-official sources including all the major ONS continuous surveys such as the Family Expenditure Survey, General Household Survey, National Food Survey plus many non-official surveys from organisations such as NOP, Gallup, Research Services etc.
Frequency	Continuous
Availability	General
Cost	On request
Comments	Data can be supplied in various formats including diskette, magnetic tape, and CD-ROM. Web site has details of services.
Address	Wivenhoe Park, University of Essex, Colchester CO4 3SO
Tel. / e-mail	01206 872001 archive@essex.ac.uk
Fax / Web site	01206 872003 www.dawww.essex.co.uk

362	**ESTATES GAZETTE**
Title	**Figures and Figures**
Coverage	General data relating to the property market including house prices, farm prices, rent index, housing starts and completions, land prices, property yields, interest rates. Based mainly on various non-official sources supported by some official statistics.
Frequency	Monthly in a weekly journal
Availability	General
Cost	£118, £2.10 for single issue
Comments	–
Address	Estates Gazette Ltd, 151 Wardour Street, London W1V 4BN
Tel. / e-mail	0171 437 0141 info@egi.co.uk
Fax / Web site	0171 437 0295 www.egi.co.uk

363	**EULER TRADE INDEMNITY**
Title	**Half-Yearly Economic Bulletin**
Coverage	Economic trends and forecasts up to two years ahead. Based on research by the company.
Frequency	Twice per annum
Availability	General
Cost	Twice yearly
Comments	–
Address	1 Canada Square, London E14 5DX
Tel. / e-mail	0171 512 9333
Fax / Web site	0171 512 9186 www.tradeindemnity.com

364

Title	**EULER TRADE INDEMNITY** **Monthly Economic Bulletin**
Coverage	The UK economy and industrial performance by major sectors. Commentary and statistics from Central Government and the company.
Frequency	Monthly
Availability	General
Cost	Free
Comments	–
Address	1 Canada Square, London E14 5DX
Tel. / e-mail	0171 512 9333
Fax / Web site	0171 512 9186 www.tradeindemnity.com

365

Title	**EULER TRADE INDEMNITY** **Quarterly Financial Trends Survey**
Coverage	Financial review of major sectors with details of late payments. Based on data collected by the company.
Frequency	Quarterly
Availability	General
Cost	Free
Comments	–
Address	1 Canada Square, London E14 5DX
Tel. / e-mail	0171 512 9333
Fax / Web site	0171 512 9186 www.tradeindemnity.com

366

Title	**EUREST** **Eurest Lunchtime Report**
Coverage	An annual review of the eating habits of workers and other activities during lunch times. Based on commissioned research.
Frequency	Annual
Availability	General
Cost	Free
Comments	–
Address	Queen's Wharf, Queen Caroline Street, London W6 9RJ
Tel. / e-mail	0181 741 1541
Fax / Web site	0181 600 2687

367	EURODIRECT DATABASE MARKETING
Title	**Demograf/CAMEO UK**
Coverage	Demograf is a Windows-based GIS marketing system incorporating demographic data. CAMEO UK is a demographic classification system based on 1991 Census data with additional information from the electoral roll.
Frequency	Continuous
Availability	General
Cost	On application, and depending on the range and nature of the information required
Comments	–
Address	Onward House, 2 Baptist Place, Bradford BD1 2PS
Tel. / e-mail	01274 737144 sales@eddm.demon-co.uk
Fax / Web site	01274 741126 www.eurodirect.co.uk

368	EUROMONITOR
Title	**Euromonitor Market and Media Guide**
Coverage	A compilation of statistics covering economic trends, regional data, consumer trends, advertising, labour market data, transport, key markets etc. Based on Euromonitor data and statistics from other sources.
Frequency	Monthly
Availability	General
Cost	£450 (annual subscription to 'Market Research Great Britain')
Comments	Included as part of 'Market Research Great Britain'. Various consumer reports on international markets also produced.
Address	60-61 Britton Street, London EC1M 5NA
Tel. / e-mail	0171 251 8024 info@euromonitor.com
Fax / Web site	0171 608 3149 www.euromonitor.com

EUROPEAN COSMETIC MARKETS

369

Title	**Market Reviews**
Coverage	Market reports are scheduled throughout the year and each report has a review of UK trends, alongside reviews of the other major European markets. The 1995 schedule is bathroom products (January), skin care (February), men's lines (March), sun care (April), women's fragrances (May), body care (June), deodorants (August), hair care (September), hair styling (October), colour cosmetics (November), oral hygiene (December). Mainly based on original consumer research.
Frequency	Monthly in a monthly journal
Availability	General
Cost	£550
Comments	–
Address	Wilmington Publishing Ltd, Wilmington House, Church Hill, Wilmington, Dartford DA2 7EF
Tel. / e-mail	01322 277788 wbp@wilmington.co.uk
Fax / Web site	01322 276474 www.cosmeticsbusiness.com

EUROPEAN PLASTICS NEWS

370

Title	**UK Plastics Annual Review**
Coverage	A commentary on the market performance of plastics raw materials in the UK with tables on the consumption of major plastics. A general outlook for the coming year is given.
Frequency	Annual in a monthly journal
Availability	General
Cost	£120, £13 per issue
Comments	–
Address	EMAP Maclaren Ltd, 19th Floor, Leon House, 233 High Street, Croydon CR0 9XT
Tel. / e-mail	0181 688 7788
Fax / Web site	0181 688 8375 www.maclaren.emap.co.uk

EXHIBITION VENUES ASSOCIATION

371

Title	**UK Exhibition Facts**
Coverage	Survey of exhibition visitors, exhibitor spending, exhibition numbers, international tourism. Data usually covers the last three years.
Frequency	Annual
Availability	General
Cost	£95
Comments	Produced by Exhibition Audience Audits Ltd.
Address	Mallards, Five Ashes, Mayfield TN20 6NN
Tel. / e-mail	01435 872244 eva@martex.co.uk
Fax / Web site	01435 872696

372	**EXPERIAN LTD**
Title	**Corporate Health Check**
Coverage	A review of corporate trends in the UK and the financial well-being of UK industry. Based on data collected by CCN from the financial statements of the UK's top 1,000 companies.
Frequency	Regular
Availability	General
Cost	On request
Comments	–
Address	Abbey House, Abbeyfield Road, Nottingham NG7 2SW
Tel. / e-mail	0115 9860801
Fax / Web site	0115 9610888 www.experian.com

373	**FACTORS AND DISCOUNTERS ASSOCIATION**
Title	**Annual Review**
Coverage	Revenues for UK factors and discounters from both their domestic and international businesses.
Frequency	Annual
Availability	General
Cost	Free
Comments	Statistics freely available on the web site and the Annual Review can be downloaded.
Address	Boston House, The Little Green, Richmond TW9 1QE
Tel. / e-mail	0181 332 9955 Christine.tout@factors.org.uk
Fax / Web site	0181 332 2585 www.factors.org.uk

374	**FACTS INTERNATIONAL LTD**
Title	**Telefacts**
Coverage	An omnibus survey of 1,000 adults each month. It is a telephone survey covering the whole of the UK.
Frequency	Monthly
Availability	General
Cost	Varies according to questions and analysis
Comments	Results available on disc.
Address	Facts Centre, Kennington Road, Ashford TN24 0TD
Tel. / e-mail	01233 643551 100141.322@compuserve.com
Fax / Web site	01233 626950 www.Facts.International.Ltd.uk

FARMERS' WEEKLY

375

Title	**Farmers' Weekly**
Coverage	Land value prices analysed over the previous six months. Includes a county-by-county analysis and the report is based on various sources.
Frequency	Weekly
Availability	General
Cost	£1.40 per issue
Comments	The publication is produced jointly by 'Farmers' Weekly' and the Royal Institution of Chartered Surveyors.
Address	Quadrant House, The Quadrant, Sutton SM2 5AS
Tel. / e-mail	0181 652 4911 farmers.weekly@rbi.co.uk
Fax / Web site	0181 652 4005 www.fwi.co.uk

FAST FACTS LTD

376

Title	**Factfinder**
Coverage	CD-ROM data base allowing access to all surveys published in 'Fast Food Facts' since 1985.
Frequency	Monthly
Availability	General
Cost	£2,200 (overall service cost)
Comments	–
Address	Lower Green, Walgrave NN6 9QF
Tel. / e-mail	01604 781 392 fastfacts@btinternet.com
Fax / Web site	01604 781 392

FAST FACTS LTD

377

Title	**Fast Food Facts**
Coverage	Regular reports on various food sectors including meat, bakery products, savoury products, chocolate and sugar confectionery. Food sectors can be added when specified by the client.
Frequency	Monthly
Availability	General
Cost	£2,200 (overall service cost)
Comments	–
Address	Lower Green, Walgrave NN6 9QF
Tel. / e-mail	01604 781 392 fastfacts@btinternet.com
Fax / Web site	01604 781 392

378	**FAST FACTS LTD**
Title	**Food Trends**
Coverage	Household consumption trends over the last ten years for over 200 product categories. Also includes projections for the next two years.
Frequency	Quarterly
Availability	General
Cost	£2,200 (overall service cost)
Comments	–
Address	Lower Green, Walgrave NN6 9QF
Tel. / e-mail	01604 781 392 fastfacts@btinternet.com
Fax / Web site	01604 781 392

379	**FEDERATION OF BAKERS**
Title	**Annual Report**
Coverage	Includes a section with statistics on production trends in the UK bakery industry.
Frequency	Annual
Availability	General
Cost	Free
Comments	–
Address	20 Bedford Square, London WC1B 3HF
Tel. / e-mail	0171 580 4252
Fax / Web site	0171 255 1389

380	**FEDERATION OF BRITISH CREMATION AUTHORITIES**
Title	**Annual Report**
Coverage	Includes cremation statistics for individual crematoria over a five year period. Based on the federation's own survey. A large amount of supporting text accompanies the data.
Frequency	Annual
Availability	General
Cost	Free
Comments	–
Address	41 Salisbury Road, Carshalton SM5 3HA
Tel. / e-mail	0181 669 4521
Fax / Web site	

381	**FEDERATION OF MASTER BUILDERS**
Title	**FMB State of Trade Survey**
Coverage	Results of a survey of member firms in England and Wales with data on workload for the previous quarter and predictions for the coming quarter. Various topical questions are also included in each survey. Text supports the data.
Frequency	Quarterly
Availability	Members only
Cost	On application
Comments	Also produces irregular factsheets.
Address	14 Great James Street, London WC1N 3DP
Tel. / e-mail	0171 242 7583
Fax / Web site	0171 404 0296 www.fmb.org.uk

382	**FEDERATION OF OPTHALMIC & DISPENSING OPTICIANS**
Title	**Optics at a Glance**
Coverage	General statistics on optics including the number of opticians, average spectacle prices. Based on a combination of the federation's own survey and Central Government data. Some supporting commentary.
Frequency	Annual
Availability	General
Cost	Free
Comments	Produced as a double-sided A4 page.
Address	113 Eastbourne Mews, London W2 6LQ
Tel. / e-mail	0171 258 0240 fod@btinternet.com
Fax / Web site	0171 724 1175 www.fodo.com

383	**FEDERATION OF RECRUITMENT AND EMPLOYMENT SERVICES**
Title	**FRES Recruitment Industry Survey**
Coverage	UK sales by the recruitment industry and total industry turnover. Also data broken down by temporary/permament workers. Based on a survey by the federation.
Frequency	Annual
Availability	General
Cost	On request
Comments	Some basic statistics from the survey freely available on the web site.
Address	36-38 Mortimer Street, London W1N 7RB
Tel. / e-mail	0171 323 4300 info@fres.co.uk
Fax / Web site	0171 255 2878 www.fres.co.uk

384	**FEDERATION OF SMALL BUSINESSES**
Title	**Small Business Surveys**
Coverage	Various regular surveys of the small business sector including a crime and small business survey and payment survey. Based mainly on member surveys.
Frequency	Regular
Availability	On request
Cost	On request
Comments	A range of small business statistics on the web site.
Address	2 Catherine Place, London SW1E 6HF
Tel. / e-mail	0171 233 7900 london@fsb.org.uk
Fax / Web site	0171 233 7899 www.fsb.org.uk

385	**FEDERATION OF THE ELECTRONICS INDUSTRY (FEI)**
Title	**Interface**
Coverage	Contains regular statistics on the electronics industry and markets in the UK based on the federation's own survey plus government data.
Frequency	6 issues per year
Availability	Usually only available to members
Cost	Free
Comments	The federation was only established in 1993.
Address	Russell Square House, 10-12 Russell Square, London WC1B 5EE
Tel. / e-mail	0171 331 2000 feedback@fei.org.uk
Fax / Web site	0171 331 2040 www.fei.org.uk/fei

386	**FEDERATION OF THE ELECTRONICS INDUSTRY (FEI)**
Title	**The FEI Review**
Coverage	Mainly text describing the activities of the federation but the 'Focus on the Industry' section includes graphs and tables on sector value, and data on the components and business equipment sectors. Based on data collected by the federation.
Frequency	Annual
Availability	General
Cost	Free
Comments	The federation was only established in 1993.
Address	Russell Square House, 10-12 Russell Square, London WC1B 5EE
Tel. / e-mail	0171 331 2000 feedback@fei.org.uk
Fax / Web site	0171 331 2040 www.fei.org.uk/fei

387

FERTILISER MANUFACTURERS' ASSOCIATION

Title	**Fertiliser Review**
Coverage	Covers area of crops, consumption of inorganic fertilisers, straight fertilisers, and compound fertilisers. Also concentration, application rates, and usage of compound fertilisers. Based mainly on the association's own research with additional data from Central Government. Most of the review is made up of text.
Frequency	Annual
Availability	General
Cost	£5
Comments	Basic statistics covering consumption, prices on the web site.
Address	Greenhill House, Thorpe Wood, Peterborough PE3 6GT
Tel. / e-mail	01733 331303
Fax / Web site	01733 333617 www.fma.org.uk

388

FINANCE AND LEASING ASSOCIATION

Title	**Annual Report**
Coverage	Contains commentary and statistics on trends in the credit and leasing market with most tables giving figures for the last two years. Based on transactions by FLA members.
Frequency	Annual
Availability	General
Cost	Free
Comments	–
Address	18 Upper Grosvenor Street, London W1X 9PB
Tel. / e-mail	0171 491 2783
Fax / Web site	0171 629 0396

389

FISH TRADER

Title	**Imports and Exports**
Coverage	Imports and exports of fish by volume and value broken down by type of fish. A short commentary accompanies the data which is based on official statistics.
Frequency	Quarterly in a monthly journal
Availability	General
Cost	£49.95
Comments	–
Address	Oban Times Ltd, Royston House, Caroline Park, Edinburgh EH5 1QJ
Tel. / e-mail	0131 551 2942 editor@specialpublications.co.uk
Fax / Web site	0131 551 2938

390		FLETCHER RESEARCH
Title		**Internet Adwatch**
Coverage		Tracking survey of over 1,500 advertisers on major UK-focused web sites.
Frequency		Ad-hoc
Availability		General
Cost		On application
Comments		Available as a subscription service or bespoke research.
Address		17 Rathbone Street, London W1P 1AF
Tel. / e-mail		0171 631 0202 info@fletch.co.uk
Fax / Web site		0171 631 5252 www.fletch.co.uk
391		FLETCHER RESEARCH
Title		**UK Internet Survey 1999**
Coverage		Survey of 300 prominent UK commercial web sites.
Frequency		Annual
Availability		General
Cost		£495
Comments		–
Address		17 Rathbone Street, London W1P 1AF
Tel. / e-mail		0171 631 0202 info@fletch.co.uk
Fax / Web site		0171 631 5252 www.fletch.co.uk
392		FLETCHER RESEARCH
Title		**UK Internet User Monitor**
Coverage		Industry standard data on internet users in the UK.
Frequency		Ad-hoc
Availability		General
Cost		On application
Comments		Available as a full market research report, a site specific report or bespoke market research.
Address		17 Rathbone Street, London W1P 1AF
Tel. / e-mail		0171 631 0202 info@fletch.co.uk
Fax / Web site		0171 631 5252 www.fletch.co.uk

393

	FLOUR ADVISORY BUREAU
Title	**Flour**
Coverage	A guide to flour in the UK with some basic data.
Frequency	Regular
Availability	General
Cost	Free
Comments	–
Address	21 Arlington Street, London SW1A 1RN
Tel. / e-mail	0171 493 2521 info@fabflour.co.uk
Fax / Web site	0171 493 6785 www.fabflour.co.uk

394

	FLOWER BUSINESS INTERNATIONAL
Title	**Annual Statistics**
Coverage	Cultivation and production data on non-edible horticultural products. Based on trade association data.
Frequency	Annual in a monthly journal
Availability	General
Cost	£41, or £2.50 per issue
Comments	–
Address	Harling House, 47-51 Great Suffolk Street, London SE1 0BS
Tel. / e-mail	0171 261 0717
Fax / Web site	0171 261 9252

395

	FLYMO LTD
Title	**Power Lawnmower Statistics**
Coverage	Tables and graphs on the power lawnmower market with data on total market size, by type of lawnmower, brand shares, price trends, and lawn numbers. Based on data from market research sources.
Frequency	Annual
Availability	General
Cost	Free
Comments	–
Address	Aycliffe Industrial Estate, Preston Road, Newton Aycliffe DL5 6UP
Tel. / e-mail	01325 300303
Fax / Web site	01325 310339

	FOOD FROM BRITAIN
396	
Title	**Annual Report**
Coverage	Includes statistics on food exports and the key export markets for UK food companies plus general details of trends in the industry. Based primarily on official statistics.
Frequency	Annual
Availability	General
Cost	Free
Comments	Summary trade data on the web site.
Address	123 Buckingham Palace Road, London SW1W 9SA
Tel. / e-mail	0171 233 5111 uk@foodfrombritain.com
Fax / Web site	0171 233 9515 www.foodfrombritain.com

	FOODSERVICE INTELLIGENCE
397	
Title	**Catering Forecasts**
Coverage	Short-term forecasts for the UK catering industry based on research carried out amongst 700 caterers with trends given sector by sector.
Frequency	Annual
Availability	General
Cost	On request
Comments	Also publishes various one-off and occasional reports on the catering market.
Address	84 Uxbridge Road, London W13 8RA
Tel. / e-mail	0181 840 5252 scampoin@foodserviceintell.com
Fax / Web site	0181 840 6173 www.foodserviceintell.com

	FOODSERVICE INTELLIGENCE
398	
Title	**Catering Industry Population File**
Coverage	A study of the structure of the catering industry giving number of outlets, value of caterers' food purchases, outlet sizes, number of meals served, sector buying concentration, and a regional analysis. Eleven catering sectors are covered in detail with historical trends over a ten-year period. Based on Marketpower research, non-official sources, and some official statistics.
Frequency	Annual
Availability	General
Cost	On request
Comments	A disc containing key data can also be supplied with the report for an additional £25. Various other one-off and occasional reports on the catering market are also published.
Address	84 Uxbridge Road, London W13 8RA
Tel. / e-mail	0181 840 5252 scampion@foodserviceintell.com
Fax / Web site	0181 840 6173 www.foodserviceintell.com

399		FOODSERVICE INTELLIGENCE
Title		**Foodservice Barometer**
Coverage		A survey of meals served by caterers in each of nine sectors: hotels, restaurants, public houses, cafes, take-aways, leisure, staff catering, health care, education. Also includes a 'balance of confidence' indicator and a special feature in each issue.
Frequency		Monthly
Availability		General
Cost		On request
Comments		Also publishes various one-off and occasional reports on the catering market.
Address		84 Uxbridge Road, London W13 8RA
Tel. / e-mail		0181 799 3200 scampion@foodserviceintell.com
Fax / Web site		0181 566 2100 www.foodserviceintell.com

400		FOOTBALL TRUST
Title		**Digest of Football Statistics**
Coverage		Details of attendances, match receipts, other financial data, miscellaneous data. Separate section on Scottish football and section also on the Football Trust. Many tables have historical series. Based mainly on non-official sources.
Frequency		Annual
Availability		General
Cost		On request
Comments		–
Address		Centre for Football Research, University of Leicester, University Road, Leicester LE1 7RH
Tel. / e-mail		01533 522741
Fax / Web site		

401		FORUM FOR PRIVATE BUSINESS
Title		**Banks' Attitudes to Borrowing**
Coverage		A regular survey of UK banks' attitudes to borrowings with a review of general attitudes torwards specific sectors. Data for the latest quarter and earlier quarters.
Frequency		Quarterly
Availability		General
Cost		On request
Comments		Also publishes a regular Crime and Small Business report.
Address		Ruskin Chambers, Drury Lane, Knutsford WA16 6HA
Tel. / e-mail		01565 634467 fpbltdcommercial@fpb.co.uk
Fax / Web site		01565 650059 www.fpbltd.co.uk

402 FORVUS

Title	**UK Imports and Exports**
Coverage	Detailed statistics on UK product imports and exports, with data on total trade, trading partners, port of entry and exit. Appointed as an official agent of HM Customs and Excise.
Frequency	Monthly
Availability	General
Cost	Depends on the amount of information required
Comments	Available in various machine readable formats.
Address	Forvus House, 53 Clapham Common, South Side, London SW4 9BX
Tel. / e-mail	0171 498 2602
Fax / Web site	0171 498 1939

403 FOUNDRY TRADE JOURNAL

Title	**Metal Prices**
Coverage	Prices of ferro-alloy and other metals and non-ferrous metals by type in the UK. Based on various non-official sources.
Frequency	Twice a month in a twice-monthly journal
Availability	General
Cost	£144.53, £16.50 per issue
Comments	–
Address	DMG Business Media Ltd, 2 Queensway, Redhill RH1 1QS
Tel. / e-mail	01737 768611 jmitchell@dmg.co.uk
Fax / Web site	01737 855476 www.dmg.co.uk

404 FRASER OF ALLENDER INSTITUTE

Title	**Quarterly Economic Bulletin**
Coverage	Trends and outlook for the Scottish economy with individual reviews of industrial performance, service sector, labour market, and the regions. Also some feature articles. Based mainly on Central Government data and a supporting commentary.
Frequency	Quarterly
Availability	General
Cost	£60
Comments	–
Address	Strathclyde University, 100 Cathedral Street, Glasgow G4 0LN
Tel. / e-mail	0141 552 4400
Fax / Web site	

405	FRASER OF ALLENDER INSTITUTE
Title	**Scottish Chambers' Business Survey**
Coverage	Trends in the Scottish economy and business sectors based on returns from a sample of members of Scottish chambers of commerce.
Frequency	Quarterly
Availability	General
Cost	On request
Comments	–
Address	Strathclyde University, Cathedral Street, Glasgow G4 0LN
Tel. / e-mail	0141 552 4400
Fax / Web site	

406	FREIGHT TRANSPORT ASSOCIATION
Title	**Manager's Guide to Distribution Costs**
Coverage	Statistics on road transport costs including wages, vehicle operating costs, haulage rates. Actual costs and indices are included. Based on the association's own survey with supporting commentary.
Frequency	Annual
Availability	Members
Cost	£100
Comments	–
Address	Hermes House, St John's Road, Tunbridge Wells TN4 9UZ
Tel. / e-mail	01892 526171 inquiries@fta.org.uk
Fax / Web site	01892 534989 www.fta.co.uk

407	FREIGHT TRANSPORT ASSOCIATION
Title	**Quarterly Transport Activity Survey**
Coverage	A review of freight transport by air, road, sea, and rail with data on demand, markets, prices, costs, safety, accidents, and forecasts. Based on Census returns from members, data from the Department of Transport, and other sources.
Frequency	Quarterly
Availability	General
Cost	Free
Comments	–
Address	Hermes House, St John's Road, Tunbridge Wells TN4 9UZ
Tel. / e-mail	01892 526171 inquiries@fta.org.uk
Fax / Web site	01892 534989 www.fta.co.uk

	408	FRESH FRUIT AND VEGETABLE INFORMATION BUREAU
Title		**UK Fresh Fruit and Vegetable Market Review**
Coverage		Commentary and statistics on the fresh produce market with sections on specific fruits and vegetables.
Frequency		Annual
Availability		General
Cost		Free
Comments		Latest issue produced in association with 'Checkout Fresh' magazine. Available from public relations consultants, Cameron Choat & Partners, at the address below.
Address		126-128 Cromwell Road, London SW7 4ET
Tel. / e-mail		0171 373 7734
Fax / Web site		0171 373 3926 www.ffvib.co.uk

	409	FTSE INTERNATIONAL
Title		**UK Monthly Review**
Coverage		Data regularly updated on indices, securities, sector weightings etc.
Frequency		Monthly
Availability		General
Cost		On request
Comments		–
Address		St Alphage House, Podium Floor, 2 Fore Street, London EC2Y 5DA
Tel. / e-mail		0171 448 1810 info@ftse.com
Fax / Web site		0171 448 1804 www.ftse.com

	410	FULLERMARKETS LTD
Title		**Commodities**
Coverage		Trends and prices in UK and USA futures markets. Covers over 30 different commodities in the food, grain, livestock/meat, industrial, metals, and finance sectors. Based on the company's data.
Frequency		Weekly and monthly
Availability		General
Cost		£835 weekly, £250 monthly, £33 per issue
Comments		–
Address		7 Swallow Street, London W1R 7HD
Tel. / e-mail		0171 439 4961 research@fullermarkets.com
Fax / Web site		0171 439 4966 www.fullermarkets.com

411

	FULLERMARKETS LTD
Title	**UK Point and Figure Library**
Coverage	Comprehensive coverage of the UK Stock Market by market sector. Over 500 charts and tables cover industry group performance, share indices, British funds, money rates, and general indicators. Based on various sources and analysis by the company.
Frequency	Weekly and monthly
Availability	General
Cost	£1,315 weekly, £575 monthly
Comments	–
Address	7 Swallow Street, London W1R 7HD
Tel. / e-mail	0171 439 4961 research@fullermarkets.com
Fax / Web site	0171 439 4966 www.fullermarkets.com

412

	FURNITURE INDUSTRY RESEARCH ASSOCIATION
Title	**FIRA Bulletin**
Coverage	Includes statistics updating the annual publication (see previous entry) including sales, imports, exports, prices etc. Mainly based on Central Government data.
Frequency	Quarterly
Availability	General
Cost	On request
Comments	Also produces statistics on the international furniture market.
Address	Maxwell Road, Stevenage SG1 2EW
Tel. / e-mail	01438 777700 fira@ttlchiltern.co.uk
Fax / Web site	01438 777800 www.fira.co.uk

413

	FURNITURE INDUSTRY RESEARCH ASSOCIATION
Title	**Furniture Industry in the UK - A Statistical Digest**
Coverage	Statistics include turnover, sales, deliveries, consumption, imports, exports, prices, and advertising. Mainly based on Central Government data, supplemented by association and non-official sources.
Frequency	Annual
Availability	General
Cost	£30, reduced price to members
Comments	Also produces statistics on the international market.
Address	Maxwell Road, Stevenage SG1 2EW
Tel. / e-mail	01438 777700 fira@ttlchiltern.co.uk
Fax / Web site	01438 777800 www.fira.co.uk

414	GALLUP ORGANISATION
Title	**Gallup Omnibus**
Coverage	Sample surveys of around 1,000 adults form the basis of this omnibus survey. Based on face-to-face interviews with adults.
Frequency	2 or 3 times a week
Availability	General
Cost	On request
Comments	Results available in various machine-readable formats.
Address	Drapers Court, Kingston Hall Road, Kingston-upon-Thames KT1 2BG
Tel. / e-mail	0181 939 7000
Fax / Web site	0181 939 7039

415	GALLUP ORGANISATION
Title	**Gallup Political Index**
Coverage	Summary data on the various opinion polls carried out by Gallup on political, economic, and social issues.
Frequency	Monthly
Availability	General
Cost	On application
Comments	Gallup data also available in machine readable formats.
Address	Drapers Court, Kingston Hall Road, Kingston-upon-Thames KT1 2BG
Tel. / e-mail	0181 939 7000
Fax / Web site	0181 939 7039

416	GARDNER MERCHANT
Title	**Gardner Merchant Survey of Children's Eating Habits**
Coverage	A survey of eating habits of children including eating at school, snacks etc. Based on commissioned research.
Frequency	Regular
Availability	General
Cost	£75
Comments	The latest edition was published in 1998.
Address	Kenley House, Kenley Lane, Kenley CR8 5ED
Tel. / e-mail	01793 512112
Fax / Web site	01793 615075 www.gardnermerchant.com

417

Title	**Geoplan**

GEOPLAN (UK) LTD

Coverage — A service supplying statistical and geographical data, and the provision of Geographical Information Systems. Based on Census data and the postcode address file.

Frequency — Continuous

Availability — General

Cost — On application, and depending on the range and nature of the information required

Comments — –

Address — 14-15 Regent Parade, Harrogate HG1 5AW

Tel. / e-mail — 01423 569538

Fax / Web site — 01423 525545

418

GFK GREAT BRITAIN LTD

Title — **DIY-Trak**

Coverage — A retail audit covering products sold in DIY outlets in the UK, mainly DIY and gardening products. Research carried out by the company.

Frequency — Continuous

Availability — Participants

Cost — On request

Comments — –

Address — 22 Stephenson Way, London NW1 2HZ

Tel. / e-mail — 0171 383 2939

Fax / Web site — 0171 383 2833   www.gfkms.co.uk

419

GFK GREAT BRITAIN LTD

Title — **Home Audit**

Coverage — A quarterly survey of around 35,000 households examining ownership and purchasing of consumer durables. Based on research by the company.

Frequency — Quarterly

Availability — General

Cost — On request

Comments — –

Address — 22 Stephenson Way, London NW1 2HZ

Tel. / e-mail — 0171 383 2939

Fax / Web site — 0171 383 2833   www.gfkms.co.uk

420

Title	GFK GREAT BRITAIN LTD **Home Trak**
Coverage	A monthly survey of around 6,000 households based on a diary kept by the households. Data on purchasing and household spending.
Frequency	Monthly
Availability	General
Cost	On request
Comments	–
Address	22 Stephenson Way, London NW1 2HZ
Tel. / e-mail	0171 383 2939
Fax / Web site	0171 383 2833 www.gfkms.co.uk

421

Title	GFK GREAT BRITAIN LTD **LEK-Trak**
Coverage	A retail audit covering electrical products and domestic electronic appliances. Research carried out by the company.
Frequency	Monthly
Availability	Participants
Cost	On request
Comments	–
Address	22 Stephenson Way, London NW1 2HZ
Tel. / e-mail	0171 383 2939
Fax / Web site	0171 383 2833 www.gfkms.co.uk

422

Title	GFK GREAT BRITAIN LTD **Office Trak**
Coverage	A retail audit of the office consumables markets.
Frequency	Monthly
Availability	General
Cost	On request
Comments	–
Address	22 Stephenson Way, London NW1 2HZ
Tel. / e-mail	0171 383 2939
Fax / Web site	0171 383 2833 www.gfkms.co.uk

423	**GFK GREAT BRITAIN LTD**
Title	**Photo-Trak**
Coverage	A continuous audit of the photographic market in the UK. Research by the company.
Frequency	Monthly
Availability	Participants
Cost	On request
Comments	–
Address	22 Stephenson Way, London NW1 2HZ
Tel. / e-mail	0171 383 2939
Fax / Web site	0171 383 2833 www.gfkms.co.uk

424	**GIN AND VODKA ASSOCIATION OF GREAT BRITAIN**
Title	**Annual Report**
Coverage	Gives production of gin, home trade sales and export sales to EU countries and non-EU countries for the last four six-month periods. Based on returns from members.
Frequency	Annual
Availability	Members
Cost	Free
Comments	–
Address	Winchester House, Winchester Street, Andover SP10 2ET
Tel. / e-mail	01264 337011 ginvodka@lineone.net
Fax / Web site	01264 350219

425	**GLOBUS OFFICE WORLD**
Title	**Office World Quarterly Small Business Survey**
Coverage	A survey of investment and financial arrangements and trends for small businesses in the UK. Based on a survey commissioned by the company.
Frequency	Quarterly
Availability	General
Cost	On request
Comments	–
Address	WSM Wordsworth, 37-39 London End, Beaconsfield HP9 2HW
Tel. / e-mail	01494 674101
Fax / Web site	01494 674202

426	GMAP LTD
Title	**GMAP**
Coverage	A geodemographic service based primarily on the 1991 Census population data.
Frequency	Continuous
Availability	General
Cost	On application, and depending on the range and nature of the information required
Comments	–
Address	Cromer Terrace, Leeds LS2 9JU
Tel. / e-mail	0113 2446164
Fax / Web site	0113 2433173

427	GROCER
Title	**Grocer Price List**
Coverage	A supplement usually produced on the first Saturday of each month giving detailed prices for various foods and grocery products.
Frequency	Monthly supplement to a weekly journal
Availability	General
Cost	£45 (subscription to The Grocer)
Comments	'The Grocer' also has regular market surveys of the main food and non-food markets.
Address	William Reed Publishing Ltd, Broadfield Park, Crawley RH11 9RT
Tel. / e-mail	01293 613400
Fax / Web site	01293 610310

428	GROCER
Title	**Market Figures**
Coverage	Prices of various foods including vegetables, meat, salad, cheese, egg, butter, lard etc. Based on various non-official sources with some supporting text.
Frequency	Weekly in a weekly journal
Availability	General
Cost	£45
Comments	'The Grocer' also has regular market surveys of the main food and non-food markets.
Address	William Reed Publishing Ltd, Broadfield Park, Crawley RH11 9RT
Tel. / e-mail	01293 613400
Fax / Web site	01293 613156

429

	HALIFAX
Title	**Halifax House Price Index**
Coverage	Commentary plus indices and average values for different types of houses. Also includes a regional analysis and additional data for first time buyers, mortgage demand etc. Based on Halifax records.
Frequency	Quarterly
Availability	General
Cost	Free
Comments	The separate regional price index publication is now included in this publication.
Address	Trinity Road, Halifax HX1 2RG
Tel. / e-mail	01422 333333
Fax / Web site	01422 332043

430

	HARDWARE TODAY
Title	**Today's Trading Trends**
Coverage	Performance trends in various hardware sectors based on a summary of the results of a survey of members of the British Hardware Federation.
Frequency	Quarterly in a monthly journal
Availability	General
Cost	On request
Comments	–
Address	Indices Publications Ltd, 18 Cornbrook, Warwick CV35 9HP
Tel. / e-mail	01926 641700 htoday@indices.moose.co.uk
Fax / Web site	01926 641700

431

	HARRIS RESEARCH
Title	**55+ Omnibus**
Coverage	A quarterly face-to-face survey based on a sample of 1,500 adults aged 55 and over. A specialist service for those whose products and services are targeted at the 'grey' market.
Frequency	Quarterly
Availability	General
Cost	On application
Comments	–
Address	34-38 Hill Rise, Richmond TW10 6UA
Tel. / e-mail	0181 332 9898 general@harris-research.co.uk
Fax / Web site	0181 948 6335 www.harrisuk@org.1.demon.co.uk

432

HARRIS RESEARCH

Harris Response

Title	**Harris Response**
Coverage	A weekly omnibus survey involving face-to-face interviews with 1,000 adults. Demographic breakdowns and detailed information on purchasing, consumer attitudes etc.
Frequency	Weekly
Availability	General
Cost	On application
Comments	–
Address	34-38 Hill Rise, Richmond TW10 6UA
Tel. / e-mail	0181 332 9898 general@harris-research.co.uk
Fax / Web site	0181 948 6335 www.harrisuk@org.1.demon.co.uk

433

HARRIS RESEARCH

Young Persons' Omnibus

Title	**Young Persons' Omnibus**
Coverage	A quarterly omnibus survey of 1,500 young people aged between 12 and 24. Face-to-face interviews collect information on the purchasing trends, attitudes, and preferences of this consumer group.
Frequency	Quarterly
Availability	General
Cost	On application
Comments	–
Address	34-38 Hill Rise, Richmond TW10 6UA
Tel. / e-mail	0181 332 9898 general@harris-research.co.uk
Fax / Web site	0181 948 6335 www.harrisuk@org.1.demon.co.uk

434

HAY MANAGEMENT CONSULTANTS LTD

Accountants and Taxation Specialists

Title	**Accountants and Taxation Specialists**
Coverage	A salary and benefits survey of accountants and related professionals based around 19 job levels and sampling over 500 organisations. Based on a survey by the company.
Frequency	Annual
Availability	Participants
Cost	£925
Comments	–
Address	52 Grosvenor Gardens, London SW1W 0AU
Tel. / e-mail	0171 881 7000 uk_infobus@haygroup.com
Fax / Web site	0171 881 7100 www.haygroup.com

435	HAY MANAGEMENT CONSULTANTS LTD
Title	**Boardroom Guide - A Survey of Directors' Remuneration**
Coverage	A survey focusing on the remuneration of top management and directors with data on over 4,000 top jobs from over 400 companies. Based on salary data collected by the company with additional data on share options, cars, pensions and other benefits.
Frequency	Annual
Availability	Participants
Cost	£1,750
Comments	–
Address	52 Grosvenor Gardens, London SW1W 0AU
Tel. / e-mail	0171 881 7000 uk_infobus@haygroup.com
Fax / Web site	0171 881 7100 www.haygroup.com

436	HAY MANAGEMENT CONSULTANTS LTD
Title	**Consumer Sector Salesforce Survey**
Coverage	A survey of salaries and benefits in fast-moving consumer goods (FMCG) companies. Based on a range of jobs in over 60 organisations.
Frequency	Annual
Availability	Participants
Cost	£700
Comments	–
Address	52 Grosvenor Gardens, London SW1W 0AU
Tel. / e-mail	0171 881 7000 uk_infobus@haygroup.com
Fax / Web site	0171 881 7100 www.haygroup.com

437	HAY MANAGEMENT CONSULTANTS LTD
Title	**Employee Benefits Reports**
Coverage	Two reports on Industrial & Service Organisations and Financial Organisations.
Frequency	Regular
Availability	General
Cost	£1,400 or £925 each if purchased separately
Comments	–
Address	52 Grosvenor Gardens, London SW1W 0AU
Tel. / e-mail	0171 881 7200 uk_infobase@haygroup.com
Fax / Web site	0171 881 7104 www.haygroup.com

438	HAY MANAGEMENT CONSULTANTS LTD
Title	**Engineers' Remuneration**
Coverage	A survey of salaries and benefits for engineers based on 22 job levels. Based on a survey by the company of over 300 organisations.
Frequency	Annual
Availability	Participants
Cost	£675
Comments	–
Address	52 Grosvenor Gardens, London SW1W 0AU
Tel. / e-mail	0171 881 7000 uk_infobus@haygroup.com
Fax / Web site	0171 881 7100 www.haygroup.com

439	HAY MANAGEMENT CONSULTANTS LTD
Title	**Hay Compensation Report**
Coverage	Statistics and analysis on the salaries and main benefits of executive, managerial, and supervisory positions. Analysis by major industrial and service sector, location, and function. Based on a quarterly updated database of over 500 companies and thousands of jobs.
Frequency	Quarterly
Availability	Participants
Cost	£1,000, or £375 per quarterly report
Comments	–
Address	52 Grosvenor Gardens, London SW1W 0AU
Tel. / e-mail	0171 881 7000 uk_infobus@haygroup.com
Fax / Web site	0171 881 7100 www.haygroup.com

440	HAY MANAGEMENT CONSULTANTS LTD
Title	**HAY/PA Publishers' Survey**
Coverage	A survey of salaries and benefits in the book and magazine publishing sectors. Based on data collected by the company and the Publishers' Association.
Frequency	Annual
Availability	Participants
Cost	£860
Comments	–
Address	52 Grosvenor Gardens, London SW1W 0AU
Tel. / e-mail	0171 881 7000 uk_infobus@haygroup.com
Fax / Web site	0171 881 7100 www.haygroup.com

441	HAY MANAGEMENT CONSULTANTS LTD
Title	**Health Service Survey**
Coverage	A survey of salaries and benefits for 17 job levels in the health service. Based on a survey of around 70 hospitals.
Frequency	Annual
Availability	Participants
Cost	£365
Comments	–
Address	52 Grosvenor Gardens, London SW1W 0AU
Tel. / e-mail	0171 881 7000 uk_infobus@haygroup.com
Fax / Web site	0171 881 7100 www.haygroup.com
442	HAY MANAGEMENT CONSULTANTS LTD
Title	**Human Resources and Personnel Remuneration**
Coverage	A survey of salaries and benefits for personnel and human resources managers and related jobs. Based on a survey of over 600 organisations.
Frequency	Annual
Availability	Participants
Cost	£720
Comments	–
Address	52 Grosvenor Gardens, London SW1W 0AU
Tel. / e-mail	0171 881 7000 uk_infobus@haygroup.com
Fax / Web site	0171 881 7100 www.haygroup.com
443	HAY MANAGEMENT CONSULTANTS LTD
Title	**Information Technology Remuneration**
Coverage	A survey of salaries and benefits for IT staff in over 400 organisations. Based on a survey by the company.
Frequency	Annual
Availability	Participants
Cost	£720
Comments	–
Address	52 Grosvenor Gardens, London SW1W 0AU
Tel. / e-mail	0171 881 7000 uk_infobus@haygroup.com
Fax / Web site	0171 881 7100 www.haygroup.com

444

Title	**HAY MANAGEMENT CONSULTANTS LTD**
	Investment Fund Remuneration
Coverage	Covers the pay and benefits of investment fund managers and related jobs down to the level of investment analysts. Analyses available by sector, and geographical location. Based on data collected by the company.
Frequency	Annual
Availability	Participants
Cost	£675
Comments	–
Address	52 Grosvenor Gardens, London SW1W 0AU
Tel. / e-mail	0171 881 7000 uk_infobus@haygroup.com
Fax / Web site	0171 881 7100 www.haygroup.com

445

Title	**HAY MANAGEMENT CONSULTANTS LTD**
	Local Authority Survey
Coverage	A survey of salaries and benefits for various levels of local authority staff based on a survey of around 70 local authorities.
Frequency	Annual
Availability	Participants
Cost	£675
Comments	–
Address	52 Grosvenor Gardens, London SW1W 0AU
Tel. / e-mail	0171 881 7000 uk_infobus@haygroup.com
Fax / Web site	0171 881 7100 www.haygroup.com

446

Title	**HAY MANAGEMENT CONSULTANTS LTD**
	Retail Survey
Coverage	A survey of salaries and benefits for various jobs in the retailing sector. Based on a survey of almost 100 organisations.
Frequency	Annual
Availability	Participants
Cost	£720
Comments	–
Address	52 Grosvenor Gardens, London SW1W 0AU
Tel. / e-mail	0171 881 7000 uk_infobus@haygroup.com
Fax / Web site	0171 881 7100 www.haygroup.com

HAY MANAGEMENT CONSULTANTS LTD

Title	**Solicitors and Legal Executives' Remuneration**
Coverage	A survey of salaries and benefits of solicitors and related professionals based on data collected by the company.
Frequency	Annual
Availability	Participants
Cost	£720
Comments	–
Address	52 Grosvenor Gardens, London SW1W 0AU
Tel. / e-mail	0171 881 7000 uk_infobus@haygroup.com
Fax / Web site	0171 881 7100 www.haygroup.com

HAYS ACCOUNTANCY PERSONNEL

Title	**Guide to Salaries in Accountancy**
Coverage	Covers accountancy salaries and merchant and international banking salaries. Information based on surveys carried out in various regional centres in England and Wales. A general commentary accompanies the data.
Frequency	Twice yearly
Availability	General
Cost	£35
Comments	–
Address	4th Floor, 141 Moorgate, London EC2M 6TX
Tel. / e-mail	0171 628 6655 marketing@hays-ap.co.uk
Fax / Web site	0171 628 4736 www.hays-ap.com

HCIS

Title	**Fitzhugh Directory of Independent Healthcare and Long Term Care**
Coverage	A directory of the independent healthcare sector which includes statistical data on market size and trends, plus details of the number of mergers and acquisitions.
Frequency	Annual
Availability	General
Cost	£240
Comments	–
Address	12 Riverview Grove, London W4 3QJ
Tel. / e-mail	0181 995 1752
Fax / Web site	0181 742 2418

450	
Title	HEALEY AND BAKER
	Prime
Coverage	Commentary and statistics on the trends in property rents with data for industrial, office, and retail property. Figures for the standard regions and a table of summary data covering a ten-year period. Based on the company's own research with supporting text.
Frequency	Annual
Availability	General
Cost	Free
Comments	–
Address	29 St George Street, Hanover Square, London W1A 3BG
Tel. / e-mail	0171 514 2290
Fax / Web site	0171 514 2366

451	
Title	HEALEY AND BAKER
	Quarterly Market Report
Coverage	Data on investment trends in the retail, office, and industrial property sectors. Commentary supported by various tables.
Frequency	Quarterly
Availability	General
Cost	Free
Comments	–
Address	29 St George Street, Hanover Square, London W1A 3BG
Tel. / e-mail	0171 514 2290
Fax / Web site	0171 514 2366

452	
Title	HEWITT ASSOCIATES
	Salary Increase Survey Report - UK
Coverage	A survey of salary increases for various categories of jobs based on a sample of around 250 companies.
Frequency	Annual
Availability	Clients
Cost	On application
Comments	The company carries out various specialist salary surveys, eg consumer electronics, consumer finance, and also maintains a salaries database. These services are available to clients only.
Address	Prospect House, Abbeyview, St Albans AL1 2QU
Tel. / e-mail	01727 888200
Fax / Web site	01727 888333 www.hewitt.com

453	HIGHER EDUCATION CAREERS SERVICES UNIT
Title	**Graduate Market Trends**
Coverage	An analysis of graduate vacancies and salaries arranged by work type, employer type, subject of study, and location. Based on data collected by CSU. A commentary is included with the data.
Frequency	Quarterly
Availability	General
Cost	Free
Comments	–
Address	Booth Street East, Manchester M13 9EP
Tel. / e-mail	0161 2775325 D.Johnson@csu.ac.uk
Fax / Web site	0161 2775250 www.prospects.csu.ac.uk

454	HIGHER EDUCATION CAREERS SERVICES UNIT
Title	**What do Graduates Do?**
Coverage	Supply of graduates and those entering employment by employer, type of work and field of study. Comparative figures for earlier years. Based on data supplied by various institutions and some supporting text.
Frequency	Annual
Availability	General
Cost	£8.95
Comments	–
Address	Booth Street East, Manchester M13 9EP
Tel. / e-mail	0161 2775325 D.Johnson@csu.ac.uk
Fax / Web site	0161 2775250 www.prospects.csu.ac.uk

455	HOME GROWN CEREALS AUTHORITY
Title	**Annual Report**
Coverage	Mainly a general commentary on the cereals sector but includes some general statistics on production, supplies etc.
Frequency	Annual
Availability	General
Cost	Free
Comments	Some statistics on the web site.
Address	Caledonia House, 223 Pentonville Road, London N1 9NG
Tel. / e-mail	0171 263 3391 mi@hgca.com
Fax / Web site	0171 520 3918 www.hgca.co.uk

456	
Title	HOME GROWN CEREALS AUTHORITY
	Cereal Statistics
Coverage	Production and supplies of specific types of cereals plus data on prices and imports and exports. Some international comparisons are included and there is a section of historical statistics. Based mainly on Central Government data with additional material from the authority and other non-official sources.
Frequency	Annual
Availability	General
Cost	£75, discounted prices for levy holders
Comments	Some statistics on the web site.
Address	Caledonia House, 223 Pentonville Road, London N1 9NG
Tel. / e-mail	0171 263 3391 mi@hgca.com
Fax / Web site	0171 520 3918 www.hgca.co.uk

457	
Title	HOME GROWN CEREALS AUTHORITY
	MI Bulletin
Coverage	Statistics on prices, imports, exports, and the futures market for cereals. International data is also included.
Frequency	Weekly
Availability	General
Cost	£300, discounted prices for levy holders
Comments	Posted, faxed, emailed on Mondays. Some statistics on the web site.
Address	Caledonia House, 223 Pentonville Road, London N1 9NG
Tel. / e-mail	0171 263 3391 mi@hgca.com
Fax / Web site	0171 520 3918 www.hgca.co.uk

458	
Title	HOME GROWN CEREALS AUTHORITY
	MI Prospects
Coverage	Statistics and comments on grain market trends and policies. Based on a combination of Central Government statistics, data from the Authority, and other non-official sources.
Frequency	Weekly
Availability	General
Cost	£250, discounted prices for levy holders
Comments	Some statistics on the web site.
Address	Caledonia House, 223 Pentonville Road, London N1 9NG
Tel. / e-mail	0171 263 3391 mi@hgca.com
Fax / Web site	0171 520 3918 www.hgca.co.uk

459

HOME GROWN CEREALS AUTHORITY

Title	**MI Saturday**
Coverage	A two-page summary outlining key market trends and statistics in the cereals and grain markets.
Frequency	Weekly
Availability	General
Cost	£249, discounted prices for levy holders.
Comments	Some statistics on the web site.
Address	Caledonia House, 223 Pentonville Road, London N1 9NG
Tel. / e-mail	mi@hgca.com
Fax / Web site	0171 520 3918 www.hgca.co.uk

460

HOTEL CATERING AND INSTITUTIONAL MANAGEMENT ASSOCIATION

Title	**Hospitality Yearbook**
Coverage	Includes an Annual Review section with commentary and statistics on developments over the previous 12 months.
Frequency	Annual
Availability	General
Cost	On request
Comments	–
Address	William Reed Publishing Ltd, Broadfield Park, Crawley RH11 9RT
Tel. / e-mail	01293 610301
Fax / Web site	01293 613304

461

HOUSEBUILDERS' FEDERATION AND HOUSEBUILDER PUBLICATIONS

Title	**Housing Market Report**
Coverage	Includes a survey of housebuilding and a survey of confidence and affordability in the market. Also data on housing market activity, building, labour market trends, mortgages. News items on the housing market are also included and historical data is included in many tables.
Frequency	Monthly
Availability	General
Cost	£36
Comments	Survey data on the web site.
Address	PO Box 2, Ellesmere Port, South Wirral L65 3EA
Tel. / e-mail	0151 3557175
Fax / Web site	0151 357 2813 www.hbf.co.uk/hbf/index.html

462	HOUSEWARES BUSINESS CENTRE (HBC)
Title	**UK Housewares Datapack**
Coverage	Market information on 85 product sectors classified as non-electrical housewares used in the kitchen. Over 900 pages of analysis and data based on research by the company.
Frequency	Annual
Availability	General
Cost	On application
Comments	Also undertakes commissioned research on the housewares sector. Summary data from the Housewares Datapack included in 'DIY Week'.
Address	45 Parkfield Road, Coleshill, Birmingham B46 3LD
Tel. / e-mail	01675 464216 hbc@easynet.co.uk
Fax / Web site	01675 467524

463	HP FOODS LTD
Title	**HP Retail Sauce Report**
Coverage	Commentary and statistics on market trends, brands, product developments etc based on commissioned research.
Frequency	Annual
Availability	General
Cost	On request
Comments	–
Address	45 Northampton Road, Market Harborough LE16 9BQ
Tel. / e-mail	01858 410144
Fax / Web site	01858 410053

464	HSBC ECONOMICS AND INVESTMENT STRATEGY
Title	**Keynotes**
Coverage	Weekly economic indicators presented in tabular and graphic form with supporting commentary.
Frequency	Weekly
Availability	Researchers and clients
Cost	Free
Comments	–
Address	Thames Exchange, 10 Queen Street Place, London EC4R 1BL
Tel. / e-mail	0171 336 2000
Fax / Web site	0171 336 4231 www.hsbcmarkets.com

465	HSBC ECONOMICS AND INVESTMENT STRATEGY
Title	**UK Economic**
Coverage	Data for the current year, quarters and forecasts. Topics covered include inflation, PSBR, trade, earnings, banking etc.
Frequency	Monthly
Availability	Researchers and clients
Cost	Free
Comments	–
Address	Thames Exchange, 10 Queen Street Place, London EC4R 1BL
Tel. / e-mail	0171 336 2000
Fax / Web site	0171 336 4231 www.hsbcmarkets.com

466	HSBC ECONOMICS AND INVESTMENT STRATEGY
Title	**UK Economic Watch**
Coverage	Statistics and commentary on UK economic trends and prospects.
Frequency	Weekly
Availability	Researchers and clients
Cost	Free
Comments	–
Address	Thames Exchange, 10 Queen Street Place, London EC4R 1BL
Tel. / e-mail	0171 336 2000
Fax / Web site	0171 336 4231 www.hsbcmarkets.com

467	HUNT MARKETING RESEARCH
Title	**The UK Paint Market**
Coverage	An analysis of trends in various sectors of the paint market including DIY paints, motor vehicle paints, industrial coatings, trade paints, high performance coatings, vehicle refinishes. Based on research by the company.
Frequency	Regular
Availability	General
Cost	£195
Comments	Usually published every two years.
Address	Old Mill, Mill Street, Wantage OX12 9AB
Tel. / e-mail	01235 772001
Fax / Web site	01235 772002

468	ICD MARKETING SERVICES
Title	**The National Lifestyle Report**
Coverage	ICD is a geodemographic service and the National Lifestyle Report is a customer profile analysis allocating every record on ICD's database into one of 100 cells, based on 280 lifestyle variables.
Frequency	Continuous
Availability	General
Cost	On application, and depending on the range and nature of the information required
Comments	–
Address	Bain House, 16 Connaught Place, London W2 2EP
Tel. / e-mail	0171 298 6300
Fax / Web site	

469	ICM RESEARCH
Title	**ICM Omnibus**
Coverage	An omnibus survey of 1,500 adults aged 15 and over at 103 sampling points around the country.
Frequency	Fortnightly
Availability	General
Cost	On application
Comments	–
Address	Knighton House, 56 Mortimer Street, London W1N 7DG
Tel. / e-mail	0171 436 3114
Fax / Web site	0171 436 3179

470	IMPERIAL CHEMICAL INDUSTRIES PLC
Title	**Dulux Paints Review**
Coverage	A review of the UK paints market with data on sales, distribution, and key brands. Based largely on market research sources.
Frequency	Regular
Availability	General
Cost	On request
Comments	–
Address	9 Millbank, London SW1P 3JF
Tel. / e-mail	0171 834 4444
Fax / Web site	0171 834 2042

		IMS (UK) LTD
471		
	Title	**IMS Databases**
	Coverage	IMS has access to a range of media and consumer databases including the British Business Survey produced by the Business Media Research Committee.
	Frequency	Continuous
	Availability	General
	Cost	On request
	Comments	–
	Address	Grosvenor House, Grosvenor Gardens, London SW1W 0BS
	Tel. / e-mail	0171 630 5033
	Fax / Web site	0171 828 3642

		INBUCON LTD
472		
	Title	**UK Survey of Executive Salaries and Benefits**
	Coverage	A survey of salaries and benefits covering 56 executive job titles based in over 20 industrial groupings. Based on a survey carried out by the company.
	Frequency	Annual
	Availability	General
	Cost	£550, £175 to participants
	Comments	–
	Address	34 Paradise Road, Richmond TW9 1FE
	Tel. / e-mail	0181 334 5727 tbt@inbucon.co.uk
	Fax / Web site	0181 334 5739

		INCOMES DATA SERVICES
473		
	Title	**Datable**
	Coverage	General statistics on retail prices and average earnings, in index form, with historical data for previous months. Based on Central Government data.
	Frequency	Twice monthly in a twice monthly journal
	Availability	General
	Cost	On request
	Comments	Published in the IDS journal, 'IDS Report'. IDS publishes a range of reports on the UK and European labour market and conditions.
	Address	77 Bastwick Street, London EC1V 3TT
	Tel. / e-mail	0171 250 3434 sales@incomesdata.co.uk
	Fax / Web site	0171 324 2510 www.incomesdata.co.uk

474

	INCOMES DATA SERVICES
Title	**IDS Management Pay Review Executive Pay Report**
Coverage	A survey of salary movements for management staff in FTSE 250 companies. Additional information on bonuses, share options, benefits, and contracts. Based on a survey by the company.
Frequency	Annual
Availability	General
Cost	On request
Comments	–
Address	77 Bastwick Street, London EC1V 3TT
Tel. / e-mail	0171 250 3434 sales@incomesdata.co.uk
Fax / Web site	0171 324 2510 www.incomesdata.co.uk

475

	INCOMES DATA SERVICES
Title	**IDS Management Pay Review Pay and Progression for Graduates**
Coverage	A survey of salary and related trends in the graduate labour market based on a sample survey of over 100 organisations.
Frequency	Annual
Availability	General
Cost	£202
Comments	–
Address	77 Bastwick Street, London EC1V 3TT
Tel. / e-mail	0171 250 3434 sales@incomesdata.co.uk
Fax / Web site	0171 324 2510 www.incomesdata.co.uk

476

	INCOMES DATA SERVICES
Title	**Pay and Bargaining Prospects**
Coverage	Commentary and statistics on the outlook for pay and bargaining in the next twelve months. Based on an analysis of current and likely economic and pay trends by IDS.
Frequency	Annual
Availability	General
Cost	On request
Comments	The survey is included as a special feature in the twice-monthly 'IDS Report', usually in a September issue.
Address	77 Bastwick Street, London EC1V 3TT
Tel. / e-mail	0171 250 3434 sales@incomesdata.co.uk
Fax / Web site	0171 324 2510 www.incomesdata.co.uk

	INCOMES DATA SERVICES
477	
Title	**Pay Settlement Analysis**
Coverage	Data on trends in pay settlements with figures for changes in the level of settlements over a 12 month period. Based on data collected by IDS.
Frequency	Quarterly in a twice-monthly journal
Availability	General
Cost	On request
Comments	The survey is included as a quarterly feature in the journal, 'IDS Report'. IDS publishes a range of reports on the UK and European labour market and conditions.
Address	77 Bastwick Street, London EC1V 3TT
Tel. / e-mail	0171 250 3434 sales@incomesdata.co.uk
Fax / Web site	0171 324 2510 www.incomesdata.co.uk

	INCOMES DATA SERVICES '
478	
Title	**Public Sector Labour Market Survey**
Coverage	An IDS survey of the public sector labour market based on a survey of employers' perceptions of the market and their recent recruitment and training experiences.
Frequency	Annual
Availability	General
Cost	On request
Comments	The survey is included as a special feature in the twice-monthly 'IDS Report'. IDS publishes a range of reports on the UK and European labour market and conditions.
Address	77 Bastwick Street, London EC1V 3TT
Tel. / e-mail	0171 250 3434 sales@incomesdata.co.uk
Fax / Web site	0171 324 2510 www.incomesdata.co.uk

	INCORPORATED SOCIETY OF BRITISH ADVERTISERS LTD
479	
Title	**Exhibition Expenditure Review**
Coverage	Expenditure by UK exhibitors on trade and consumer exhibitions by venue and by media. Based on a survey of around 2,000 exhibitors at various types of exhibitions. A small amount of supporting text.
Frequency	Annual
Availability	General
Cost	On request
Comments	–
Address	44 Hertford Street, London W1Y 8AE
Tel. / e-mail	0171 499 7502
Fax / Web site	0171 629 5355 www.isba.org.uk

480	INDEPENDENT HEALTHCARE ASSOCIATION
Title	**Survey of Acute Hospitals in the Independent Sector**
Coverage	Details of the size of, and growth trends for, the private hospital market in the UK. Regional data is also included. Based on information collected by the association.
Frequency	Annual
Availability	General
Cost	£25
Comments	–
Address	22 Little Russell Street, London WC1A 2HT
Tel. / e-mail	0171 430 0537 angela.salway@iha.org.uk
Fax / Web site	0171 242 2681 www.iha.org.uk

481	INDEPENDENT SCHOOLS INFORMATION SERVICE (ISIS)
Title	**ISIS Annual Census**
Coverage	General statistical information about the number of pupils in ISIS schools, spending, current trends in independent education etc. Based on a regular ISIS survey.
Frequency	Annual
Availability	General
Cost	Free
Comments	–
Address	56 Buckingham Gate, London SW1E 6AG
Tel. / e-mail	0171 798 1500
Fax / Web site	0171 630 5013

482	INDEPENDENT TELEVISION COMMISSION (ITC)
Title	**ITC Quarterly Analysis of Cable Industry**
Coverage	A press release giving figures for the take-up, homes passed, penetration of cable TV.
Frequency	Quarterly
Availability	General
Cost	On application
Comments	Also produces an annual report with a general review of viewing trends.
Address	33 Foley Street, London W1P 7LB
Tel. / e-mail	0171 255 3000 publicaffairs@itc.org.uk
Fax / Web site	0171 306 7800 www.itc.org.uk

483

	INDEPENDENT TELEVISION COMMISSION (ITC)
Title	**Television Audience Share Figures**
Coverage	Quarterly TV viewing figures broken down by channel.
Frequency	Quarterly
Availability	General
Cost	On application
Comments	Also produces an annual report with a general review of viewing trends.
Address	33 Foley Street, London W1P 7LB
Tel. / e-mail	0171 255 3000 publicaffairs@itc.org.uk
Fax / Web site	0171 306 7800 www.itc.org.uk

484

	INDEPENDENT TELEVISION COMMISSION (ITC)
Title	**Television Audience Share Figures**
Coverage	Quarterly viewing figures broken down by TV channel.
Frequency	Quarterly
Availability	General
Cost	On application
Comments	Also produces an annual report with a general review of viewing trends.
Address	33 Foley Street, London W1P 7LB
Tel. / e-mail	0171 255 3000 publicaffairs@itc.org.uk
Fax / Web site	0171 306 7800 www.itc.org.uk

485

	INDEPENDENT TELEVISION COMMISSION (ITC)
Title	**Television: the Public's View**
Coverage	Annual survey, from 1970 onwards, of consumer opinions of television plus ownership levels. Includes data on the number of TV sets, subscriptions to cable and satellite television, programme selection, motives for choosing specific programmes, opinions on standards and quality, comments on specific types of programmes.
Frequency	Annual
Availability	General
Cost	£7.50
Comments	Also produces an annual report with a general review of viewing trends.
Address	33 Foley Street, London W1P 7LB
Tel. / e-mail	0171 255 3000 publicaffairs@itc.org.uk
Fax / Web site	0171 306 7800 www.itc.org.uk

	INDICES PUBLICATIONS LTD
486	
Title	**The New Grey List**
Coverage	Market prices for over 30,000 hardware and DIY products based on a survey by Indices Publications of prices throughout the country.
Frequency	Monthly
Availability	General
Cost	£119, £99 to British Hardware Federation members
Comments	–
Address	14-16 Church Street, Rickmansworth WD3 1WD
Tel. / e-mail	01923 711434
Fax / Web site	01923 896063

	INDUSTRIAL RELATIONS SERVICES (IRS)
487	
Title	**IRS Employment Review**
Coverage	The Employment Review comprises five journals which have been brought together under one cover. These include 'Pay' and 'Benefits Bulletin', with data on earnings, settlements, prices etc. and 'IRS Employment Trends'.
Frequency	Twice a month
Availability	General
Cost	On request
Comments	–
Address	18-20 Highbury Place, London N5 1QP
Tel. / e-mail	0171 354 5858
Fax / Web site	0171 359 4000

	INFORMATION RESEARCH NETWORK
488	
Title	**Annual Cruise Review**
Coverage	A detailed statistical analysis of the UK cruise market.
Frequency	Annual
Availability	General
Cost	On request
Comments	Produced in association with the Passenger Shipping Association. Various other cruise, and general travel reports available.
Address	Davis House, 129 Wilton Road, London SW1V 1LD
Tel. / e-mail	0171 416 8107 info@irn-research.com.
Fax / Web site	0171 828 2030 www.irn-research.com.

489	INFORMATION RESEARCH NETWORK
Title	**Ferrystat: PSA Monthly Digest of Ferry Statistics**
Coverage	Statistics on passenger, car, and coach carrying by ferries. Based on regular survey of PSA members.
Frequency	Monthly
Availability	General
Cost	£475
Comments	Produced on behalf of the Passenger Shipping Association. Various other cruise, and general travel reports available.
Address	Davis House, 129 Wilton Road, London SW1V 1LD
Tel. / e-mail	0171 416 8107 info@irn-research.com.
Fax / Web site	0171 828 2030 www.irn-research.com.

490	INFORMATION RESEARCH NETWORK
Title	**Market Resource Locator**
Coverage	Web site offering links to over 600 non-governmental sites providing statistics or market data. Mainly UK but also European, US, and international sites.
Frequency	Continuous
Availability	General
Cost	Free
Comments	–
Address	Davis House, 129 Wilton Road, London SW1V 1LD
Tel. / e-mail	0171 416 8107 info@irn-research.com.
Fax / Web site	0171 828 2030 www.irn-research.com.

491	INFORMATION RESEARCH NETWORK
Title	**Travelstat**
Coverage	Detailed statistics covering inbound and outbound tourist profiles, tourist flows by origin and destination, tourist flows by purpose of visit, expenditure breakdowns, traffic by mode of transport, market shares etc. Based primarily on Central Government's International Passenger Survey plus IRN's own database of travel and tourism data.
Frequency	Continuous
Availability	General
Cost	Varies according to the nature and range of data required
Comments	Available in hard copy or disc formats.
Address	Davis House, 129 Wilton Road, London SW1V 1LD
Tel. / e-mail	0171 416 8107 info@irn-research.com
Fax / Web site	0171 828 2030 www.irn-research.com

492	INGLEBY TRICE KENNARD
Title	**City Floorspace Survey**
Coverage	Details of floorspace in the centre of London with a geographical breakdown into three areas: city, central city, city fringe. Based on data held by the company.
Frequency	Monthly
Availability	General
Cost	£180 per annum
Comments	Ingleby Trice was previously Richard Saunders & Partners.
Address	11 Old Jewry, London EC2R 8DU
Tel. / e-mail	0171 606 7461 m.trice@inglebytk.co.uk
Fax / Web site	0171 726 2578

493	INSTITUTE FOR EMPLOYMENT STUDIES
Title	**IES Graduate Review**
Coverage	Statistics on graduates and the graduate recruitment market, plus characteristics of the student population. Also examines major issues relevant to graduate recruitment. Based on data collected and analysed by the institute.
Frequency	Annual
Availability	General
Cost	£27.50
Comments	Various other reports on the labour market produced and a publications catalogue is available.
Address	Mantell Building, University of Sussex, Falmer, Brighton BN1 9RF
Tel. / e-mail	01273 686751 enquiries@employment-studies.co.uk
Fax / Web site	01273 690430 www.employment-studies.co.uk

494

INSTITUTE OF GROCERY DISTRIBUTION

Title **Food Industry Statistics Digest**

Coverage Food retailing trends by sector, company, region and the number and size of outlets. Also includes data on costs, profits, employment , stocks, capital, wholesaling, cash and carry, along with consumption and expenditure patterns plus key economic indicators. Details of the leading operators are also included. A compilation from various sources.

Frequency Monthly

Availability General

Cost £120, £90 to members

Comments Produced in a loose-leaf format each month with a binder provided. Various other occasional and one-off reports are produced on the grocery sector.

Address Grange Lane, Letchmore Heath, Watford WD2 8DQ

Tel. / e-mail 01923 857141 igd@igd.org.uk

Fax / Web site 01923 852531

495

INSTITUTE OF GROCERY DISTRIBUTION

Title **Grocery Market Bulletin**

Coverage News items, features and statistics covering trends in the UK grocery market. Based on various sources.

Frequency Monthly

Availability General

Cost £75, for both members and non-members

Comments Various other occasional and one-off reports are produced on the grocery sector.

Address Grange Lane, Letchmore Heath, Watford WD2 8DQ

Tel. / e-mail 01923 857141 igd@igd.org.uk

Fax / Web site 01923 852531

496

INSTITUTE OF GROCERY DISTRIBUTION

Title **Grocery Retailing**

Coverage A regularly updated report on grocery retailing in the UK with details of sales and sectors, companies, consumer trends, and new developments. Based on various sources.

Frequency Regular

Availability General

Cost £260, £190 for members

Comments Various other occasional and one-off reports are produced on the grocery sector.

Address Grange Lane, Letchmore Heath, Watford WD2 8DQ

Tel. / e-mail 01923 857141 igd@igd.org.uk

Fax / Web site 01923 852531

497	INSTITUTE OF GROCERY DISTRIBUTION
Title	**Grocery Wholesaling**
Coverage	A regularly updated report on grocery wholesaling with commentary and statistics covering sales, wholesaling sectors, companies, employment, and new developments. Based on various sources.
Frequency	Regular
Availability	General
Cost	£230, £175 for members
Comments	Various other occasional and one-off reports are produced on the grocery sector.
Address	Grange Lane, Letchmore Heath, Watford WD2 8DQ
Tel. / e-mail	01923 857141 igd@igd.org.uk
Fax / Web site	01923 852531

498	INSTITUTE OF GROCERY DISTRIBUTION
Title	**Retail Distribution**
Coverage	A review of UK retailing trends with commentary and statistics by sector.
Frequency	Annual
Availability	General
Cost	£150, £200 non-members
Comments	–
Address	Grange Lane, Letchmere Heath, Watford WD2 8DQ
Tel. / e-mail	01923 857141 igd@igd.org.uk
Fax / Web site	01923 852531

499	INSTITUTE OF INFORMATION SCIENTISTS (IIS)
Title	**IIS Remuneration Survey**
Coverage	Salary statistics for institute members in full time employment. Analysis by grade of membership, age, and sectors of employment. A commentary accompanies the data.
Frequency	Every 2 years
Availability	General
Cost	£15, free to members
Comments	–
Address	44 Museum Street, London WC1A 1LY
Tel. / e-mail	0171 831 8003 iis@dial.pipex.com
Fax / Web site	0171 430 1270 www.iis.org.uk

500	INSTITUTE OF PERSONNEL AND DEVELOPMENT (IPD)
Title	**IPD Labour Turnover Survey**
Coverage	A survey of employee turnover and job tenure with analysis by type of job, sectors, and manual/non-manual workers. Based on a survey by IPD.
Frequency	Annual
Availability	General
Cost	Free
Comments	–
Address	IPD House, Camp Road, Wimbledon, London SW19 4UX
Tel. / e-mail	0181 971 9000 ipd@ipd.co.uk
Fax / Web site	0181 263 3333 www.ipd.co.uk

501	INSTITUTE OF PETROLEUM
Title	**IP Statistical Service**
Coverage	A folder with data sheets providing summary information on the main indicators relating to the UK petroleum sector. Based largely on the institute's own data.
Frequency	Regular
Availability	General
Cost	£50 annual subscription
Comments	Also produces the monthly 'Petroleum Review' which contains some statistics.
Address	61 New Cavendish Street, London W1M 8AR
Tel. / e-mail	0171 467 7100 ip@petroleum.co.uk
Fax / Web site	0171 255 1472 www.petroleum.co.uk

502	INSTITUTE OF PETROLEUM
Title	**Petroleum Review: Retail Marketing Survey**
Coverage	Statistics and commentary on the retail market for petrol with data on sites, sales, company performance, and new developments and sites. Also data on forecourt retailing.
Frequency	Annual
Availability	General
Cost	£80
Comments	Also publishes the monthly 'Petroleum Review' which contains some statistics.
Address	61 New Cavendish Street, London W1M 8AR
Tel. / e-mail	0171 467 7100 ip@petroleum.co.uk
Fax / Web site	0171 255 1472 www.petroleum.co.uk

503

	INSTITUTE OF PETROLEUM
Title	**UK Consumption and Refining Production: Ten-Year Cumulation**
Coverage	Historical statistics covering the key indicators in the UK petroleum sector.
Frequency	Annual
Availability	General
Cost	£8 members, £12 non-members
Comments	Also publishes the monthly 'Petroleum Review' which contains some statistics.
Address	61 New Cavendish Street, London W1M 8AR
Tel. / e-mail	0171 467 7100 ip@petroleum.co.uk
Fax / Web site	0171 255 1472 www.petroleum.co.uk

504

	INSTITUTE OF PHYSICS
Title	**Remuneration Survey**
Coverage	Analysis of salaries of members by class of membership, age, sex, type of work etc. Based on a survey of members and supported by a brief commentary.
Frequency	Annual
Availability	General
Cost	£20
Comments	Available in the house journal Physics World.
Address	47 Belgrave Square, London SW1X 8QX
Tel. / e-mail	0171 470 4800 john.brindley@iop.org
Fax / Web site	0171 470 4848 www.physicsweb.org

505

	INSTITUTE OF PRACTITIONERS IN ADVERTISING
Title	**IPA Agency Census**
Coverage	Estimated number of people employed in IPA member advertising agencies categorised by location, staff category, size of agency. Based on the IPA's own survey with some supporting text. Usually published early in the year following a survey in autumn of the previous year.
Frequency	Annual
Availability	General
Cost	£15
Comments	Also produces surveys of agency costs usually only available to members.
Address	44 Belgrave Square, London SW1X 8QS
Tel. / e-mail	0171 235 7020 dawn@ipa.co.uk
Fax / Web site	0171 245 9904 www.ipa.co.uk

506	
Title	INSTITUTE OF PRACTITIONERS IN ADVERTISING
	IPA Monitor of Attitudes to Advertising Effectiveness
Coverage	A survey of perceptions of advertising awareness.
Frequency	Regular
Availability	General
Cost	£15
Comments	–
Address	44 Belgrave Square, London SW1X 8QS
Tel. / e-mail	0171 235 7020 dawn@ipa.co.uk
Fax / Web site	0171 245 9904 www.ipa.co.uk

507	
Title	INSTITUTION OF CHEMICAL ENGINEERS
	Salary Survey
Coverage	Remuneration and employment trends for members of the institution based on the organisation's own survey.
Frequency	Every 2 years
Availability	General
Cost	£105, free to members
Comments	–
Address	Davis Building, 165-171 Railway Terrace, Rugby CV21 3HQ
Tel. / e-mail	01788 578214
Fax / Web site	01788 560833 www.icheme.org

508	
Title	INSTITUTION OF CIVIL ENGINEERS
	ICE Salary Survey
Coverage	An analysis by employer, age, type of work, overtime payments, location, firm size, qualifications etc. Based on a survey of members.
Frequency	Annual
Availability	General
Cost	£130
Comments	Produced in association with 'New Civil Engineer'.
Address	Thomas Telford Ltd, 1 Heron Quay, London E14 4JD
Tel. / e-mail	0171 987 6999
Fax / Web site	0171 538 4101

509 INSTITUTION OF ELECTRICAL ENGINEERS (IEE)

Title	**IEE Salary Survey**
Coverage	A random sample of members, analysed by age, position, class, type of work, levels of responsibility, size of work, qualifications, location of employment, fringe benefits etc. A small amount of supporting text.
Frequency	Annual
Availability	General
Cost	£50, £30 to members
Comments	–
Address	Michael Faraday House, Six Hills Way, Stevenage SG1 2SD
Tel. / e-mail	01438 313311
Fax / Web site	01438 313465

510 INSTITUTION OF MECHANICAL ENGINEERS

Title	**Salary Survey**
Coverage	Salary survey of the members of the institution with data by type of work, sector, type of member, and geographical location. Also includes data on fringe benefits and overtime.
Frequency	Every 2 years
Availability	General
Cost	£60
Comments	Latest survey - September 1998.
Address	1 Birdcage Walk, London SW1H 9JJ
Tel. / e-mail	0171 222 7899 s_macdonald@imeche.org.uk
Fax / Web site	0171 973 0439 www.imeche.org.uk

511 INSTITUTIONAL FUND MANAGERS' ASSOCIATION

Title	**Fund Management Survey**
Coverage	A survey of IFMA members with data on fund ownership, funds under management, client analysis, overseas earnings, and staff.
Frequency	Regular
Availability	General
Cost	On request
Comments	First published in 1992.
Address	Roman House, Wood Street, London EC2Y 5BA
Tel. / e-mail	0171 588 0588
Fax / Web site	0171 588 7100

512

Title	INVESTMENT PROPERTY DATABANK **IPD Annual Review**
Coverage	Presents and interprets statistics about current trends in the commercial property market. Utilises records of over 9,000 properties on the IPD and includes ten-years worth of data on total returns, capital growth, income return, value growth, fund strategies etc. A large amount of text accompanies the data.
Frequency	Annual
Availability	General
Cost	On request
Comments	Also offers a telephone inquiry service.
Address	7-8 Greenland Place, London NW1 0AP
Tel. / e-mail	0171 482 5149
Fax / Web site	0171 267 0208

513

Title	INVESTMENT PROPERTY DATABANK **Monthly Index**
Coverage	A monthly index examining the trends in the value of commercial property analysed by region and sector. Based on data collected by IPD.
Frequency	Monthly
Availability	General
Cost	£250
Comments	–
Address	7-8 Greenland Place, London NW1 0AP
Tel. / e-mail	0171 482 5149
Fax / Web site	0171 267 0208

514

Title	INVESTMENT PROPERTY DATABANK **Quarterly Review**
Coverage	A quarterly review of the trends in the value of commercial property with an analysis by region and sector. Based on data collected by IPD.
Frequency	Quarterly
Availability	General
Cost	£750
Comments	–
Address	7-8 Greenland Place, London NW1 0AP
Tel. / e-mail	0171 482 5149
Fax / Web site	0171 267 0208

515	INVESTMENT PROPERTY DATABANK/SAVILLS
Title	**IPD/Savills Agricultural Performance Analysis**
Coverage	Data on institutional investment in farmland including rental growth, capital growth, total returns, and the future. A number of tables and graphs give historical trends. Data by land grade and type of tenancy and some regional figures. Based on IPD's records of investments with some supporting text.
Frequency	Annual
Availability	General
Cost	On request
Comments	Published in association with Savills (see separate entry).
Address	7-8 Greenland Place, London NW1 0AP
Tel. / e-mail	0171 482 5149
Fax / Web site	0171 267 0208

516	IPSOS-RSL LTD
Title	**Capibus**
Coverage	A weekly omnibus survey of 2,000 adults based on face-to-face interviews in the home.
Frequency	Weekly
Availability	General
Cost	On application
Comments	Capibus was the UK's first computer assisted face-to-face omnibus, launched in 1992. RSL also publish the British Business Survey for the Business Media Research Committee (see other entry).
Address	Kings House, Kymberley Road, Harrow HA1 1PT
Tel. / e-mail	0181 861 8099 information@ipsos-rsl.com
Fax / Web site	0181 863 6647 www.ipsos.rslmedia.com

517	IPSOS-RSL LTD
Title	**Flexifarm Livestock Omnibus**
Coverage	An omnibus survey of 800 cattle farmers, 500 sheep farmers, and 400 pig farmers based on telephone and face-to-face interviews.
Frequency	Annual and twice yearly
Availability	General
Cost	On application
Comments	RSL also publish the British Business Survey for the Business Media Research Committee (see other entry).
Address	Kings House, Kymberley Road, Harrow HA1 1PT
Tel. / e-mail	0181 861 8099 information@ipsos-rsl.com
Fax / Web site	0181 863 6647 www.ipsos.rslmedia.com

518

	IPSOS-RSL LTD
Title	**Signpost**
Coverage	A monthly monitor of the effectiveness of outdoor advertising posters based on a consumer survey by the company.
Frequency	Monthly
Availability	General
Cost	On application
Comments	RSL also publish the British Business Survey for the Business Media Research Committee (see other entry).
Address	Kings House, Kymberley Road, Harrow HA1 1PT
Tel. / e-mail	0181 861 8099 information@ipsos-rsl.com
Fax / Web site	0181 863 6647 www.ipsos.rslmedia.com

519

	ISSB LTD
Title	**UK Iron and Steel Industry: Annual Statistics**
Coverage	Figures on production, consumption, trade of iron and steel products. Also details of raw materials consumed, cokemaking, iron foundries, and manpower. Historical figures given in most tables and based almost entirely on the bureau's own data.
Frequency	Annual
Availability	General
Cost	£150
Comments	Also publishes regular statistics on steel in specific countries. Name changed from UK Iron and Steel Statistics Bureau.
Address	Millbank Tower, 21/24 Millbank, London SW1P 4QP
Tel. / e-mail	0171 343 3933
Fax / Web site	0171 343 3903 www.issb.co.uk

520

	ISSB LTD
Title	**UK Steel Exports**
Coverage	A monthly volume showing cumulative exports for the year to date. Covering 190 products in 100 countries.
Frequency	Monthly
Availability	General
Cost	£350 annual subscription
Comments	Also publishes regular statistics on steel in specific countries. Name changed from UK Iron and Steel Statistics Bureau.
Address	Millbank Tower, 21-24 Millbank, London SW1P 4QP
Tel. / e-mail	0171 343 3933
Fax / Web site	0171 343 3903 www.issb.co.uk

521		ISSB LTD
Title		**UK Steel Imports**
Coverage		Published in two separate versions either showing individual months or cumulative figures. Series covers 190 products from 38 countries.
Frequency		Monthly
Availability		General
Cost		£350 per series
Comments		Also publishes regular statistics on steel in specific countries. Name changed from UK Iron and Steel Statistics Bureau.
Address		Millbank Tower, 21-24 Millbank, London SW1P 4QP
Tel. / e-mail		0171 343 3933
Fax / Web site		0171 343 3903 www.issb.co.uk

522		JOINT INDUSTRY COMMITTEE FOR REGIONAL PRESS RESEARCH (JICRPR)
Title		**Readership Surveys**
Coverage		Regular readership surveys relating to regional and local newspapers.
Frequency		Regular
Availability		General
Cost		On request
Comments		–
Address		Bloomsbury House, 74-77 Great Russell Street, London WC1B 3DA
Tel. / e-mail		0171 636 7014
Fax / Web site		0171 631 5119

523		JONES LANG LASALLE
Title		**50 Centres: Office, Industrial and Retail Rents**
Coverage		Statistics on 50 main urban centres based on JLW's Centres database which records transactions at the top end of the prime property market. Some supporting text.
Frequency		Twice yearly
Availability		General
Cost		On request
Comments		Publications also cover London City offices and West End offices.
Address		22 Hanover Square, London W1A 2BN
Tel. / e-mail		0171 493 6040 info@jlw.co.uk
Fax / Web site		0171 408 0220 www.joneslanglassale.com

	JONES LANG LASALLE
524	
Title	**JLW Property Index**
Coverage	Analysis of the returns to property by type and comparisons with other investments. Figures given over a ten-year period and portfolio statistics by region. Data calculated from various sources and some supporting text.
Frequency	Quarterly
Availability	General
Cost	On request
Comments	Publications also cover London City offices and West End offices.
Address	22 Hanover Square, London W1A 2BN
Tel. / e-mail	0171 493 6040 info@jlw.co.uk
Fax / Web site	0171 408 0220 www.joneslanglassale.com

	JONES, ALAN & ASSOCIATES
525	
Title	**Charities Salary Survey**
Coverage	A survey by the company of salaries for various jobs in 30 charities.
Frequency	Annual
Availability	General
Cost	On request
Comments	–
Address	Apex House, Wonastow Road, Monmouth NP5 4YE
Tel. / e-mail	01600 716916
Fax / Web site	

	JOSEPH ROWNTREE FOUNDATION
526	
Title	**Housing Finance Review**
Coverage	A compendium of data on the housing sector with 150 tables covering key housing issues. Based on data collected from various sources.
Frequency	Annual
Availability	General
Cost	£17.50
Comments	–
Address	The Homestead, 40 Water End, York YO3 6LP
Tel. / e-mail	01904 629241
Fax / Web site	01904 620072 www.jrf.org.uk

527	JOSEPH ROWNTREE FOUNDATION
Title	**Monitoring Poverty and Social Exclusion**
Coverage	A review of poverty trends.
Frequency	Regular
Availability	General
Cost	£16.95
Comments	First published in 1999 with a view to updating every two years.
Address	The Homestead, 40 Water End, York YO3 6LP
Tel. / e-mail	01904 629241
Fax / Web site	01904 620072 www.jrf.org.uk

528	KADENCE (UK) LTD
Title	**Corporate and Financial Omnibus**
Coverage	Omnibus survey of the professional business and corporate financial markets based on telephone interviews.
Frequency	Quarterly
Availability	General
Cost	On request
Comments	–
Address	Kadence House, 748 Fulham Road, London SW6 5SN
Tel. / e-mail	0171 610 6464
Fax / Web site	0171 610 6565

529	KADENCE (UK) LTD
Title	**Retail and Hospitality Omnibus**
Coverage	Omnibus surveys of specific retailing and hospitality sectors.
Frequency	Quarterly
Availability	General
Cost	On request
Comments	–
Address	Kadence House, 748 Fulham Road, London SW6 5SN
Tel. / e-mail	0171 610 6464
Fax / Web site	0171 610 6565

530	KEY NOTE PUBLICATIONS
Title	**Key Note Market Reviews**
Coverage	These are reviews of general market sectors in the UK, such as food, drinks, catering, clothing, leisure and recreation, and travel and tourism. Within each report, the market sector is broken down into its main segments. There is also a section profiling the major companies in the sector and, normally, some original consumer data. Most market reviews are updated regularly and there are approximately 40 titles in the series.
Frequency	Regular
Availability	General
Cost	£375
Comments	Executive summaries of reports available on the web site.
Address	Field House, 72 Oldfield Road, Hampton TW12 2HQ
Tel. / e-mail	0181 481 8750
Fax / Web site	0181 783 1940 www.keynote.co.uk

531	KEY NOTE PUBLICATIONS
Title	**Key Note Reports**
Coverage	A range of over 200 reports on UK markets and sectors, with many of the reports updated every 12 to 18 months. Each report follows a standard format with sections on market definition, market size, industry background, competitor analysis, SWOT analysis, buying behaviour, outside suppliers, current issues, forecasts, and company profiles. Based on various sources including official statistics, trade association data, company reports, TGI data, and, occasionally, commissioned research.
Frequency	Regular
Availability	General
Cost	£185 each
Comments	Executive summaries of reports available on the web site.
Address	Field House, 72 Oldfield Road, Hampton TW12 2HQ
Tel. / e-mail	0181 481 8750
Fax / Web site	0181 783 1940 www.keynote.co.uk

532	KING STURGE & CO
Title	**Industrial Floorspace Today**
Coverage	Commentary on the industrial floorspace market with data sheets giving statistics by region.
Frequency	3 issues a year
Availability	General
Cost	Free
Comments	–
Address	7 Stratford Place, London W1N 9AE
Tel. / e-mail	0171 493 4933
Fax / Web site	0171 409 0469 www.kingsturge.co.uk

533	KNIGHT FRANK & RUTLEY
Title	**Central London**
Coverage	Property development trends, including rents and floorspace, in Central London.
Frequency	Quarterly
Availability	General
Cost	Free
Comments	–
Address	20 Hanover Square, London WIR 0AH
Tel. / e-mail	0171 629 8171
Fax / Web site	0171 629 1610 www.knightfrank.com

534	KNIGHT FRANK & RUTLEY
Title	**Quarterly UK Investment Commentary**
Coverage	An economic overview is followed by data on property investment trends and a property overview.
Frequency	Quarterly
Availability	General
Cost	Free
Comments	–
Address	20 Hanover Square, London W1R 0AH
Tel. / e-mail	0171 629 8171
Fax / Web site	0171 629 1610 www.knightfrank.com

535	KNIGHT FRANK & RUTLEY
Title	**UK Industrial Focus**
Coverage	A review of industrial property trends with a regional assessment.
Frequency	Twice yearly
Availability	General
Cost	Free
Comments	–
Address	20 Hanover Square, London W1R 0AH
Tel. / e-mail	0171 629 8171
Fax / Web site	0171 629 1610 www.knightfrank.com

536	KPMG
Title	**Building Society Database**
Coverage	Mainly information on specific societies but there is also a statistical section with eight-year industry trends.
Frequency	Annual
Availability	General
Cost	On request
Comments	–
Address	1 The Embankment, Leeds LS1 4DW
Tel. / e-mail	0113 231 3000
Fax / Web site	0113 231 3139

537	KPMG CORPORATE FINANCE
Title	**Alternative Investment Market (AIM)**
Coverage	Commentary and statistics on trends in the alternative investment market including total size, companies etc.
Frequency	Quarterly
Availability	General
Cost	On request
Comments	–
Address	8 Salisbury Square, London EC4Y 8BB
Tel. / e-mail	0171 236 8805
Fax / Web site	0171 248 6552 www.kpmg.co.uk

538	KPMG CORPORATE FINANCE
Title	**Management Buy-Out Commentary**
Coverage	A detailed review of buy-outs with historical data by region and for Europe.
Frequency	Regular
Availability	General
Cost	On request
Comments	–
Address	8 Salisbury Square, London EC4Y 8BB
Tel. / e-mail	0171 236 8805
Fax / Web site	0171 248 6552 www.kpmg.co.uk

539	KPMG CORPORATE FINANCE
Title	**Management Buyout Bulletin**
Coverage	Commentary and statistics on the total value of buy-outs plus data by category, size of buy-out.
Frequency	Quarterly
Availability	General
Cost	On request
Comments	–
Address	8 Salisbury Square, London EC4Y 8BB
Tel. / e-mail	0171 236 8805
Fax / Web site	0171 248 6552 www.kpmg.co.uk

540	KPMG CORPORATE FINANCE
Title	**New Issue Statistics**
Coverage	Commentary and statistics on UK flotations, new issues by quarter. Also contains details of specific new issues. Based on an analysis of Stock Exchange data.
Frequency	Quarterly
Availability	General
Cost	On request
Comments	–
Address	8 Salisbury Square, London EC4Y 8BB
Tel. / e-mail	0171 236 8805
Fax / Web site	0171 248 6552 www.kpmg.co.uk

541	LABOUR RESEARCH
Title	**Bargaining Report**
Coverage	News and articles on bargaining issues plus 'Bargaining - Key Statistics' with economic, labour market, and earnings data.
Frequency	11 issues a year
Availability	General
Cost	£160
Comments	Also publishes reports on directors' pay and bargaining plus a monthly journal, 'Labour Research'.
Address	78 Blackfriars Road, London SE1 8HF
Tel. / e-mail	0171 928 3649 lrd@geo2.poptel.org.uk
Fax / Web site	0171 928 0621 www.lrd.org.uk

542	LABOUR RESEARCH
Title	**Labour Research Fact Service**
Coverage	A weekly pamphlet containing news and statistics relating to the labour market. Based on various sources.
Frequency	Weekly
Availability	General
Cost	£46.95
Comments	Also publishes reports on directors' pay and bargaining plus a monthly journal, 'Labour Research'.
Address	78 Blackfriars Road, London SE1 8HF
Tel. / e-mail	0171 928 3649 lrd@geo2.poptel.org.uk
Fax / Web site	0171 928 0621 www.lrd.org.uk

543	LAING & BUISSON PUBLICATIONS LTD
Title	**Laing's Review of Private Healthcare**
Coverage	Analysis and statistics covering the private healthcare market with information on three sectors: acute healthcare services, medical insurance, and long-term care of the elderly. Based on research by the company.
Frequency	Annual
Availability	General
Cost	£120
Comments	–
Address	29 Angel Gate, City Road, London EC1V 2PT
Tel. / e-mail	0171 833 9123 info@laingbuisson.co.uk
Fax / Web site	0171 833 9129

LEATHER MAGAZINE

Title	**Leather Magazine**
Coverage	Leather and hide prices in the UK based on data collected from leather markets.
Frequency	Monthly in a monthly journal
Availability	General
Cost	£75 annual subscription, £8.50 single copy
Comments	The journal also has regular surveys of the UK leather industry and similar surveys of European and international markets.
Address	Miller Freeman UK Ltd, Miller Freeman House, Sovereign Way, Tonbridge TN9 1RW
Tel. / e-mail	01732 377485 abell@unmf.com
Fax / Web site	01732 361534

544

LEATHERHEAD FOOD RA

Title	**UK Food and Drinks Report**
Coverage	A two-volume report reviewing the UK food market, industry, and new product trends by sector. Based on a combination of original research and various published sources.
Frequency	Regular
Availability	General
Cost	£525, £350 to members
Comments	Also publishes various one-off reports on the UK and European food industry.
Address	Randalls Road, Leatherhead KT22 7RY
Tel. / e-mail	01372 376761 market@lfra.co.uk
Fax / Web site	01372 386228 www.lfra.co.uk

545

LEISURE INDUSTRIES RESEARCH CENTRE

Title	**Leisure Forecasts**
Coverage	Published in two volumes with the first volume covering leisure away from the home and the second volume relating to leisure in the home. Forecasts are given for five years ahead for consumer spending, prices, and key market indicators. Based largely on the company's own research with some supporting commentary.
Frequency	Annual
Availability	General
Cost	£120 for each volume
Comments	Published in association with Leisure Consultants.
Address	Unit 1, Sheffield Science Park, Howard Street, Sheffield S1 2LX
Tel. / e-mail	01787 375777
Fax / Web site	01787 375777

546

547	LEX SERVICE PLC
Title	**LEX Report on Motoring**
Coverage	A sample survey of approximately 1,500 drivers providing information on purchasing, ownership, attitudes etc. It also includes forecasts relating to the motoring sector.
Frequency	Annual
Availability	General
Cost	Volume 1 £295, Consumer Edition, Volume 2 £150, Company Edition
Comments	–
Address	Lex House, Boston Drive, Bourne End SL8 5YS
Tel. / e-mail	01628 843888 alo@lex.co.uk
Fax / Web site	01628 810613

548	LIBRARY AND INFORMATION STATISTICS UNIT (LISU)
Title	**Average Prices of British Academic Books**
Coverage	A survey of thousands of published titles with prices analysed by various subject categories, and academic and calender year indexing.
Frequency	Twice yearly
Availability	General
Cost	£11
Comments	The survey is published in February and August each year and there is a companion publication on academic book prices in the USA. LISU also publishes a range of occasional and one-off surveys of the library and publishing sectors.
Address	Loughborough University of Technology, Loughborough LE11 3TU
Tel. / e-mail	01509 223071 lisu@lboro.ac.uk
Fax / Web site	01509 223072 www.lboro.ac.uk/departments/dils/lisu

549	**LIBRARY AND INFORMATION STATISTICS UNIT (LISU)**
Title	**LISU Annual Library Statistics**
Coverage	A compendium of statistics on UK libraries including public libraries, university libraries, the national libraries, and the book trade. Historical statistics are included for the last ten years and the data is based on returns to CIPFA, UFC, and SCONUL supplemented by some special surveys.
Frequency	Annual
Availability	General
Cost	£27.50
Comments	LISU also publishes a range of occasional and one-off surveys of the library and publishing sectors.
Address	Loughborough University of Technology, Loughborough LE11 3TU
Tel. / e-mail	01509 223071 lisu@lboro.ac.uk
Fax / Web site	01509 223072 www.lboro.ac.uk/departments/dils/lisu

550	**LIBRARY AND INFORMATION STATISTICS UNIT (LISU)**
Title	**Statistics from the NHS Regional Librarians' Group**
Coverage	A survey of the operations and performance of NHS libraries with data on expenditure, funding sources, user populations, stocks, loans, electronic searches.
Frequency	Regular
Availability	General
Cost	£25
Comments	The second survey was published in October 1998.
Address	Loughborough University, Loughborough LE11 3TU
Tel. / e-mail	01509 223071 lisu@lboro.ac.uk
Fax / Web site	01509 223072 www.lboro.ac.uk/departments/dils/lisu/

551	LIBRARY AND INFORMATION STATISTICS UNIT (LISU)
Title	**Survey of Public Library Services to Schools and Children in the UK**
Coverage	An analysis of services based on a questionnaire survey carried out with guidance from AMDECL, SOCCEL, and other groups of specialist librarians. It includes tables of detailed information by authority with explanatory comments, summaries, and per capita indicators. The delegation effect of local management of schools on the Schools Library Service is monitored.
Frequency	Annual
Availability	General
Cost	£19.50, £16.50 to contributing institutions
Comments	LISU also publishes a range of occasional and one-off surveys of the library and publishing sectors.
Address	Loughborough University of Technology, Loughborough LE11 3TU
Tel. / e-mail	01509 223071 lisu@lboro.ac.uk
Fax / Web site	01509 223072 www.lboro.ac.uk/departments/dils/lisu

552	LIBRARY AND INFORMATION STATISTICS UNIT (LISU)
Title	**UK Public Library Materials Fund and Budget Survey**
Coverage	Originally concentrating on public library book funds, this survey now also covers audio and video material, service points, opening hours, and staffing levels. Comparisons are presented between individual authorities responding to the survey, and the latest year's budgets are compared to the previous year.
Frequency	Annual
Availability	General
Cost	£22.50, £17.50 to contributing institutions
Comments	Published in July each year. LISU also publishes a range of occasional and one-off surveys of the library and publishing sectors.
Address	Loughborough University of Technology, Loughborough LE11 3TU
Tel. / e-mail	01509 223071 lisu@lboro.ac.uk
Fax / Web site	01509 223072 www.lboro.ac.uk/departments/dils/lisu

553

LIBRARY ASSOCIATION RECORD	
Title	**Annual Periodical Prices**
Coverage	Brief commentary and statistics of periodical prices arranged by subject, with figures for the latest year and the previous year. Based on data collected by Blackwells from a broad selection of journals.
Frequency	Annual
Availability	General
Cost	£79.50
Comments	Usually published in July.
Address	7 Ridgmount Street, London WC1E 7AE
Tel. / e-mail	0171 636 7543 record@la-hq.org.uk
Fax / Web site	0171 323 6675 www.la-hq.org.uk/record

554

LIVERPOOL COTTON ASSOCIATION LTD	
Title	**Raw Cotton Report**
Coverage	The Liverpool market for cotton, UK cotton supply and consumption, futures market, conference freight rates to Liverpool, and world raw cotton markets.
Frequency	26 issues per year
Availability	General
Cost	£30 members, £41 non-members
Comments	–
Address	620 Cotton Exchange Building, Edmund Street, Liverpool L3 9LH
Tel. / e-mail	0151 236 6041
Fax / Web site	0151 255 0174

555

LIVERPOOL MACROECONOMIC RESEARCH LTD	
Title	**Quarterly Economic Review**
Coverage	Quarterly commentary on economic trends supported by statistics and forecasts of future trends.
Frequency	Quarterly
Availability	General
Cost	£300 subscription (corporate subscribers), £80 subscription (personal subscribers)
Comments	–
Address	Liverpool Macroeconomic Research Ltd, 131 Mount Pleasant, Liverpool L3 5TF
Tel. / e-mail	0151 709 2221
Fax / Web site	07070 769822

556	**LLOYDS OF LONDON**
Title	**Lloyds' Nautical Yearbook**
Coverage	Includes a section on the 'Year in Shipping', plus casualty statistics, port statistics, and country information. Based on various sources.
Frequency	Annual
Availability	General
Cost	On request
Comments	Publishes various regular statistical reports on international shipping trends.
Address	Lloyds of London Press Ltd, Sheepen Place, Colchester CO3 3LP
Tel. / e-mail	01206 772277
Fax / Web site	01206 46273

557	**LONDON BUSINESS SCHOOL, CENTRE FOR ECONOMIC FORECASTING**
Title	**Economic Outlook**
Coverage	Detailed forecasts of the UK economy, along with other major world economies. Summary articles and features on trends.
Frequency	Quarterly
Availability	General
Cost	£346, £104 per issue
Comments	Published by Blackwell Publishing Ltd at the address below. A summary of the forecast is on the LBS web site at the address below..
Address	108 Cowley Road, , Oxford OX4 1JF
Tel. / e-mail	01865 791100 jnlsamples@blackwellpublishers.co.uk
Fax / Web site	01865 791347 www.lbs.ac.uk/cef/outlook.htm/

558	**LONDON CHAMBER OF COMMERCE**
Title	**Annual Review of the London Economy**
Coverage	A review of economic trends in the capital based on data from the chamber and other sources.
Frequency	Annual
Availability	General
Cost	On request
Comments	–
Address	33 Queen Street, London EC4R 1AP
Tel. / e-mail	0171 248 4444 lc@londonchamber.co.uk
Fax / Web site	0171 489 0391 www.londonchamber.co.uk

559	LONDON CHAMBER OF COMMERCE
Title	**Quarterly Review of the London Economy**
Coverage	A review of economic and business trends in London including statistics on domestic business, investment, profits, exports, labour. Based on a survey of around 250 companies in the capital with additional data from official sources.
Frequency	Quarterly
Availability	General
Cost	On request
Comments	–
Address	33 Queen Street, London EC4R 1AP
Tel. / e-mail	0171 248 4444 lc@londonchamber.co.uk
Fax / Web site	0171 489 0391 www.londonchamber.co.uk

560	LONDON CLEARING HOUSE
Title	**London Clearing House Statistics**
Coverage	Statistics relating to cleared volumes with monthly figures for the latest year. Based on data collected by the clearing house.
Frequency	Monthly
Availability	General
Cost	On request
Comments	–
Address	Roman Wall House, 1-2 Crutched Friars, London EC3N 2AN
Tel. / e-mail	0171 265 2000
Fax / Web site	0171 265 2056

561	LONDON CORN CIRCULAR
Title	**Market Prices**
Coverage	Prices of cereals and various other crops with some forecasts of future prices.
Frequency	Weekly in a weekly journal
Availability	General
Cost	£80
Comments	–
Address	Palace Hall, Darthill Road, March PE35 8HP
Tel. / e-mail	01354 661976
Fax / Web site	01354 660055

562	**LONDON METAL EXCHANGE**
Title	**Statistics at a Glance**
Coverage	A regular market report including data on price movements, liquidity, and volume. Based on the exchange's own data.
Frequency	Monthly
Availability	General
Cost	£100
Comments	–
Address	56 Leadenhall Street, London EC3A 2BJ
Tel. / e-mail	0171 264 5555 james.oliver@lme.co.uk
Fax / Web site	0171 680 0505 www.lme.co.uk

563	**LONDON STOCK EXCHANGE**
Title	**AIM Market Statistics**
Coverage	Statistics covering trends in the recently established AIM market based on information maintained by the Stock Exchange.
Frequency	Monthly
Availability	General
Cost	Part of the annual subscription to the Economic and Market Information Service
Comments	–
Address	Stock Exchange, London EC2N 1HP
Tel. / e-mail	0171 797 1000
Fax / Web site	0891 437052 www.londonstockex.co.uk

564	**LONDON STOCK EXCHANGE**
Title	**Primary Market Fact Sheet**
Coverage	News, statistics on new issues, shares, equity values, market trends.
Frequency	Monthly
Availability	General
Cost	Part of the annual subscription to the Economic and Market Information Service.
Comments	–
Address	Stock Exchange, London EC2N 1HP
Tel. / e-mail	0171 797 1000
Fax / Web site	0891 437052 www.londonstockex.co.uk

565	
Title	LONDON STOCK EXCHANGE **Secondary Market Fact Sheet**
Coverage	News, statistics on turnover, market movements etc.
Frequency	Monthly
Availability	General
Cost	Part of the annual subscription to the Economic and Market Information Service
Comments	–
Address	Stock Exchange, London EC2N 1HP
Tel. / e-mail	0171 797 1000
Fax / Web site	0891 437052 www.londonstockex.co.uk

566	
Title	LONDON STOCK EXCHANGE **Stock Exchange Fact Book**
Coverage	Commentary, graphs, and tables providing summary information on the workings of the Stock Exchange. Based on statistics maintained by the Stock Exchange.
Frequency	Annual
Availability	General
Cost	Part of the annual subscription to the Economic and Market Information Service
Comments	–
Address	Stock Exchange, London EC2N 1HP
Tel. / e-mail	0171 797 1000
Fax / Web site	0891 437052 www.londonstockex.co.uk

567	
Title	LYONS WADDELL **Premier Beverages Hot Beverages Report**
Coverage	A review of the UK hot beverages market with commentary and statistics on market size, brands, products etc.
Frequency	Annual
Availability	General
Cost	On request
Comments	–
Address	11-12 Bouverie Street, London EC4Y 8AH
Tel. / e-mail	0171 583 2523
Fax / Web site	

568	M.A.C.E.
Title	**Information Systems in HM Government**
Coverage	A review of IT developments in the UK government.
Frequency	Twice yearly
Availability	General
Cost	£225
Comments	–
Address	Brenfield House, Bolney Road, Ansty RH17 5AW
Tel. / e-mail	01444 459151 sales@mace.demon.co.uk
Fax / Web site	01444 454061 www.mace.demon.co.uk/mace.html

569	M.A.C.E.
Title	**Information Systems in Other Financial Institutions**
Coverage	A review of IT developments in various financial institutions with data on budgets, IT trends, and IT outlook. Based on research by the company.
Frequency	Annual
Availability	General
Cost	£245
Comments	–
Address	Brenfield House, Bolney Road, Ansty RH17 5AW
Tel. / e-mail	01444 459151 sales@mace.demon.co.uk
Fax / Web site	01444 454061 www.mace.demon.co.uk/mace.html

570	M.A.C.E.
Title	**Information Systems in the Food, Drink and Tobacco Industries**
Coverage	A review of IT developments in the UK food, drink and tobacco sectors.
Frequency	Twice yearly
Availability	General
Cost	£195
Comments	–
Address	Brenfield House, Bolney Road, Ansty RH17 5AW
Tel. / e-mail	01444 459151 sales@mace.demon.co.uk
Fax / Web site	01444 454061 www.mace.demon.co.uk/mace.html

571	M.A.C.E.
Title	**Information Systems in the UK Construction Industry**
Coverage	A review of IT developments in the UK construction sector.
Frequency	Occasional
Availability	General
Cost	£185
Comments	–
Address	Brenfield House, Bolney Road, Ansty RH17 5AW
Tel. / e-mail	01444 459151 sales@mace.demon.co.uk
Fax / Web site	01444 454061 www.mace.demon.co.uk/mace.html

572	M.A.C.E.
Title	**Information Systems in the UK Energy Industries**
Coverage	A review of IT developments in the UK energy sector.
Frequency	Twice yearly
Availability	General
Cost	£195
Comments	–
Address	Brenfield House, Bolney Road, Ansty RH17 5AW
Tel. / e-mail	01444 459151 sales@mace.demon.co.uk
Fax / Web site	01444 454061 www.mace.demon.co.uk/mace.html

573	M.A.C.E.
Title	**Information Systems in the UK Physical Distribution Industry**
Coverage	A review of IT developments in the UK physical distribution sector.
Frequency	Occasional
Availability	General
Cost	On application
Comments	–
Address	Brenfield House, Bolney Road, Ansty RH17 5AW
Tel. / e-mail	01444 459151 sales@mace.demon.co.uk
Fax / Web site	01444 454061 www.mace.demon.co.uk/mace.html

574	M.A.C.E.
Title	**Information Systems in the UK Publishing Industries**
Coverage	A review of IT developments in the UK publishing industries including paper, manufacturing and printig.
Frequency	Occasional
Availability	General
Cost	£195
Comments	–
Address	Brenfield House, Bolney Road, Ansty RH17 5AW
Tel. / e-mail	01444 459151 sales@mace.demon.co.uk
Fax / Web site	01444 454061 www.mace.demon.co.uk/mace.html

575	M.A.C.E.
Title	**Information Systems in the UK Retail Sector**
Coverage	A review of IT developments in the UK retail sector.
Frequency	Occasional
Availability	General
Cost	£245
Comments	–
Address	Brenfield House, Bolney Road, Ansty RH17 5AW
Tel. / e-mail	01444 459151 sales@mace.demon.co.uk
Fax / Web site	01444 454061 www.mace.demon.co.uk/mace.html

576	M.A.C.E.
Title	**Information Systems in the UK Transport Insdustry**
Coverage	A review of IT developments in the UK transport sector.
Frequency	Occasional
Availability	General
Cost	£195
Comments	–
Address	Brenfield House, Bolney Road, Ansty RH17 5AW
Tel. / e-mail	01444 459151 sales@mace.demon.co.uk
Fax / Web site	01444 454061 www.mace.demon.co.uk/mace.html

577

	M.A.C.E.
Title	**Information Systems in the UK Utility Companies**
Coverage	A review of IT developments in UK utilities - water, electricity, gas and telecoms with data on branches, budgets, IT trends, and IT outlook. Based on research by the company.
Frequency	Twice yearly
Availability	General
Cost	£195
Comments	–
Address	Brenfield House, Bolney Road, Ansty RH17 5AW
Tel. / e-mail	01444 459151 sales@mace.demon.co.uk
Fax / Web site	01444 454061 www.mace.demon.co.uk/mace.html

578

	M.A.C.E.
Title	**Information Systems in the UK Utility Companies**
Coverage	A review of IT developments in the utilities sector with data on budgets, IT trends, and IT outlook. Based on research by the company.
Frequency	Annual
Availability	General
Cost	£245
Comments	–
Address	Brenfield House, Bolney Road, Ansty RH17 5AW
Tel. / e-mail	01444 459151 sales@mace.demon.co.uk
Fax / Web site	01444 454061

579

	M.A.C.E.
Title	**Information Systems in UK Local Government**
Coverage	A review of IT developments in UK local government.
Frequency	Twice yearly
Availability	General
Cost	£245
Comments	–
Address	Brenfield House, Bolney Road, Ansty RH17 5AW
Tel. / e-mail	01444 459151 sales@mace.demon.co.uk
Fax / Web site	01444 454061 www.mace.demon.co.uk/mace.html

580

	M.A.C.E.
Title	**Information Systems in UK Tourism and Leisure**
Coverage	A review of IT developments in UK tourism and leisure.
Frequency	Occasional
Availability	General
Cost	£180
Comments	–
Address	Brenfield House, Bolney Road, Ansty RH17 5AW
Tel. / e-mail	01444 459151 sales@mace.demon.co.uk
Fax / Web site	01444 454061 www.mace.demon.co.uk/mace.html

581

	M.A.C.E.
Title	**Information Technology in Financial and Commodity Exchanges**
Coverage	A review of IT developments in financial and commodity exchanges with data on budgets, IT trends, and IT outlook. Based on research by the company.
Frequency	Annual
Availability	General
Cost	£195
Comments	–
Address	Brenfield House, Bolney Road, Ansty RH17 5AW
Tel. / e-mail	01444 459151 sales@mace.demon.co.uk
Fax / Web site	01444 454061 www.mace.demon.co.uk/mace.html

582

	M.A.C.E.
Title	**Information Technology in the UK Banks and Building Societies**
Coverage	A review of IT developments in UK building societies with data on branches, budgets, IT trends, and IT outlook. Based on research by the company.
Frequency	Annual
Availability	General
Cost	£395
Comments	–
Address	Brenfield House, Bolney Road, Ansty RH17 5AW
Tel. / e-mail	01444 459151 sales@mace.demon.co.uk
Fax / Web site	01444 454061 www.mace.demon.co.uk/mace.html

583

	M.A.C.E.
Title	**Information Technology in the UK Chemical Industry**
Coverage	A review of IT developments in the UK chemical industry.
Frequency	Occasional
Availability	General
Cost	£195
Comments	–
Address	Brenfield House, Bolney Road, Ansty RH17 5AW
Tel. / e-mail	01444 459151 sales@mace.demon.co.uk
Fax / Web site	01444 454061 www.mace.demon.co.uk/mace.html

584

	M.A.C.E.
Title	**Information Technology in the UK Insurance Industry**
Coverage	A review of IT developments in the insurance industry with data on budgets, IT trends, and IT outlook. Based on research by the company.
Frequency	Annual
Availability	General
Cost	£295
Comments	–
Address	Brenfield House, Bolney Road, Ansty RH17 5AW
Tel. / e-mail	01444 459151 sales@mace.demon.co.uk
Fax / Web site	01444 454061 www.mace.demon.co.uk/mace.html

585

	M.A.C.E.
Title	**Information Technology in UK & Eire Healthcare Sectors**
Coverage	A review of IT developments in UK and Eire healthcare sectors.
Frequency	Twice yearly
Availability	General
Cost	£245
Comments	–
Address	Brenfield House, Bolney Road, Ansty RH17 5AW
Tel. / e-mail	01444 459151 sales@mace.demon.co.uk
Fax / Web site	01444 454061 www.mace.demon.co.uk/mace.html

MACHINE TOOL TECHNOLOGIES ASSOCIATION

Title	**Basic Facts**
Coverage	Basic figures on production, sales, investment, imports, exports, and consumption over a ten-year period. Also information on the leading export markets and leading import sources plus the UK's share of total world production and exports. Based on a mixture of Central Government and non-official sources.
Frequency	Annual
Availability	General
Cost	Free
Comments	Produced in pocketbook format.
Address	62 Bayswater Road, London W2 3PS
Tel. / e-mail	0171 402 6671 mtta@:mtta.co.uk
Fax / Web site	0171 724 7250 www.mtta.co.uk

MACHINE TOOL TECHNOLOGIES ASSOCIATION

Title	**MTTA Press Release**
Coverage	Review of machine tool import/export trends.
Frequency	Quarterly
Availability	General
Cost	Free
Comments	–
Address	62 Bayswater Road, London W2 3PS
Tel. / e-mail	0171 402 6671 mtta@:mtta.co.uk
Fax / Web site	0171 724 7250 www.mtta.co.uk

MACHINE TOOL TECHNOLOGIES ASSOCIATION

Title	**Statistical Report on Trade Figures**
Coverage	Detailed import and export statistics accompanying the regular press release on overseas trade.
Frequency	Quarterly
Availability	General
Cost	Free
Comments	–
Address	62 Bayswater Road, London W2 3PS
Tel. / e-mail	0171 402 6671 mtta@:mtta.co.uk
Fax / Web site	0171 724 7250 www.mtta.co.uk

		MACMILLAN DAVIES HODES
589	*Title*	**The Value of Safety and Health**
	Coverage	An annual survey of salaries and attitudes of health and safety practitioners.
	Frequency	Annual
	Availability	General
	Cost	£75, £20 for members of the Institute of Occupational Safety and Health
	Comments	Produced in association with the Institute of Occupational Safety and Health.
	Address	Television House, Mount Street, Manchester M2 5WS
	Tel. / e-mail	01992 552552
	Fax / Web site	

		MALSTERS' ASSOCIATION OF GREAT BRITAIN
590	*Title*	**Malting Statistics**
	Coverage	Some statistics available to members and basic statistics on the web site.
	Frequency	Regular
	Availability	On request
	Cost	On request
	Comments	–
	Address	31B Castle Gate, Newark NG24 1AZ
	Tel. / e-mail	01636 700781
	Fax / Web site	01636 701836 www.breworld.com/malsters/magb/ht

		MANAGEMENT CONSULTANCIES ASSOCIATION
591	*Title*	**President's Statement and Annual Report**
	Coverage	Includes five pages of statistical data with details of total turnover, numbers of clients, number of consultants employed, and a breakdown of turnover by service category. Based on a survey of members.
	Frequency	Annual
	Availability	General
	Cost	Free
	Comments	The annual report is available from the web site and there are also some press releases with data on the site.
	Address	11 West Halkin Street, London SW1X 8JL
	Tel. / e-mail	0171 235 3897 mca@mca.org.uk
	Fax / Web site	0171 235 0825 www.mca.org.uk

MANAGEMENT CONSULTANCY

Title	**Surveys**
Coverage	Regular surveys of the management consultancy sector with surveys of particular types of consultants and specific work areas. Based on various sources and some research by the journal.
Frequency	Regular in a monthly journal
Availability	General
Cost	£45
Comments	–
Address	VNU Business Publications, VNU House, 32-34 Broadwick Street, London W1A 2HG
Tel. / e-mail	0171 316 9000
Fax / Web site	0171 316 9250

MANAGEMENT CONSULTANCY INFORMATION SERVICE

Title	**Management Consultancy Fee Rate Survey**
Coverage	The survey analyses fees charged by management consultants ranging in size from sole practitioners to major international practices. The results are analysed by seven different practice areas and by four sector groups, as well as geographical variations, analysis by size of consultancy, fees charged for different levels of consultant, recruitment charges, and terms of working. Based on original research.
Frequency	Every 2 years
Availability	General
Cost	£27, £50 with Salary Survey
Comments	A relatively new survey, first published in 1992.
Address	38 Blenheim Avenue, Gants Hill, Ilford IG2 6JQ
Tel. / e-mail	0181 554 4695
Fax / Web site	0181 554 4695

MANAGEMENT CONSULTANCY INFORMATION SERVICE

Title	**Management Consultancy Salary Survey**
Coverage	A survey of consultancy salaries across different functions, different consultancy sizes etc.
Frequency	Every 2 years
Availability	General
Cost	£27, £50 with Fee Rate Survey
Comments	–
Address	38 Blenheim Avenue, Gants Hill, Ilford IG2 6JQ
Tel. / e-mail	0181 554 4695
Fax / Web site	0181 554 4695

595	MANAGEMENT TODAY
Title	**Johnson Controls UK Office Costs Index**
Coverage	Tracking index of cost trends for property operations costs and office services costs.
Frequency	Twice yearly
Availability	General
Cost	On application
Comments	–
Address	Johnson Controls IFM, Camargue House, Wellington Road, Cheltenham GL52 2AG
Tel. / e-mail	01242 577277
Fax / Web site	01242 527277

596	MANPOWER PLC
Title	**Survey of Employment Prospects**
Coverage	Short-term forecasts of employment for specific sectors in manufacturing, services, and the public sector based on the stated intentions of over 2,000 companies and organisations. Data by region is included and a commentary accompanies the statistics.
Frequency	Quarterly
Availability	General
Cost	Free
Comments	–
Address	International House, 66 Chiltern Street, London W1M 1PR
Tel. / e-mail	0171 224 6688
Fax / Web site	0171 224 5267

597	MANUFACTURING CHEMIST
Title	**Aerosol Review**
Coverage	Listing of all aerosols filled in the UK and imported. Also lists all types of aerosols filled by company, brand name, type etc. Based on non-official sources.
Frequency	Annual and as a separate item from the journal
Availability	General
Cost	£24
Comments	–
Address	Miller Freeman Technical Ltd, 30 Calderwood Street, Woolwich, London SE18 6QH
Tel. / e-mail	0181 855 7777 shoulton@unmf.com
Fax / Web site	0181 316 3545 www.dotfinechem.com

598

Title	MARKET ASSESSMENT INTERNATIONAL **Market Forecasts**
Coverage	Forecasts over a five-year period of trends in 150 markets covered in the MAPS market research report series.
Frequency	Annual
Availability	General
Cost	£350 (combined subscription with Top Markets - £550)
Comments	–
Address	Field House, 72 Oldfield Road, Hampton TW12 2HQ
Tel. / e-mail	0181 481 8710 marketassessment@compuserve.com
Fax / Web site	0181 783 0310

599

Title	MARKET ASSESSMENT INTERNATIONAL **Market Reports**
Coverage	Over 100 regular reports are published on UK consumer markets with data and analysis on market value, brands, market segments, consumers, advertising, companies, distribution, and forecasts. Based on various sources.
Frequency	Regular
Availability	General
Cost	On request
Comments	–
Address	Field House, 72 Oldfield Road, Hampton TW12 2HQ
Tel. / e-mail	0181 481 8710 marketassessment@compuserve.com
Fax / Web site	0181 783 0310

600

Title	MARKET ASSESSMENT INTERNATIONAL **Top Markets**
Coverage	A digest of statistics and commentary on the top 150 markets covered in the MAPS market research report series. Each market summary has data on value, trade, brands, advertising, and general trends.
Frequency	Annual
Availability	General
Cost	£350 (combined subscription with Market Forecasts - £550)
Comments	–
Address	Field House, 72 Oldfield Road, Hampton TW12 2HQ
Tel. / e-mail	0181 481 8710 marketassessment@compuserve.com
Fax / Web site	0181 783 0310

601	**MARKET LOCATION LTD**
Title	**Industry Analysis**
Coverage	Tables giving the distribution of industry by region and SIC classification. Based on Market Location's database of establishments.
Frequency	Regular
Availability	General
Cost	On request
Comments	–
Address	1 Warwick Street, Leamington Spa CV32 5LW
Tel. / e-mail	01926 450388
Fax / Web site	01926 450592

602	**MARKET RESEARCH SCOTLAND**
Title	**Scottish Consumer Omnibus**
Coverage	An omnibus survey based around a sample of 1,000 consumers in Scotland.
Frequency	Monthly
Availability	General
Cost	On application
Comments	–
Address	9 Park Quadrant, Glasgow G3 6BS
Tel. / e-mail	0141 332 5751
Fax / Web site	0141 332 3035

603	**MARKETING WEEK**
Title	**Ball and Hoolahan Salary Survey**
Coverage	Volume 1 supplies key information on average salary levels by industry sector. Volume 2 supplies more detailed information on 11 different job titles from marketing director through to marketing executive.
Frequency	Annual
Availability	General
Cost	£129
Comments	–
Address	Freepost 39, 50 Poland Street, London W1E 6JZ
Tel. / e-mail	0171 970 6301
Fax / Web site	0171 970 6722 www.marketing-week.co.uk

604	MASTER FOODS
Title	**Wet Cooking Sauces Market Report**
Coverage	A review of the market based on market research sources and some commissioned research. Includes a general review of the market plus sections on specific sauces - Italian, Indian, Oriental, Mexican, traditional and other sauces. Figures for the last five years are usually given. Further information on the leading brands, manufacturers, TV advertising, trade sectors, merchandising, and demographics.
Frequency	Annual
Availability	General
Cost	Free
Comments	–
Address	Hansa Road, Kings Lynn PE30 4JE
Tel. / e-mail	01553 692222
Fax / Web site	01553 697920

605	MDS TRANSMODAL
Title	**Overseas Trade Data**
Coverage	Detailed product information for imports and exports plus details of trading partners and port of entry and exit. Appointed as an official agent of HM Customs and Excise.
Frequency	Monthly
Availability	General
Cost	Depends on amount of information required
Comments	Available in various machine readable formats. The company is also an agent for the International Passenger Survey.
Address	6 Hunter's Walk, Canal Street, Chester CH1 4EB
Tel. / e-mail	01244 348301 queries@mdst.co.uk
Fax / Web site	01244 348471 www.mdst.co.uk

606	MEAT TRADES JOURNAL
Title	**Market Prices**
Coverage	Wholesale and retail prices for different types of meat and livestock and the data usually refers to prices at the end of the previous week.
Frequency	Weekly in a weekly journal
Availability	General
Cost	£60, £1.20 per week
Comments	–
Address	Quantum Publishing, Quantum House, 19 Scarbrook Road, Croydon CR9 1LX
Tel. / e-mail	0181 565 4255 freda:qpp.co.uk
Fax / Web site	0181 565 4250

607 METAL BULLETIN PLC

Title	**Metal Bulletin**
Coverage	Every issue contains 800 prices for metals, ferro-alloys, ores, steel, scrap.
Frequency	Twice a week
Availability	General
Cost	£460
Comments	Price information can also be supplied electronically via the Internet at www.metalnet.co.uk. Various other market reports on metals and geographical markets.
Address	Park House, Park Terrace, Worcester Park KT4 7HY
Tel. / e-mail	0171 827 9977 subscriptions@metalbulletin.plc.uk
Fax / Web site	0171 337 8943 www.metalnet.co.uk

608 METAL PACKAGING MANUFACTURERS' ASSOCIATION

Title	**Annual Report**
Coverage	Includes a review of the year with statistics on sales of packaging materials, sales by end-user sector, sales by type of packaging, exports, and employees. Based mainly on data collected by the association.
Frequency	Annual
Availability	General
Cost	Free
Comments	A good set of statistics is included on the web site.
Address	19 Elmshott Lane, Chippenham 3LI JQ5
Tel. / e-mail	01628 605203 mpma.enquiries@btinternet.com
Fax / Web site	01628 665597 www.mpma.org.uk

609 METALWORKING PRODUCTION

Title	**Survey of Machine Tools and Production Equipment**
Coverage	Trends in sales and use of the various types of machine tools with a detailed breakdown by industrial sector and a regional analysis. Based on returns from over 4,000 companies. A detailed commentary introduces the statistics.
Frequency	Every 5 years, published separately from the journal
Availability	General
Cost	On request
Comments	–
Address	Morgan Grampian, 30 Calderwood Street, Woolwich, London SE18 6QH
Tel. / e-mail	0181 855 7777
Fax / Web site	0181 855 7913

610	MIL MOTORING RESEARCH
Title	**MIL Motoring Telephone Omnibus**
Coverage	An omnibus survey of a national representative sample of motorists in Great Britain. Based on a sample of 500 and the results include a wide range of motoring demographics plus consumer results.
Frequency	Weekly
Availability	General
Cost	On application
Comments	–
Address	1-2 Berners Street, London W1P 3AG
Tel. / e-mail	0171 612 0265
Fax / Web site	0171 612 0263

611	MILLS, ROWENA & ASSOCIATES LTD
Title	**Statistical and Economic Review of UK Packaging Industries**
Coverage	A detailed commentary plus a statistical analysis of the industry covering the last five years with data on production, imports, exports, industrial structure, consumption, prices. Also forecasts for the next few years. Based on official statistics and various non-official sources.
Frequency	Regular
Availability	General
Cost	£495 plus p+p
Comments	Published in association with 'Packaging Week'.
Address	Peart Hall, Spaxton, Bridgewater TA5 1DA
Tel. / e-mail	01278 671343
Fax / Web site	01278 671209

612	MILPRO
Title	**Pharmaceutical Development Service**
Coverage	A monthly omnibus survey of 200 NHS general practitioners with data on prescribing trends for various products and therapeutic groups. Analysis available by regional health authority, practice size, date of qualification, practice type etc.
Frequency	Monthly
Availability	General
Cost	On request
Comments	–
Address	NOP Research Group, Evelyn House, 62 Oxford Street, London W1N 9LD
Tel. / e-mail	0171 612 0153
Fax / Web site	0171 612 0159

613	MINTEL
Title	**Finance Subscription**
Coverage	A series of regular reports on the UK financial services sector with basic data updated regularly and analytical articles updated every few years.
Frequency	Regular
Availability	General
Cost	On request
Comments	Special reports, services covering specific markets, ad-hoc reports and analyses are also available. Mintel is available online and via CD-ROM.
Address	18-19 Long Lane, London EC1A 9HE
Tel. / e-mail	0171 606 6000 enquiries@mintel.co.uk
Fax / Web site	0171 606 5932 www.mintel.co.uk

614	MINTEL
Title	**Leisure Subscription**
Coverage	A series of regular reports on the UK leisure sector with basic data updated regularly and analytical articles updated every few years.
Frequency	Regular
Availability	General
Cost	On request
Comments	Special reports, services covering specific markets, ad-hoc reports and analyses are also available. Mintel is available online and via CD-ROM.
Address	18-19 Long Lane, London EC1A 9HE
Tel. / e-mail	0171 606 6000 enquiries@mintel.co.uk
Fax / Web site	0171 606 5932 www.mintel.co.uk

615	MINTEL
Title	**Mintel Market Intelligence Subscription**
Coverage	A series of regular reports on the UK food, drink, white/brown goods sectors with detailed market data and forecasts in addition to key consumer trends.
Frequency	Monthly
Availability	General
Cost	On request
Comments	Special reports, services covering specific markets, ad-hoc reports and analyses are also available. Mintel reports are available online and via CD-ROM.
Address	18-19 Long Lane, London EC1A 9HE
Tel. / e-mail	0171 606 6000 enquiries@mintel.co.uk
Fax / Web site	0171 606 5932 www.mintel.co.uk

MINTEL

Title **Retailing Subscription**

Coverage A series of regular reports on the UK retailing sector with basic retailing data updated regularly and specific reports updated every few years.

Frequency Regular

Availability General

Cost On request

Comments Special reports, services covering specific markets, ad-hoc reports and analyses are also available. Mintel is available online and via CD-ROM.

Address 18-19 Long Lane, London EC1A 9HE

Tel. / e-mail 0171 606 6000   enquiries@mintel.co.uk

Fax / Web site 0171 606 5932   www.mintel.co.uk

MONEYFACTS GROUP

Title **Business Money Facts**

Coverage A range of economic and monetary statistics including retail prices, annual inflation rates, average earnings, base rates, tax and price index, finance house base rates, commercial rents, employment statistics, and house price data from the Halifax. Based on various official and non-official sources.

Frequency Regular

Availability General

Cost £59.80, £14.95 per issue

Comments –

Address Moneyfacts House, 66-70 Thorpe Road, Norwich   NR1 1BJ

Tel. / e-mail 01603 476476   mfacts:dircon.co.uk

Fax / Web site 01603 476477

MONKS PARTNERSHIP

Title **Board and Senior Management Remuneration in Smaller Companies**

Coverage Pay and benefits of managers and board members in a sample of smaller companies. Based on original research by the company.

Frequency Regular

Availability General

Cost £75

Comments Other reports available on remuneration in specific sectors.

Address The Mill House, Wendens Ambo, Saffron Walden   CB11 4JX

Tel. / e-mail 01799 54222

Fax / Web site 01799 541805

619

	MONKS PARTNERSHIP
Title	**Board Earnings in FTSE 100 Companies**
Coverage	A survey of salary trends based on an analysis of company annual reports and other published data.
Frequency	Annual
Availability	General
Cost	£215
Comments	Other reports available on remuneration in specific sectors.
Address	The Mill House, Wendens Ambo, Saffron Walden CB11 4JX
Tel. / e-mail	01799 54222
Fax / Web site	01799 541805

620

	MONKS PARTNERSHIP
Title	**Board Earnings UK**
Coverage	Published in two volumes with the first covering earnings in UK quoted companies. The second has details of company incentive agreements. Based on a survey of around 1,200 companies.
Frequency	Annual
Availability	General
Cost	£125 for each volume, or £225 combined
Comments	Other reports available on remuneration in specific sectors.
Address	The Mill House, Wendens Ambo, Saffron Walden CB11 4JX
Tel. / e-mail	01799 54222
Fax / Web site	01799 541805

621

	MONKS PARTNERSHIP
Title	**Management Remuneration in UK**
Coverage	Pay and benefits of directors and managers in various industries and sectors. Also details of incentives, company cars. Based on the company's own research.
Frequency	Twice yearly
Availability	General
Cost	£300
Comments	Usually published in March and October. Other reports available on remuneration in specific sectors.
Address	The Mill House, Wendens Ambo, Saffron Walden CB11 4JX
Tel. / e-mail	01799 54222
Fax / Web site	01799 541805

622	MONKS PARTNERSHIP
Title	**Survey of Non-Executive Director Practices and Fees**
Coverage	A survey of non-executive director salaries and benefits, and other issues, based on a survey by the company.
Frequency	Annual
Availability	Participants
Cost	£100
Comments	Other reports available on remuneration in specific sectors.
Address	The Mill House, Wendens Ambo, Saffron Walden CB11 4JX
Tel. / e-mail	01799 54222
Fax / Web site	01799 541805

623	MONKS PARTNERSHIP
Title	**UK Company Car Policy**
Coverage	Details of policies, benefits, changes based on a survey by the company.
Frequency	Annual
Availability	General
Cost	£150
Comments	Other reports available on remuneration in specific sectors.
Address	The Mill House, Wendens Ambo, Saffron Walden CB11 4JX
Tel. / e-mail	01799 54222
Fax / Web site	01799 541805

624	MORI
Title	**British Public Opinion**
Coverage	A digest of some of the major polls carried out by MORI in previous weeks.
Frequency	10 issues a year
Availability	General
Cost	£100
Comments	Various other research services available.
Address	95 Southwark Street, London SE1 0HX
Tel. / e-mail	0171 928 5955 mori@mori.com
Fax / Web site	0171 955 0670 www.mori.com

625	MORI
Title	**MORI Omnibus**
Coverage	Face-to-face omnibus survey of 2,000 adults in the UK. Detailed analysis of results covering purchasing trends, consumer attitudes, consumer awareness etc.
Frequency	Fortnightly
Availability	General
Cost	On application
Comments	Various other research services available.
Address	95 Southwark Street, London SE1 0HX
Tel. / e-mail	0171 928 5955 mori@mori.com
Fax / Web site	0171 955 0670 www.mori.com

626	MORTGAGE FINANCE GAZETTE
Title	**Loans Figures and Figures/Indicators**
Coverage	Details of the number of mortgage loans by type of loan and other indicators of the housing market. Based on various sources.
Frequency	Monthly in a monthly journal
Availability	General
Cost	£54
Comments	Incorporates the previously published 'Building Societies Gazette'.
Address	Charterhouse Communications Ltd, Arnold House, 36-41 Holywood Lane, London EC2A 3SF
Tel. / e-mail	0171 827 5454 chartcom@dircon.co.uk
Fax / Web site	0171 827 0567

627	MOTOR CYCLE INDUSTRY ASSOCIATION
Title	**Annual Report**
Coverage	The annual report contains some basic statistics on the motor cycle industry.
Frequency	Annual
Availability	General
Cost	On application
Comments	–
Address	Starley House, Eaton Road, Coventry CV6 2GH
Tel. / e-mail	01203 334772 mcia@mcia.co.uk
Fax / Web site	01203 229175 www.mcia.co.uk

628	MOTOR CYCLE INDUSTRY ASSOCIATION
Title	**New Powered Two Wheeler Registrations - UK**
Coverage	A monthly review of new registrations by model, type etc.
Frequency	Monthly
Availability	Members and bona-fide researchers
Cost	Free to members, £160 annual subscription, non-members
Comments	–
Address	Starley House, Eaton Road, Coventry CV6 2GH
Tel. / e-mail	01203 334772 mcia@mcia.co.uk
Fax / Web site	01203 229175 www.mcia.co.uk

629	MOTOR CYCLE INDUSTRY ASSOCIATION
Title	**UK Industry Statistics**
Coverage	Statistics to order on production, registrations etc.
Frequency	Monthly
Availability	General
Cost	On application
Comments	–
Address	Starley House, Eaton Road, Coventry CV6 2GH
Tel. / e-mail	01203 334772 mcia@mcia.co.uk
Fax / Web site	01203 229175 www.mcia.co.uk

630	MOTOR TRANSPORT
Title	**199- Road Transport Market Survey**
Coverage	A survey of companies, vehicles, haulage trends in the road transport sector carried out for Motor Transport by NOP. The survey also includes comparative data for previous years.
Frequency	Annual in a weekly journal
Availability	General
Cost	£70
Comments	–
Address	Reed Business Publishing, The Quadrant, Sutton SM2 5AS
Tel. / e-mail	0181 652 3500
Fax / Web site	0181 652 8932

631	MOTOR TRANSPORT
Title	**Market Intelligence**
Coverage	Summary statistics and news covering vehicles and road transport with data collected from various sources.
Frequency	Weekly in a weekly journal
Availability	General
Cost	£70
Comments	–
Address	Reed Business Publishing, The Quadrant, Sutton SM2 5AS
Tel. / e-mail	0181 652 3500
Fax / Web site	0181 652 8932

632	MSI MARKETING RESEARCH FOR INDUSTRY
Title	**MSI Data Reports/MSI Data Briefs**
Coverage	MSI publishes over a 100 reports per year on UK consumer and industrial sectors and many of these are updated on a regular basis. Based primarily on research by the company supported by data from official non-official sources.
Frequency	Regular
Availability	General
Cost	£245 - £645 depending on type of report
Comments	–
Address	Viscount House, Riverside Business Park, River Lane, Saltney, Chester CH4 8QY
Tel. / e-mail	01244 681424 msi_marketingresearch@compuserve.com
Fax / Web site	01244 681457

633	MSL INTERNATIONAL
Title	**Survey of the Remuneration of Corporate Treasurers**
Coverage	A survey of average salaries for corporate treasurers analysed by turnover group, region, type of work etc. Based on a survey by the company.
Frequency	Annual
Availability	General
Cost	£20
Comments	–
Address	32 Aybrook Street, London W1M 3JL
Tel. / e-mail	0171 872 1500
Fax / Web site	

634	MUSHROOM GROWERS' ASSOCIATION
Title	**Industry Survey**
Coverage	Production and manpower figures for the sector plus a cost analysis, methods of growing, and industry yield figures. Based on a survey of members, and accompanied by a commentary.
Frequency	Annual
Availability	Members
Cost	
Comments	–
Address	2 St Pauls Street, Stamford PE9 2BE
Tel. / e-mail	01780 766888
Fax / Web site	01780 766558

635	MUSIC PUBLISHERS' ASSOCIATION LTD
Title	**Music Sales Statistics**
Coverage	Sales statistics in the UK and overseas.
Frequency	Twice yearly
Availability	Members
Cost	Free
Comments	–
Address	3rd Floor Strandgate, 18-20 York Buildings, London WC2N 6JU
Tel. / e-mail	0171 839 7779 mpa@musicpublishers.co.uk
Fax / Web site	0171 839 7776

636	NATIONAL ASSOCIATION OF ESTATE AGENTS
Title	**Market Trends**
Coverage	A review of trends in the housing market based on a survey of a sample of members, plus data from other sources.
Frequency	Monthly
Availability	Members only
Cost	On request
Comments	–
Address	Arbon House, 21 Jury Street, Warwick CV34 4EH
Tel. / e-mail	01926 496800 naea@dial.pipex.com
Fax / Web site	01926 403958 www.naea.co.uk

	NATIONAL ASSOCIATION OF PAPER MERCHANTS
637	
Title	**Merchanting Statistics**
Coverage	Detailed statistics on sales based on returns from member companies.
Frequency	Regular
Availability	Members
Cost	On request
Comments	The web site has some basic data for non-members plus member access to 'Merchanting Statistics'.
Address	Hamilton Court, Cogmore Lane, Chertsey KT16 9AP
Tel. / e-mail	01932 569797 info@napm.org.uk
Fax / Web site	01932 569749 www.napm.org.uk

	NATIONAL ASSOCIATION OF PENSION FUNDS LTD
638	
Title	**Annual Survey of Occupational Pension Schemes**
Coverage	A survey of various schemes with data on income, expenditure, size of fund, the nature of the schemes, benefits provided. The data is collected via a postal survey to all members of the association. A supporting commentary is included with the statistics.
Frequency	Annual
Availability	General
Cost	£75 members, £125 non-members
Comments	The web site has some useful links to statistical sources.
Address	12-18 Grosvenor Gardens, London SW1W 0DH
Tel. / e-mail	0171 730 0585 jeremy.gibson@napf.co.uk
Fax / Web site	0171 730 2595 www.napf.co.uk

	NATIONAL COMPUTING CENTRE LTD (NCC)
639	
Title	**Business Information Security Survey**
Coverage	A review of security issues related to the use of IT.
Frequency	Annual
Availability	General
Cost	On request
Comments	–
Address	Oxford House, Oxford Road, Manchester M1 7ED
Tel. / e-mail	0161 242 2200 enquiries@ncc.co.uk
Fax / Web site	0161 242 2400 www.ncc.co.uk

640

Title	NATIONAL COMPUTING CENTRE LTD (NCC) **Salaries and Staff Issues in IT**
Coverage	A survey of salaries and benefits for 34 IT job titles based on questionnaires sent to 12,000 individuals in 600 organisations.
Frequency	Annual
Availability	General
Cost	£250, £155 to members
Comments	Produced in association with 'Computer Weekly'.
Address	Oxford House, Oxford Road, Manchester M1 7ED
Tel. / e-mail	0161 228 6333 enquiries@ncc.co.uk
Fax / Web site	0161 242 2345 www.ncc.co.uk

641

Title	NATIONAL COMPUTING CENTRE LTD (NCC) **Survey of IT Users**
Coverage	A regular survey of IT users based on research by the organisation.
Frequency	Annual
Availability	General
Cost	Free to members
Comments	–
Address	Oxford House, Oxford Road, Manchester M1 7ED
Tel. / e-mail	0161 242 2200 enquiries@ncc.co.uk
Fax / Web site	0161 242 2400 www.ncc.co.uk

642

Title	NATIONAL COUNCIL OF BUILDING MATERIAL PRODUCERS **BMP State of Trade Survey**
Coverage	A survey of the UK building materials industry based on an opinion survey of members.
Frequency	Twice yearly
Availability	General
Cost	£95 annual subscription - members, £150 annual subscription - non-members, £95 per issue
Comments	–
Address	26 Store Street, London WC1E 7BT
Tel. / e-mail	0171 323 3770 pr@building-materials.org.uk
Fax / Web site	0171 323 0307 www.building-materials.org.uk

643

NATIONAL COUNCIL OF BUILDING MATERIAL PRODUCERS

Title **BMP Statistical Bulletin**

Coverage Covers housebuilding starts and completions, renovations, prices, mortgages, value of new orders and output, capital expenditure, trade, and building materials. Based on a combination of Central Government data and non-official sources.

Frequency Monthly

Availability General

Cost £125 annual subscription - members, £200 annual subscription - non-members, £21 per issue

Comments –

Address 26 Store Street, London WC1E 7BT

Tel. / e-mail 0171 323 3770   pr@building-materials.org.uk

Fax / Web site 0171 323 0307

644

NATIONAL COUNCIL OF BUILDING MATERIAL PRODUCERS

Title **Construction Forecasts**

Coverage Forecasts three years ahead for housing starts and completions, other new work and repair, maintenance and improvement. Based on BMP's own forecasts with a large amount of supporting commentary.

Frequency 3 issues per year

Availability General

Cost £250 annual subscription - members, £375 annual subscription - non-members, £165 per issue

Comments Published in April, August, December.

Address 26 Store Street, London WC1E 7BT

Tel. / e-mail 0171 323 3770   pr@building-materials.org.uk

Fax / Web site 0171 323 0307   www.building-materials.org.uk

645

NATIONAL DAIRY COUNCIL

Title **Dairy Industry**

Coverage Statistics covering the prices, consumption, and general market for milk and other dairy products. Data from various sources with a significant amount of supporting text.

Frequency Annual

Availability General

Cost On request

Comments –

Address 5-7 John Princes Street, London W1M 0AP

Tel. / e-mail 0171 499 7822

Fax / Web site 0171 487 4734   www.milk.co.uk

646	NATIONAL FARMERS' UNION
Title	**National Weekly Egg Market Intelligence Report**
Coverage	Weekly report on egg production and output trends.
Frequency	Weekly
Availability	General
Cost	On request
Comments	Also publishes an annual review of farm incomes. Basic statistics on the web site.
Address	Agriculture House, Pynes Hill, Rydon Lane, Exeter EX2 5ST
Tel. / e-mail	01392 440700
Fax / Web site	01392 440701 www.nfu.org.uk

647	NATIONAL HOUSE BUILDING COUNCIL
Title	**New House-Building Statistics**
Coverage	Covers dwelling starts and completions, prices, market share of timber frame, first time buyers' ability to buy, and some regional trends. Largely based on the council's own survey plus some Central Government data. Usually published two to three weeks after the quarter to which it relates, and some historical data is included.
Frequency	Quarterly
Availability	General
Cost	£50 subscription, £12.50 per issue
Comments	–
Address	Buildmark House, Chiltern Avenue, Amersham HP6 5AP
Tel. / e-mail	01494 434477
Fax / Web site	01494 735201 www.nhbc.co.uk

648	NATIONAL INSTITUTE OF ECONOMIC AND SOCIAL RESEARCH (NIESR)
Title	**National Institute Economic Review**
Coverage	General analysis of the UK and world economy with forecasts usually up to 18 months ahead. Special articles on relevant topics. A separate statistical section is included in each issue along with some tables in the text.
Frequency	Quarterly
Availability	General
Cost	£80
Comments	Macroeconomic analysis package available in machine-readable format.
Address	2 Dean Trench Street, Smith Square, London SW1P 3HE
Tel. / e-mail	0171 222 7665 g.disham@niesr.ac.uk
Fax / Web site	0171 654 1900 www.niesr.ac.uk

NATIONAL ON-LINE MANPOWER INFORMATION SYSTEM (NOMIS)

Title	**NOMIS**
Coverage	A database of approximately 19 billion monthly, quarterly, annual, and triennial population and labour statistics and, with the appropriate software, users can access the data, manipulate it, and produce graphs, charts etc. Based on data supplied by Central Government departments.
Frequency	Regular
Availability	A 'Public Domain' file is available generally but the complete file is only available to authorised users.
Cost	On request
Comments	–
Address	Unit 3, Mountjoy Research Centre, Durham University DH1 3SW
Tel. / e-mail	0191 374 2468
Fax / Web site	0191 374 3741

NATIONAL READERSHIP SURVEY

Title	**National Readership Survey**
Coverage	Statistics on the readership of national newspapers and various consumer magazines based on a stratified random sample of over 28,000 individuals. Results are published a few months after the survey. Some commentary supports the text.
Frequency	Annual
Availability	General
Cost	On request
Comments	Top line data from the survey can be accessed freely on the web site.
Address	Garden Studios, 11-15 Betterton Street, Covent Garden, London WC2H 9BP
Tel. / e-mail	0171 379 0344
Fax / Web site	0171 240 4399 www.nrs.co.uk

651	**NATIONAL TYRE DISTRIBUTORS' ASSOCIATION**
Title	**Quarterly Tyre Statistics**
Coverage	Statistics on sales of new tyres, retreads, exhausts, and batteries. Based on research by the association.
Frequency	Quarterly
Availability	General
Cost	On request
Comments	Basic data from the quarterly series is available free on the web site.
Address	Elsinore House, Buckingham Street, Aylesbury HP20 2NQ
Tel. / e-mail	01296 395933 ntda@ndirect.co.uk
Fax / Web site	01296 488675 www.ntda.co.uk

652	**NATIONAL WESTMINSTER BANK/SMALL BUSINESS RESEARCH TRUST**
Title	**NATWEST/SBRT Quarterly Survey of Small Businesses in Britain**
Coverage	A survey of small businesses in the UK, 95% of which employ less than 50 people. Information on turnover, employment, sales, exports, and business problems plus features on the sector.
Frequency	Quarterly
Availability	General
Cost	£75, £20 per issue
Comments	–
Address	Small Business Research Trust, Open University Business School, Walton Hall, Milton Keynes MK7 6AA
Tel. / e-mail	01908 655831 oubs-sbrt@open.ac.uk
Fax / Web site	

653	NATIONWIDE
Title	**Housing Finance Review**
Coverage	A review of the UK housing market with commentary and statistics on house prices, types of houses purchased, mortgage lending, regional house prices, and house prices by type of house. Based on data collected and analysed by the building society.
Frequency	Quarterly
Availability	General
Cost	Free
Comments	Nationwide also has summary sheets of house price data available back to 1952 for national data and back to 1973 for regional data. A guide to the house price methodology used by Nationwide is available free from the address below.
Address	Nationwide House, Pipers Way, Swindon SN38 1NW
Tel. / e-mail	01793 455196
Fax / Web site	01793 455903 www.nationwide.co.uk
654	NDL INTERNATIONAL
Title	**NDL Lifestyle Data**
Coverage	The NDL database contains information on over 16 million consumers and the original sources used include the 1991 Census, postcode address file, and electoral roll data.
Frequency	Continuous
Availability	General
Cost	On application, and depending on the range and nature of the information required
Comments	–
Address	Po Box 362, , London SW11 3LD
Tel. / e-mail	0171 738 0522
Fax / Web site	0171 738 0415

NESTLE (UK) LTD
National Drinks Survey

Title	**National Drinks Survey**
Coverage	A review of the drinks market covering tea, coffee, chocolate, food drinks, carbonates, fruit juices, alcoholic drinks. Includes details of market value, brands, retailing, and new developments.
Frequency	Annual
Availability	General
Cost	Free
Comments	A multi-volume report with specific volumes on individual markets.
Address	St George,s House, Park Lane, Croydon CR9 1NR
Tel. / e-mail	0181 667 5616
Fax / Web site	0181 668 9471

NET PROFIT PUBLICATIONS
Net Figures

Title	**Net Figures**
Coverage	Figures on web site use and Internet use customised to the client's requirements.
Frequency	Continuous
Availability	General
Cost	On request
Comments	Part of a European survey of Internet use. Other ad-hoc surveys on Internet use produced.
Address	PO Box 11155, London SE22 0LY
Tel. / e-mail	0181 516 4630 figures@net-profit.co.uk
Fax / Web site	www.net-profit.co.uk

NEW LEISURE MARKETS
Key Leisure Trends

Title	**Key Leisure Trends**
Coverage	A review of trends in the core leisure sectors with commentary and market data. Based largely on original research by the company.
Frequency	Regular
Availability	General
Cost	On request
Comments	Reports on specific leisure sectors are also produced. In 1999, reports on seven leisure markets plus Key Leisure Trends were available for £2,995.
Address	5th Floor, 29-30 Warwick Street, London W1R 5RD
Tel. / e-mail	0171 727 3443 marketscape@dial.pipex.com
Fax / Web site	www.ds.dial.pipex.com/marketscape

658	NOP CONSUMER MARKET RESEARCH
Title	**NOP Quota Omnibus**
Coverage	An omnibus survey covering a sample of 1,500 adults carried out face-to-face in households.
Frequency	Twice monthly
Availability	General
Cost	On application
Comments	–
Address	Ludgate House, 245 Blackfriars Road, London SE1 9UL
Tel. / e-mail	0171 890 9000 nopinfo@nopres.co.uk
Fax / Web site	0171 890 9362 www.nopres.co.uk

659	NOP CONSUMER MARKET RESEARCH
Title	**NOP Random Omnibus Survey**
Coverage	A weekly omnibus survey covering 2,000 adults and based around face-to-face in-home interviews. Demographic and lifestyle analysis plus details of purchasing trends, consumer habits etc.
Frequency	Weekly
Availability	General
Cost	On application
Comments	–
Address	Ludgate House, 245 Blackfriars Road, London SE1 9UL
Tel. / e-mail	0171 890 9000 nopinfo@nopres.co.uk
Fax / Web site	0171 890 9362 www.nopres.co.uk

660	NOP CONSUMER MARKET RESEARCH
Title	**NOP Telebus**
Coverage	A weekly omnibus survey of 1,000 adults based on telephone interviews. The data analysis follows the same breakdown as the Random Omnibus Survey (see previous entry).
Frequency	Weekly
Availability	General
Cost	On application
Comments	–
Address	Ludgate House, 245 Blackfriars Road, London SE1 9UL
Tel. / e-mail	0171 890 9000 nopinfo@nopres.co.uk
Fax / Web site	0171 890 9362 www.nopres.co.uk

661

	NOP CORPORATE AND FINANCIAL
Title	**National Architects' Survey**
Coverage	A survey of a sample of architects with results covering journal readership, information sources used, etc.
Frequency	6 issues per year
Availability	General
Cost	On application
Comments	–
Address	Ludgate House, 245 Blackfriars Road, London SE1 9UL
Tel. / e-mail	0171 890 9000 nopinfo@nopres.co.uk
Fax / Web site	0171 890 9362 www.nopres.co.uk

662

	NOP CORPORATE AND FINANCIAL
Title	**NOP Financial Research Survey (FRS)**
Coverage	An omnibus survey monitoring trends in the personal finance sector based on a regular sample of 2,000 people. Analysis of customer bases, products, and cross holdings.
Frequency	32 surveys per year
Availability	General
Cost	On application
Comments	–
Address	Ludgate House, 245 Blackfriars Road, London SE1 9UL
Tel. / e-mail	0171 890 9000 nopinfo@nopres.co.uk
Fax / Web site	0171 890 9362 www.nopres.co.uk

663

	NOP CORPORATE AND FINANCIAL
Title	**Office Equipment Dealer Omnibus**
Coverage	A survey of 300 office equipment dealers covering products such as copiers, computers, telecommunications equipment, office furniture, and other office supplies.
Frequency	Regular
Availability	General
Cost	On application
Comments	–
Address	Ludgate House, 245 Blackfriars Road, London SE1 9UL
Tel. / e-mail	0171 890 9000 nopinfo@nopres.co.uk
Fax / Web site	0171 890 9362 www.nopres.co.uk

NOP HEALTHCARE

Title	**Healthcare Surveys**
Coverage	Various continuous surveys of the healthcare sector usually based on interviews with medical staff.
Frequency	Continuous
Availability	General
Cost	On application
Comments	–
Address	Ludgate Houe, 245 Blackfriars Road, London SE1 9UL
Tel. / e-mail	0171 890 9000 nopinfo@nopres.co.uk
Fax / Web site	0171 890 9362 www.nopres.co.uk

664

NTC PUBLICATIONS LTD

Title	**Drink Pocket Book**
Coverage	Basic data on the drinks sector including general statistics on the market followed by sections on specific drinks and drink outlets. Some international data is included. Based on various sources but a strong reliance on data from Stats MR.
Frequency	Annual
Availability	General
Cost	£35
Comments	Published in association with Stats MR.
Address	Farm Road, Henley-on-Thames RG9 1EJ
Tel. / e-mail	01491 411000 email@admap.co.uk
Fax / Web site	01491 571188 www.warc.com

665

NTC PUBLICATIONS LTD

Title	**Financial Marketing Pocket Book**
Coverage	Published in association with NOP Financial, a guide to the UK personal finance sector. Includes data from NOP research and covers personal incomes, wealth and savings, consumers' expenditure, personal investments, life assurance, general insurance, consumer credit, mortgages, banking, credit cards, and advertising.
Frequency	Regular
Availability	General
Cost	£32
Comments	–
Address	Farm Road, Henley-on-Thames RG9 1EJ
Tel. / e-mail	01491 411000 email@admap.co.uk
Fax / Web site	01491 571188 www.warc.com

666

667   NTC PUBLICATIONS LTD

Title	**Food Pocket Book**
Coverage	Basic data on the food market with a general overview followed by sections on specific foods, food retailing, food companies. Some European data. Based on various sources.
Frequency	Annual
Availability	General
Cost	£28
Comments	–
Address	Farm Road, Henley-on-Thames RG9 1EJ
Tel. / e-mail	01491 411000 email@admap.co.uk
Fax / Web site	01491 571188 www.warc.com

668   NTC PUBLICATIONS LTD

Title	**Geodemographic Pocket Book**
Coverage	A profile of Britain's towns, counties, products, and consumer spending patterns based primarily on data collected by CACI (see other entry).
Frequency	Annual
Availability	General
Cost	£32
Comments	Published in association with CACI.
Address	Farm Road, Henley-on-Thames RG9 1EJ
Tel. / e-mail	01491 411000 email@admap.co.uk
Fax / Web site	01491 571188 www.warc.com

669   NTC PUBLICATIONS LTD

Title	**Insurance Pocket Book**
Coverage	Basic data on the insurance sector including an overview and detailed sections on life insurance, general insurance, the London insurance market, corporate risk management, specialised insurance carriers and the international insurance market.
Frequency	Regular
Availability	General
Cost	£35
Comments	Published in association with Tillinghast, a Towers Perrin company.
Address	Farm Road, Henley-on-Thames RG9 1EJ
Tel. / e-mail	01491 411000 email@admap.co.uk
Fax / Web site	01491 571188 www.warc.com

670	**NTC PUBLICATIONS LTD**
Title	**Lifestyle Pocket Book**
Coverage	Lifestyle data for the UK with sections on shopping habits, consumption patterns, leisure, holidays, media usage, personal finance, housing and households, transport, communications, employment, education, health, crime, economics, and demographics. A final section provides some summary data on the rest of Europe. Based on various official and non-official sources.
Frequency	Annual
Availability	General
Cost	£24
Comments	Published in association with the Advertising Association.
Address	Farm Road, Henley-on-Thames RG9 1EJ
Tel. / e-mail	01491 411000 email@admap.co.uk
Fax / Web site	01491 571188 www.warc.com

671	**NTC PUBLICATIONS LTD**
Title	**Marketing Pocket Book**
Coverage	A statistical profile of the marketing, distribution, and consumption of goods and services in the UK, with some additional data on Europe and other areas. Based on various sources, including official and market research publications.
Frequency	Annual
Availability	General
Cost	£24
Comments	Published in association with the Advertising Association. A companion volume, European Marketing Pocket Book, is also available.
Address	Farm Road, Henley-on-Thames RG9 1EJ
Tel. / e-mail	01491 411000 email@admap.co.uk
Fax / Web site	01491 571188 www.warc.com

672

NTC PUBLICATIONS LTD

Title	**Media Pocket Book**
Coverage	A statistical profile of British commercial media. Coverage includes advertising spending by media and product category, circulation and readership data, publisher information, titles, stations, audiences, viewing, reach, indices of media rates and cover prices.
Frequency	Regular
Availability	General
Cost	£26
Comments	–
Address	Farm Road, Henley-on-Thames RG9 1EJ
Tel. / e-mail	01491 411000 email@admap.co.uk
Fax / Web site	01491 571188 www.warc.com

673

NTC PUBLICATIONS LTD

Title	**Parliament and Government Pocket Book**
Coverage	Information on the UK and EU parliaments with data on their spending of public money and the public's attitude to them.
Frequency	Regular
Availability	General
Cost	£32
Comments	Published in association with the Hansard Society.
Address	Farm Road, Henley-on-Thames RG9 1EJ
Tel. / e-mail	01491 411000 email@admap.co.uk
Fax / Web site	01491 571188 www.warc.com

674

NTC PUBLICATIONS LTD

Title	**Pay and Benefits Pocket Book**
Coverage	A compilation of pay and benefits data based on various sources.
Frequency	Regular
Availability	General
Cost	£22
Comments	Published in association with Bacon & Woodrow.
Address	Farm Road, Henley-on-Thames RG9 1EJ
Tel. / e-mail	01491 411000 email@admap.co.uk
Fax / Web site	01491 571188 www.warc.com

675	**NTC PUBLICATIONS LTD**
Title	**Pensions Pocket Book**
Coverage	Statistics on pension schemes, the legal background, and current pension issues.
Frequency	Regular
Availability	General
Cost	£24
Comments	Published in association with Bacon & Woodrow.
Address	Farm Road, Henley-on-Thames RG9 1EJ
Tel. / e-mail	01491 411000 email@admap.co.uk
Fax / Web site	01491 571188 www.warc.com

676	**NTC PUBLICATIONS LTD**
Title	**Regional Marketing Pocket Book**
Coverage	Statistics on consumer spending, health, media use, leisure activities, personal finance, demographics, tourism, transport, communications, economic trends, crime, education by region. Based on various sources with some additional information on Europe's regions.
Frequency	Annual
Availability	General
Cost	£24
Comments	Published in association with the Advertising Association.
Address	Farm Road, Henley-on-Thames RG9 1EJ
Tel. / e-mail	01491 411000 email@admap.co.uk
Fax / Web site	01491 571188 www.warc.com

677	**NTC PUBLICATIONS LTD**
Title	**Retail Pocket Book**
Coverage	Statistics on specific retail markets and the major retailers plus advertising trends and developments in retailing. A final section covers international retailing. Based on data collected from various sources.
Frequency	Annual
Availability	General
Cost	£28
Comments	Published in association with Nielsen.
Address	Farm Road, Henley-on-Thames RG9 1EJ
Tel. / e-mail	01491 411000 email@admap.co.uk
Fax / Web site	01491 571188 www.warc.com

NTC PUBLICATIONS LTD
The British Shopper

Coverage	A pocket book of data on British shopping patterns, consumers, and consumer purchasing behaviour. Based on various sources but a strong reliance on Nielsen data.
Frequency	Annual
Availability	General
Cost	£24
Comments	Published in association with Nielsen.
Address	Farm Road, Henley-on-Thames RG9 1EJ
Tel. / e-mail	01491 411000 email@admap.co.uk
Fax / Web site	01491 571188 www.warc.com

NTC PUBLICATIONS LTD
The Drink Forecast

Coverage	Data, analysis, and forecasts for the beer, wine, cider, spirits, and soft drinks markets of the UK. Based on a range of sources.
Frequency	Quarterly
Availability	General
Cost	£695
Comments	–
Address	Farm Road, Henley-on-Thames RG9 1EJ
Tel. / e-mail	01491 411000 email@admap.co.uk
Fax / Web site	01491 571188 www.warc.com

NTC PUBLICATIONS LTD
The Food Forecast

Coverage	Information, analysis, and forecasts for the food markets of the UK. Analysis and commentary accompanies the data.
Frequency	Quarterly
Availability	General
Cost	£595
Comments	–
Address	Farm Road, Henley-on-Thames RG9 1EJ
Tel. / e-mail	01491 411000 email@admap.co.uk
Fax / Web site	01491 571188 www.warc.com

681	NTC PUBLICATIONS LTD
Title	**The Report on Business**
Coverage	Based on a monthly opinion survey of UK purchasing managers, it provides a series of monthly economic indicators of the health of the UK economy and industry.
Frequency	Monthly
Availability	General
Cost	£175, fax service available for £395
Comments	Published in association with the Chartered Institute of Purchasing and Supply whose members are surveyed every month.
Address	Farm Road, Henley-on-Thames RG9 1EJ
Tel. / e-mail	01491 411000 email@admap.co.uk
Fax / Web site	01491 571188 www.warc.com

682	OPINION LEADER RESEARCH
Title	**Opinion Leader Panel**
Coverage	A panel survey of over 100 key opinion leaders such as directors in industry, politicians, media, trade unionists, city analysts etc.
Frequency	Regular
Availability	Participants
Cost	On application
Comments	–
Address	Alliance House, 30-32 Grays Inn Road, London WC1X 8HR
Tel. / e-mail	0171 242 2222
Fax / Web site	0171 404 7250

683	OUTDOOR ADVERTISING ASSOCIATION
Title	**OSCAR**
Coverage	The Outdoor Site Classification and Audience Research (OSCAR) measures the effectiveness and awareness of poster advertising. Based on commissioned research.
Frequency	Regular
Availability	Detailed results only available to poster industry but summary results published
Cost	On request
Comments	–
Address	77 Newman Street, London W1A 1DX
Tel. / e-mail	0171 298 8035
Fax / Web site	0171 298 8034

684	PA CONSULTING
Title	**Survey of Graduate Salaries and Recruitment Trends**
Coverage	Statistics and analysis of trends in the graduate labour market based on research by the company.
Frequency	Annual
Availability	General
Cost	£445, £295 for participants
Comments	–
Address	123 Buckingham Palace Road, London SW1
Tel. / e-mail	0171 730 9000
Fax / Web site	0171 333 5050

685	PA CONSULTING
Title	**Telesales and Customer Services Sales Survey**
Coverage	A survey of salaries in telesales and customer services based around 18 job categories. Based on a survey carried out by the company.
Frequency	Annual
Availability	General
Cost	£375
Comments	–
Address	123 Buckingham Palace Road, London SW1W 9SR
Tel. / e-mail	0171 730 9000
Fax / Web site	0171 333 5050

686	PANNELL KERR FORSTER
Title	**London Trends**
Coverage	Summary of the performance of approximately 72 London hotels with details of occupancy levels, achieved room rate, sales, and the cost of sales of food and beverage departments. Some supporting text.
Frequency	Annual
Availability	General
Cost	£100
Comments	Also publishes surveys on European and international trends.
Address	78 Hatton Garden, London EC1N 8JA
Tel. / e-mail	0171 831 7393 Hotels@uk.pkf.com
Fax / Web site	0171 404 8112

	PANNELL KERR FORSTER
687	
Title	**UK Trends**
Coverage	A review of the operating and financial characteristics of a sample of around 245 provincial hotels from AA five-star to two-star. Details of occupancy rates, revenues, costs and expenses with data for the latest year and the previous year. Some supporting text.
Frequency	Annual
Availability	General
Cost	£300
Comments	Also publishes surveys on European and international trends.
Address	78 Hatton Garden, London EC1N 8JA
Tel. / e-mail	0171 831 7393 Hotels@uk.pkf.com
Fax / Web site	0171 404 8112

	PAPER FEDERATION OF GREAT BRITAIN
688	
Title	**Annual Survey of Capacity**
Coverage	Historical data for the last few years and forecasts for three or four years ahead of capacity in the industry.
Frequency	Annual
Availability	General
Cost	£850
Comments	Enquiry service can deal with ad hoc enquiries (minimum charge £15).
Address	Papermakers House, Rivenhall Road, Swindon SN5 7BD
Tel. / e-mail	01793 886086 fedn@paper.org.uk
Fax / Web site	01793 886182 www.paper.org.uk

	PAPER FEDERATION OF GREAT BRITAIN
689	
Title	**Annual Survey of Energy Use and Costs**
Coverage	Analysis and statistics on energy use and costs in the paper and board sector.
Frequency	Annual
Availability	General
Cost	£150
Comments	Enquiry service can deal with ad hoc enquiries (minimum charge £15).
Address	Papermakers House, Rivenhall Road, Swindon SN5 7BD
Tel. / e-mail	01793 886086 fedn@paper.org.uk
Fax / Web site	01793 886182 www.paper.org.uk

PAPER FEDERATION OF GREAT BRITAIN

Title	**Consumption of Paper and Board**
Coverage	Monthly statistics and commentary on paper and board consumption in the UK.
Frequency	Monthly
Availability	General
Cost	£125
Comments	Enquiry service can deal with ad hoc enquiries (minimum charge £15).
Address	Papermakers House, Rivenhall Road, Swindon SN5 7BD
Tel. / e-mail	01793 886086 fedn@paper.org.uk
Fax / Web site	01793 886182 www.paper.org.uk

PAPER FEDERATION OF GREAT BRITAIN

Title	**Fact Card**
Coverage	Summary data on the paper and board industry based on the various statistics produced by the federation.
Frequency	Annual
Availability	General
Cost	£4 for paper edition, prices on request for transparencies, 35mm slides, electronic graphics file
Comments	Enquiry service can deal with ad hoc enquiries (minimum charge £15).
Address	Papermakers House, Rivenhall Road, Swindon SN5 7BD
Tel. / e-mail	01793 886086 fedn@paper.org.uk
Fax / Web site	01793 886182 www.paper.org.uk

PAPER FEDERATION OF GREAT BRITAIN

Title	**Imports of Paper and Board**
Coverage	Detailed monthly import statistics for paper and board based on Central Government data.
Frequency	Monthly
Availability	General
Cost	£250
Comments	Enquiry service can deal with ad hoc enquiries (minimum charge £15).
Address	Papermakers House, Rivenhall Road, Swindon SN5 7BD
Tel. / e-mail	01793 886086 fedn@paper.org.uk
Fax / Web site	01793 886182 www.paper.org.uk

693	PAPER FEDERATION OF GREAT BRITAIN
Title	**Industry Facts**
Coverage	Key figures on production and consumption plus a commentary on trends.
Frequency	Annual
Availability	General
Cost	£40 member, £50 non-member, £75 disc copy member, £80 disc copy non-member
Comments	Enquiry service can deal with ad hoc enquiries (minimum charge £15).
Address	Papermakers House, Rivenhall Road, Swindon SN5 7BD
Tel. / e-mail	01793 886086 fedn@paper.org.uk
Fax / Web site	01793 886182 www.paper.org.uk

694	PAPER FEDERATION OF GREAT BRITAIN
Title	**Market Statistics**
Coverage	Detailed tables and charts on consumption, production, sales, stocks, imports, exports of paper and board plus consumption, production, stocks and imports of raw materials. Based on a combination of sources.
Frequency	Monthly
Availability	General
Cost	£900, £100 for individual copies, individual tables and sections can also be supplied on request
Comments	Enquiry service can deal with ad hoc enquiries (minimum charge £15).
Address	Papermakers House, Rivenhall Road, Swindon SN5 7BD
Tel. / e-mail	01793 886086 fedn@paper.org.uk
Fax / Web site	01793 886182 www.paper.org.uk

695	PAPER FEDERATION OF GREAT BRITAIN
Title	**National Agreements**
Coverage	Wages and terms and conditions of employment for process workers and craftsmen in the UK paper and board industry.
Frequency	Regular
Availability	General
Cost	£400 member, £600 non-member
Comments	–
Address	Papermakers House, Rivenhall Road, Swindon SN5 7BD
Tel. / e-mail	01793 889615 fedn@paper.org.uk
Fax / Web site	01793 886182 www.paper.org.uk

696	PAPER FEDERATION OF GREAT BRITAIN
Title	**Production of Paper and Board**
Coverage	Monthly data and analysis on production, sales, and stocks of paper and board.
Frequency	Monthly
Availability	General
Cost	£250
Comments	Enquiry service can deal with ad hoc enquiries (minimum charge £15).
Address	Papermakers House, Rivenhall Road, Swindon SN5 7BD
Tel. / e-mail	01793 886086 fedn@paper.org.uk
Fax / Web site	01793 886182 www.paper.org.uk

697	PAPER FEDERATION OF GREAT BRITAIN
Title	**Pulp Consumption Stocks and Trade**
Coverage	Monthly statistics covering pulp demand, stocks, and trade based on various sources.
Frequency	Monthly
Availability	General
Cost	£250
Comments	Enquiry service can deal with ad hoc enquiries (minimum charge £15).
Address	Papermakers House, Rivenhall Road, Swindon SN5 7BD
Tel. / e-mail	01793 886086 fedn@paper.org.uk
Fax / Web site	01793 886182 www.paper.org.uk

698	PAPER FEDERATION OF GREAT BRITAIN
Title	**Recovered Fibre Consumption, Stocks and Trade**
Coverage	Monthly statistics on waste paper demand, stocks, and overseas trade based on various sources.
Frequency	Monthly
Availability	General
Cost	£250
Comments	Enquiry service can deal with ad hoc enquiries (minimum charge £15).
Address	Papermakers House, Rivenhall Road, Swindon SN5 7BD
Tel. / e-mail	01793 886086 fedn@paper.org.uk
Fax / Web site	01793 886182 www.paper.org.uk

699	**PAPER FEDERATION OF GREAT BRITAIN**
Title	**Reference Statistics**
Coverage	Ten-year series of tables and charts with data on production, consumption, sales, stocks, imports and exports of paper and board plus consumption, production, stocks, and imports of raw materials. Also data on employment, energy, and finance. Based on various sources.
Frequency	Annual
Availability	General
Cost	£100
Comments	Enquiry service can deal with ad hoc enquiries (minimum charge £15).
Address	Papermakers House, Rivenhall Road, Swindon SN5 7BD
Tel. / e-mail	01793 886086 fedn@paper.org.uk
Fax / Web site	01793 886182 www.paper.org.uk

700	**PAPER PUBLICATIONS LTD**
Title	**Paper Market Digest**
Coverage	Monthly digest which includes statistics on market trends and prices.
Frequency	Monthly
Availability	General
Cost	On request
Comments	–
Address	Church House, Church Lane, Kings Langley WD4 8JP
Tel. / e-mail	01923 261555 pplresearch@paper-pub.co.uk
Fax / Web site	01923 261118

701	**PAY AND WORKFORCE RESEARCH (PWR)**
Title	**Survey of Independent Healthcare Pay and Conditions**
Coverage	A survey of salaries, benefits, and conditions in the independent healthcare sector based on a survey of a sample of relevant organisations.
Frequency	Annual
Availability	General
Cost	£20, £15 to PWR clients
Comments	–
Address	Clarendon House, 9 Victoria Avenue, Harrogate HE1 1DY
Tel. / e-mail	01423 842684
Fax / Web site	01423 520272

702	
Title	PAY AND WORKFORCE RESEARCH (PWR)
	Terms and Conditions of Service for Healthcare Staff
Coverage	A survey of around 80 NHS organisations with data on salaries, terms, and conditions.
Frequency	Annual
Availability	General
Cost	£250, free to participants and PWR clients
Comments	–
Address	Clarendon House, 9 Victoria Avenue, Harrogate HE1 1DY
Tel. / e-mail	01423 842684
Fax / Web site	01423 520272

703	
Title	PEARSON PROFESSIONAL LTD
	Unit Trust Yearbook
Coverage	Includes a market commentary plus a statistical section on sales, total funds, performance, income from unit trusts etc. The official yearbook of the Association of Unit Trusts and Investment Funds and many figures are taken from this source.
Frequency	Annual
Availability	General
Cost	On request
Comments	An 'FT Financial Publishing' imprint.
Address	Maple House, 149 Tottenham Court Road, London W1P 9LL
Tel. / e-mail	0171 896 2222
Fax / Web site	0171 896 2274

704	
Title	PEDDER ASSOCIATES
	Applications Usage by Industry Sector
Coverage	Statistics and analysis of applications usage by companies spending £15,000 or more on data processing. Usage is broken down into 31 areas. Based on research by the company.
Frequency	Annual
Availability	General
Cost	£2,600
Comments	–
Address	34 Duncan Road, Richmond-upon-Thames TW9 2JD
Tel. / e-mail	0181 940 4300
Fax / Web site	0181 948 1531

705

Title	PEDDER ASSOCIATES **Computer Usage by Geographical Region**
Coverage	Statistics and analysis of the use of computers in companies spending £15,000 or over on data processing, broken down by region. Based on research by the company.
Frequency	Annual
Availability	General
Cost	£2,600
Comments	–
Address	34 Duncan Road, Richmond-upon-Thames TW9 2JD
Tel. / e-mail	0181 940 4300
Fax / Web site	0181 948 1531

706

Title	PEDDER ASSOCIATES **Computer Usage by Industry Sector**
Coverage	Statistics and analysis of the use of computers by companies spending over £15,000 on data processing per year. Covers 20 SIC sectors and based on research by the company.
Frequency	Annual
Availability	General
Cost	£2,600
Comments	–
Address	34 Duncan Road, Richmond-upon-Thames TW9 2JD
Tel. / e-mail	0181 940 4300
Fax / Web site	0181 94 8 1531

707

Title	PEDDER ASSOCIATES **DP Expenditure by Industry Sector**
Coverage	Statistics and analysis covering expenditure on hardware, software, and services for 20 industry sectors. Based on research by the company.
Frequency	Annual
Availability	General
Cost	£2,600
Comments	–
Address	34 Duncan Road, Richmond-upon-Thames TW9 2JD
Tel. / e-mail	0181 940 4300
Fax / Web site	0181 948 1531

708	PEDDER ASSOCIATES
Title	**General Purpose Computer Systems**
Coverage	A report detailing the ten-year installed base of computers and shipments history, broken down model by model. Also includes five-year projections of the installed base. Based on research by the company.
Frequency	Annual
Availability	General
Cost	£7,500
Comments	–
Address	34 Duncan Road, Richmond-upon-Thames TW9 2JD
Tel. / e-mail	0181 940 4300
Fax / Web site	0181 948 1531

709	PEDDER ASSOCIATES
Title	**Operating Systems Trends**
Coverage	Statistics and analysis of the usage and installed base of operating systems for companies spending more than £15,000 on data processing. Based on research by the company.
Frequency	Annual
Availability	General
Cost	£2,600
Comments	–
Address	34 Duncan Road, Richmond-upon-Thames TW9 2JD
Tel. / e-mail	0181 940 4300
Fax / Web site	0181 948 1531

710	PEDDER ASSOCIATES
Title	**Software Package Trends**
Coverage	Statistics and analysis of expenditure on software by companies spending £15,000 or more on data processing. Based on research by the company.
Frequency	Annual
Availability	General
Cost	£2,600
Comments	–
Address	34 Duncan Road, Richmond-upon-Thames TW9 2JD
Tel. / e-mail	0181 940 4300
Fax / Web site	0181 948 1531

711

PERIODICAL PUBLISHERS' ASSOCIATION

Handbook of Statistics on the Magazine Industry

Title	Handbook of Statistics on the Magazine Industry
Coverage	A compilation of data on the journal sector based on various sources.
Frequency	Regular
Availability	General
Cost	On request
Comments	Also publishes an Annual Review and various research reports on the magazine sector.
Address	15-19 Kingsway, London WC2B 6UN
Tel. / e-mail	0171 379 6268
Fax / Web site	0171 379 5661 www.ppa.co.uk

712

PET FOOD MANUFACTURERS' ASSOCIATION

PFMA Profile

Title	PFMA Profile
Coverage	Data on the market size and value for prepared pet foods plus some figures on pet ownership. Figures usually for the latest year and percentage change over the previous year. Based on the association's own survey with a general commentary on the figures.
Frequency	Regular
Availability	General
Cost	On request
Comments	–
Address	Suite 1-2, 12-13 Henrietta Street, London WC2E 8LH
Tel. / e-mail	0171 379 9009 info@pfma.org.uk
Fax / Web site	0171 379 8008

713

PETROLEUM ARGUS

Petroleum Argus Fundamentals

Title	Petroleum Argus Fundamentals
Coverage	Statistical analysis of the petroleum sector with data on prices, output, trade, consumption.
Frequency	Monthly
Availability	General
Cost	On request
Comments	–
Address	93 Shepperton Road, London N1 3DF
Tel. / e-mail	0171 359 8792 Kennington@petroleumargus.com
Fax / Web site	0171 226 0695

714	PETROLEUM ECONOMIST
Title	**Markets**
Coverage	Tables covering oil prices, world production, and tanker freight rates based on various sources.
Frequency	Monthly in a monthly journal
Availability	General
Cost	£230
Comments	Also publishes regular statistics on world oil trends.
Address	PO Box 105, Baird House, 15-17 St Cross Street, London EC1N 8VW
Tel. / e-mail	0171 831 5588 petecon@easynet.co.uk
Fax / Web site	0171 831 4567 www.petroleum-economist.com

715	PETROLEUM ECONOMIST
Title	**UK North Sea Survey**
Coverage	Statistics on North Sea oil fields with data on reserves, ownership, production etc. Compiled from a variety of sources.
Frequency	Annual in a monthly journal
Availability	General
Cost	£230
Comments	Also contains regular statistics on world oil trends.
Address	PO Box 105, Baird House, 15-17 St Cross Street, London EC1N 8VW
Tel. / e-mail	0171 831 5588 petecon@easynet.co.uk
Fax / Web site	0171 831 4567 www.petroleum-economist.com

716	PETROLEUM TIMES
Title	**Petroleum Times Energy Report**
Coverage	Provides pump prices for petrol in various towns and cities in the UK. Based on the journal's own survey with some supporting text.
Frequency	Twice monthly
Availability	General
Cost	£195 per annum
Comments	–
Address	Nexus Media Ltd, Nexus House, Azalea Drive, Swanley BR8 8HY
Tel. / e-mail	01322 660070
Fax / Web site	01322 667633 www.atelier.net/energyreport

	PHARMACEUTICAL JOURNAL
717	
Title	**Retail Sales Index for Chemists**
Coverage	General figures on the sales trends in total and for specific products sold in chemists. Based on Central Government data.
Frequency	Weekly
Availability	General
Cost	£99
Comments	Other statistics published occasionally.
Address	1 Lambeth High Street, London SE1 7JN
Tel. / e-mail	0171 735 9141 pharmpress@rpsgb.org.uk
Fax / Web site	0171 735 5085 www.pharmpress.com

	PHOTO MARKETING ASSOCIATION INTERNATIONAL (UK) LTD
718	
Title	**Industry Trends Report**
Coverage	A review of trends in the sector based on original market research.
Frequency	Annual
Availability	General
Cost	Free to members, £94 to others
Comments	–
Address	Peel Place, 50 Carver Street, Hockley, Birmingham B1 3AS
Tel. / e-mail	0121 212 0299 hattonpmauk@compuserve.com
Fax / Web site	0121 212 0298 www.pmai.org

	PIRA INTERNATIONAL
719	
Title	**Paper and Packaging Analyst**
Coverage	A review of trends in the paper and packaging sectors with articles and statistics.
Frequency	Quarterly
Availability	General
Cost	£495, £140 for a single issue
Comments	Also publishes reviews of the European printing and packaging sectors.
Address	Randalls Road, Leatherhead KT22 7RU
Tel. / e-mail	01372 802000 hattonpmauk@compuserve.com
Fax / Web site	01372 802239 www.pira.co.uk

720

	PIRA INTERNATIONAL
Title	**UK Printing Industry Statistics**
Coverage	The report includes 120 statistical tables covering production, and trends in the key sectors such as book, periodicals, and newspaper publishing. The strategic issues facing the industry are examined and company profiles are also included.
Frequency	Annual
Availability	General
Cost	£195
Comments	Also publishes reviews of the European printing and packaging sectors.
Address	Randalls Road, Leatherhead KT22 7RU
Tel. / e-mail	01372 802000 hattonpmauk@compuserve.com
Fax / Web site	01372 802239 www.pira.co.uk

721

	PMSI UK LTD
Title	**Medical Research Omnibus**
Coverage	A monthly omnibus survey of 400 general medical practitioners with face-to-face interviews in surgeries.
Frequency	Monthly
Availability	General
Cost	On application
Comments	Also carries out media advertising recall surveys and specialist omnibus surveys in the health care area.
Address	Mallard House, Peregrine Business Park, Gomm Road, High Wycombe HP13 7DL
Tel. / e-mail	01494 450098
Fax / Web site	01494 521934

722

	PRE-SCHOOL PLAY GROUP ASSOCIATION
Title	**Figures and Figures**
Coverage	Facts and figures on pre-school play based on data collected by the association and published sources.
Frequency	Regular
Availability	General
Cost	On application
Comments	Also publishes an Annual Aeport.
Address	61-63 Kings Cross Road, London WC1X 9LL
Tel. / e-mail	0171 833 0991
Fax / Web site	0171 837 4442

723	PRICE WATERHOUSE COOPERS
Title	**Price Waterhouse IT Review**
Coverage	A review of IT trends in the UK including data on expenditure, systems in place etc. Based on research by the company.
Frequency	Annual
Availability	General
Cost	Free
Comments	–
Address	Southwark Towers, 32 London Bridge Street, London SE1 9SY
Tel. / e-mail	0171 939 3000
Fax / Web site	0171 378 0647 www.pwcglobalcom/uk

724	PRICE WATERHOUSE COOPERS
Title	**UK Financial Services Information Technology**
Coverage	Based on a survey of IT directors in leading financial service companies, the report includes statistics on IT staff numbers, budgets, technologies etc. A commentary supports the tables and graphs.
Frequency	Regular
Availability	General
Cost	On request
Comments	–
Address	Southwark Towers, 32 London Bridge Street, London SE1 9SY
Tel. / e-mail	0171 939 3000
Fax / Web site	0171 378 0647 www.pwcglobalcom/uk

725	PRINTED CIRCUIT INTERCONNECTION FEDERATION (PCIF)
Title	**Quarterly Monitor**
Coverage	Basic data on sales, orders, exports with percentage changes from the previous figures. Based largely on the federation's own research.
Frequency	Quarterly
Availability	General
Cost	Free to members, £150 to others
Comments	–
Address	45 Beaufort Court, Admirals Way, South Quay, London E14 9XL
Tel. / e-mail	0171 515 1166 pcifenquiries@pcif.org.uk
Fax / Web site	0171 515 1188 www.pcif.org.uk

726	PRINTED CIRCUIT INTERCONNECTION FEDERATION (PCIF)
Title	**UK PCB Report**
Coverage	Statistics and analysis on production, imports, exports, UK market supply, employment, and a market breakdown. Based largely on original research supported by government import and export data.
Frequency	Annual
Availability	General
Cost	Free to members, £250 to others
Comments	–
Address	45 Beaufort Court, Admirals Way, South Quay, London E14 9XL
Tel. / e-mail	0171 515 1166 pcifenquiries@pcif.org.uk
Fax / Web site	0171 515 1188 www.pcif.org.uk

727	PROCESSING AND PACKAGING MACHINERY ASSOCIATION (PPMA)
Title	**UK Imports and Exports of Packaging Machinery**
Coverage	Brief commentary and graphs showing exports and imports over a three-year period. The figures are produced from Customs and Excise sources and separate intra-EU and extra-EU trade.
Frequency	Annual
Availability	
Cost	Free
Comments	–
Address	New Progress House, 34 Stafford Road, Wallington SM6 9AA
Tel. / e-mail	0181 773 8111 admin:ppma.co.uk
Fax / Web site	0181 773 0022 www.ppma.co.uk

728	PRODUCE STUDIES LTD
Title	**Omnifarm**
Coverage	An omnibus survey of 1,000 farmers in Great Britain with data on purchases, product awareness, general expenditure, readership etc.
Frequency	3 times a year
Availability	General
Cost	On application
Comments	Various other research projects and reports produced.
Address	Northcroft House, West Street, Newbury RG13 1HD
Tel. / e-mail	01635 46112
Fax / Web site	01635 43945

729	PROFESSIONAL PERSONNEL CONSULTANTS
Title	**PPC High Technology Salary Survey**
Coverage	A survey of salaries and benefits for staff in small high technology companies based on data collected by the company.
Frequency	Annual
Availability	General
Cost	£65
Comments	–
Address	Godwin House, George Street, Huntingdon PE18 6BU
Tel. / e-mail	01480 411111
Fax / Web site	01480 411111

730	PROFESSIONAL PERSONNEL CONSULTANTS
Title	**PPC Wage and Salary Survey**
Coverage	A salary and wages survey covering around 60 managerial, administrative, and manual jobs. Based on data collected by the company.
Frequency	Twice yearly
Availability	General
Cost	£75
Comments	–
Address	Godwin House, George Street, Huntingdon PE18 6BU
Tel. / e-mail	01480 411111
Fax / Web site	01480 411111

731	PROFESSIONAL PERSONNEL CONSULTANTS
Title	**Review of Directors' Remuneration and Benefits**
Coverage	A survey of directors' salaries and benefits in small- and medium-sized companies employing up to 400 staff. Based on data collected by the company.
Frequency	Annual
Availability	General
Cost	£65
Comments	–
Address	Godwin House, George Street, Huntingdon PE18 6BU
Tel. / e-mail	01480 411111
Fax / Web site	01480 411111

732	PROFESSIONAL PERSONNEL CONSULTANTS
Title	**Salary Survey for Hospitals and Nursing Homes**
Coverage	A survey of salaries and benefits covering 31 job functions in hospitals and nursing homes. Based on data collected by the company.
Frequency	Annual
Availability	General
Cost	£145, £75 for participants
Comments	–
Address	Godwin House, George Street, Huntingdon PE18 6BU
Tel. / e-mail	01480 411111
Fax / Web site	01480 411111

733	PROPERTY INTELLIGENCE PLC
Title	**UK Town and County Focus**
Coverage	A database, available online or on disc, of over 700 UK towns and cities, plus counties. For each town there is a statistical profile including demographic data, projections, employment trends, socio-economic profiles, rents, and unemployment data. Additional information on local plans, major retailers, proximity to other towns, and recent articles on the town. Based on various sources including the population Census, geodemographic data, local information, and property consultants.
Frequency	Continuous
Availability	General
Cost	On request
Comments	Property Intelligence PLC offers various property, and related databases. Also operates a European Town Focus database. Information Research Network (see other entry) and Chas E. Goad act as agents for the UK town profile database.
Address	Ingram House, 13-15 John Adam Street, London WC2N 6LD
Tel. / e-mail	0171 839 7684
Fax / Web site	0171 839 1060

734

PUBLISHERS' ASSOCIATION

Book Trade Yearbook

Title	**Book Trade Yearbook**
Coverage	Commentary followed by a statistical section covering publishers' sales, consumer expenditure, prices, exports, export prices. Statistics in the latest issue cover seven or eight years in many tables.
Frequency	Annual
Availability	General
Cost	£50, £10 to members
Comments	Also publishes various one-off reports. The web site has some useful statistics under the Key Facts and Figures pages.
Address	1 Kingsway, London WC2B 6XF
Tel. / e-mail	0171 565 7474 mail@publishers.org.uk
Fax / Web site	0171 836 4543 www.publishers.org.uk

735

PURCON CONSULTANTS LTD

The Purcon Index: A Salary Survey for the Purchasing Profession

Title	**The Purcon Index: A Salary Survey for the Purchasing Profession**
Coverage	A salary survey prepared from the Purcon Register which has records of over 10,000 candidates for jobs in purchasing.
Frequency	Twice yearly
Availability	General
Cost	£50 per copy, £90 annual subscription
Comments	–
Address	Ardenham Lane House, Aylesbury HP19 3AA
Tel. / e-mail	01296 480200 info@purcon.co.uk
Fax / Web site	01296 485899 www.purcon.co.uk

736

QUANTIME LTD

UK Labour Force Surveys

Title	**UK Labour Force Surveys**
Coverage	Quantime is an agent for the UK government's labour force statistics and it can provide data for specific requests or produce regular packages for clients. The original data is based on a sample survey of 65,000 households.
Frequency	Regular
Availability	General
Cost	Varies according to information required
Comments	Available in various formats including a dial-up database, information sheets, discs, hard copy reports etc.
Address	Maygrove House, 67 Maygrove Road, London NW6 2EG
Tel. / e-mail	0171 625 7111
Fax / Web site	0171 624 5293

737	QUARRY PRODUCTS' ASSOCIATION
Title	**QPA Statistical Yearbook**
Coverage	Statistics on the number and location of quarries, pits, and plants with additional information on the use of various types of construction materials. Based primarily on returns from members.
Frequency	Annual
Availability	General
Cost	£25
Comments	More detailed statistics are available to members.
Address	156 Buckingham Palace Road, London SW1 9TR
Tel. / e-mail	0171 730 8194 qpa@qpa.org
Fax / Web site	0171 730 4355

738	RADIO JOINT AUDIENCE RESEARCH (RAJAR)
Title	**Listener Surveys**
Coverage	Produces regular audience figures for BBC radio and national and local commercial radio.
Frequency	Regular
Availability	General
Cost	On request
Comments	Summary data on the RAJAR web site.
Address	Collier House, 163-169 Brompton Road, London SW3 1PY
Tel. / e-mail	0171 584 3003
Fax / Web site	0171 589 4004 www.rajar.co.uk

739	REED PERSONNEL SERVICES
Title	**Reed Employment Index**
Coverage	A review of trends in the jobs market with separate indices for temporary employment and permanent employment. Based on information obtained by the company.
Frequency	Monthly
Availability	General
Cost	On request
Comments	–
Address	6th Floor, Tolworth Tower, Ewell Road, Tolworth KT6 7EL
Tel. / e-mail	0181 399 5221
Fax / Web site	0181 399 4930

740	REMUNERATION ECONOMICS
Title	**A Survey of Sales and Marketing Staff**
Coverage	A salary survey covering nine levels of responsibility and broken down into various sectors. Based on data collected by the company.
Frequency	Annual
Availability	General
Cost	£370, £185 for participants
Comments	–
Address	Survey House, 51 Portland Road, Kingston-upon-Thames KT1 2SH
Tel. / e-mail	0181 549 8726 re@celre.co.uk
Fax / Web site	0181 541 5705 www.celre.co.uk

741	REMUNERATION ECONOMICS
Title	**Directors' Survey**
Coverage	A survey of salaries and benefits for chief executives, directors, and senior executives.
Frequency	Annual
Availability	General
Cost	£600
Comments	Produced in association with Bacon & Woodrow.
Address	Survey House, 51 Portland Road, Kingston-upon-Thames KT1 2SH
Tel. / e-mail	0181 549 8726 re@celre.co.uk
Fax / Web site	0181 541 5705 www.celre.co.uk

742	REMUNERATION ECONOMICS
Title	**National Management Salary Survey**
Coverage	A survey of managers to produce statistics on earnings, fringe benefits, and bonuses. Produced in three volumes: a general review of the survey, a detailed statistics volume, and a small business review.
Frequency	Annual
Availability	General
Cost	£380 for volumes 1 and 2 combined, £200 for the small business review. £470 for all three reports, discounts available to participants
Comments	Produced in association with the Institute of Management.
Address	Survey House, 51 Portland Road, Kingston-upon-Thames KT1 2SH
Tel. / e-mail	0181 549 8726 re@celre.co.uk
Fax / Web site	0181 541 5705 www.celre.co.uk

743	REMUNERATION ECONOMICS
Title	**Survey of Actuaries and Actuarial Students**
Coverage	A salary survey of actuaries and students with data by levels of responsibility, company size, age, qualifications etc.
Frequency	Annual
Availability	General
Cost	£640, £320 to participants
Comments	Produced in association with the Institute of Actuaries.
Address	Survey House, 51 Portland Road, Kingston-upon-Thames KT1 2SH
Tel. / e-mail	0181 549 8726 re@celre.co.uk
Fax / Web site	0181 541 5705 www.celre.co.uk

744	REMUNERATION ECONOMICS
Title	**Survey of Engineering Functions**
Coverage	A survey of engineering salaries covering nine levels of responsibility, by company size, type of work, qualifications, location etc. Based on the company's own survey with some supporting text.
Frequency	Annual
Availability	General
Cost	£300, £150 for participants
Comments	–
Address	Survey House, 51 Portland Road, Kingston-upon-Thames KT1 2SH
Tel. / e-mail	0181 549 8726 re@celre.co.uk
Fax / Web site	0181 541 5705 www.celre.co.uk

745	REMUNERATION ECONOMICS
Title	**Survey of Financial Functions**
Coverage	A salary survey for various levels of responsibility by company size, industry group, location, age, qualifications etc. Additional data on benefits and recruitment. Based on the company's own survey with some supporting text.
Frequency	Annual
Availability	General
Cost	£340, £185 to participants
Comments	–
Address	Survey House, 51 Portland Road, Kingston-upon-Thames KT1 2SH
Tel. / e-mail	0181 549 8726 re@celre.co.uk
Fax / Web site	0181 541 5705 www.celre.co.uk

746

	REMUNERATION ECONOMICS
Title	**Survey of Pensions Managers**
Coverage	A salary survey of pensions managers and related jobs with data by company size, industry group, location, age etc. Based on the company's own survey with some supporting text.
Frequency	Annual
Availability	General
Cost	£340, £185 for participants
Comments	–
Address	Survey House, 51 Portland Road, Kingston-upon-Thames KT1 2SH
Tel. / e-mail	0181 549 8726 re@celre.co.uk
Fax / Web site	0181 541 5705 www.celre.co.uk

747

	REMUNERATION ECONOMICS
Title	**Survey of Personnel Functions**
Coverage	A salary survey covering various levels of responsibility by size of company, industry group, location, age, qualifications etc. Additional data on benefits and recruitment. Based on the company's own survey with some supporting text.
Frequency	Annual
Availability	General
Cost	£340, £185 for participants
Comments	–
Address	Survey House, 51 Portland Road, Kingston-upon-Thames KT1 2SH
Tel. / e-mail	0181 549 8726 re@celre.co.uk
Fax / Web site	0181 541 5705 www.celre.co.uk

748

	RESEARCH AND AUDITING SERVICES LTD
Title	**National Business Omnibus**
Coverage	A regular omnibus survey of 2,000 businesses stratified by SIC code, UK region, and company size.
Frequency	Monthly
Availability	General
Cost	On application
Comments	–
Address	Monarch House, Victoria Road, London NW3 6RZ
Tel. / e-mail	0181 993 2220
Fax / Web site	0181 993 1114

	RESEARCH SURVEYS OF GREAT BRITAIN (RSGB)
749	
Title	**Baby Omnibus**
Coverage	Purchasing trends for baby products plus frequency of purchase, price paid, source of purchase, brand share. Also data on advertising awareness, and attitudes to new and existing products and images of products, services, and companies. Based on a sample of 700 mothers and analysis by age, social group, and incidence of birth.
Frequency	Quarterly
Availability	General
Cost	On request
Comments	Various other consumer surveys carried out.
Address	AGB House, West Gate, London W5 1EL
Tel. / e-mail	0181 967 4201 pam.walker@tnagb.com
Fax / Web site	0181 967 4330 www.tnagb.com

	RESEARCH SURVEYS OF GREAT BRITAIN (RSGB)
750	
Title	**Mailmonitor**
Coverage	A panel of 1,350 households is used to obtain data on the receipt of mail, including direct mail.
Frequency	Quarterly
Availability	General
Cost	On request
Comments	Various other consumer surveys carried out.
Address	AGB House, West Gate, London W5 1EL
Tel. / e-mail	0181 967 4201 pam.walker@tnagb.com
Fax / Web site	0181 967 4330 www.tnagb.com

	RESEARCH SURVEYS OF GREAT BRITAIN (RSGB)
751	
Title	**Omnibus Survey**
Coverage	A weekly omnibus survey based on face-to-face interviews with 2,000 adults. Demographic analysis and socio-economic analysis using the ACORN and MOSAIC classifications.
Frequency	Weekly
Availability	General
Cost	On application
Comments	Various other consumer surveys carried out.
Address	AGB House, West Gate, London W5 1EL
Tel. / e-mail	0181 967 4201 pam.walker@tnagb.com
Fax / Web site	0181 967 4330 www.tnagb.com

	752	RETAIL INTELLIGENCE
	Title	**The Retail Rankings**
	Coverage	Mainly financial and operating information on specific companies but it also has general statistics on retail sales, by sector, for the latest two years based on estimates produced by the company.
	Frequency	Annual
	Availability	General
	Cost	£295
	Comments	Also publishes various other reports on UK retailing sectors and European retailing.
	Address	48 Bedford Square, London WC1B 3DY
	Tel. / e-mail	0171 696 9006 sales@cior.com
	Fax / Web site	0171 696 9004 www.cior.com

	753	RETAIL INTELLIGENCE
	Title	**UK Retail Report**
	Coverage	Each report contains a number of surveys of specific retail sectors, with statistics, and most of these surveys are updated twice a year.
	Frequency	10 issues a year
	Availability	General
	Cost	£595
	Comments	Also publishes various other reports on UK retailing sectors and European retailing.
	Address	48 Bedford Square, London WC1B 3DY
	Tel. / e-mail	0171 696 9006 sales@cior.com
	Fax / Web site	0171 696 9004 www.cior.com

	754	RETAIL JEWELLER AND BRITISH JEWELLER
	Title	**British Jewellers' Yearbook**
	Coverage	A directory and handbook for the industry which includes statistics on fine gold prices for the last 15 years, including highs and lows.
	Frequency	Annual
	Availability	General
	Cost	£45
	Comments	–
	Address	EMAP Business Communications, Angle House, 338-346 Goswell Road, London EC1V 7QP
	Tel. / e-mail	0171 520 1584 rj@fashion.emap.co.uk
	Fax / Web site	0171 520 15852

	755 RETAIL JEWELLER AND BRITISH JEWELLER
Title	**Market Reports/Prices**
Coverage	Mainly news and features on the jewellery trade but some regular market reports with data on precious metal prices and fine gold prices.
Frequency	Twice monthly
Availability	General
Cost	£2.10 per issue
Comments	–
Address	EMAP Business Communications, Angle House, 338-346 Goswell Road, London EC1V 7QP
Tel. / e-mail	0171 520 1584 rj@fashion.emap.co.uk
Fax / Web site	0171 520 1582

	756 REWARD GROUP
Title	**Charity Salary Survey**
Coverage	A survey of salaries in the charity sector with analysis by job and level of charity income for full-time employees. Based on research by the company.
Frequency	Annual
Availability	General
Cost	£260
Comments	Published in September. Specific inquiries answered from Reward's data bank.
Address	Reward House, Diamond Way, Stone Business Park, Stone ST15 0SD
Tel. / e-mail	01785 813566 enquiries@reward-group.co.uk
Fax / Web site	01785 817007 www.reward-group.co.uk

	757 REWARD GROUP
Title	**Clerical and Operative Rewards**
Coverage	A review of all clerical and operative positions analysed by size of company, sector, and geographical area. Based on research by the company.
Frequency	Twice yearly
Availability	General
Cost	£445 subscription
Comments	Published in January and July. Specific inquiries answered from Reward's data bank.
Address	Reward House, Diamond Way, Stone Business Park, Stone ST15 0SD
Tel. / e-mail	01785 813566 enquiries@reward-group.co.uk
Fax / Web site	01785 817007 www.reward-group.co.uk

758

REWARD GROUP

Directors' Rewards

Title

Coverage Detailed information of salaries and benefits for chairman, managing director, and a wide range of functional directors posts, analysed by company turnover and number of employees. Based on the company's own research.

Frequency Annual

Availability General

Cost £550

Comments Produced in association with the Institute of Directors. Published in December. Specific inquiries answered from Reward's data bank.

Address Reward House, Diamond Way, Stone Business Park, Stone ST15 0SD

Tel. / e-mail 01785 813566   enquiries@reward-group.co.uk

Fax / Web site 01785 817007   www.reward-group.co.uk

759

REWARD GROUP

Distribution Rewards

Title

Coverage Salary information on management, professional, technical, and commercial jobs in the distribution sector. Based on research by the company.

Frequency Bi-annual

Availability General

Cost £500

Comments Specific inquiries answered by Reward's data bank.

Address Reward House, Diamond Way, Stone Business Park, Stone ST15 0SD

Tel. / e-mail 01785 813566   enquiries@reward-group.co.uk

Fax / Web site 01785 817007   www.reward-group.co.uk

760

REWARD GROUP

Electronics Industry Rewards

Title

Coverage Salary information on management, professional, technical, and commercial jobs in the software and electronics sector. Based on research by the company.

Frequency Bi-annual

Availability General

Cost £500

Comments Specific inquiries answered from Reward's data bank.

Address Reward House, Diamond Way, Stone Business Park, Stone ST15 0SD

Tel. / e-mail 01785 813566   enquiries@reward-group.co.uk

Fax / Web site 01785 817007   www.reward-group.co.uk

	REWARD GROUP
761	
Title	**Local Authority Survey**
Coverage	A salary survey of local authority jobs, including many which are specific to local authorities. Based on research by the company.
Frequency	Twice yearly
Availability	General
Cost	£225, £110 to participants
Comments	Published in April and November. Specific inquiries answered from Reward's data bank.
Address	Reward House, Diamond Way, Stone Business Park, Stone ST15 0SD
Tel. / e-mail	01785 813566 enquiries@reward-group.co.uk
Fax / Web site	01785 817007 www.reward-group.co.uk

	REWARD GROUP
762	
Title	**London Secretarial Salary Survey**
Coverage	A salary survey of six types of secretarial jobs in the capital. Based on research by the company.
Frequency	Twice yearly
Availability	General
Cost	£275
Comments	Published in February and August. Specific inquiries answered from Reward's data bank.
Address	Reward House, Diamond Way, Stone Business Park, Stone ST15 0SD
Tel. / e-mail	01785 813566 enquiries@reward-group.co.uk
Fax / Web site	01785 817007 www.reward-group.co.uk

	REWARD GROUP
763	
Title	**Oilfield Services**
Coverage	Salary information on management, professional, technical, and commercial jobs in oilfield services. Based on research by the company.
Frequency	Annual
Availability	General
Cost	£720, £360 to participants
Comments	Specific inquiries answered from Reward's data bank.
Address	Reward House, Diamond Way, Stone Business Park, Stone ST15 0SD
Tel. / e-mail	01785 813566 enquiries@reward-group.co.uk
Fax / Web site	01785 817007 www.reward-group.co.uk

REWARD GROUP

Pay for Senior NHS Managers

Title	
Coverage	A review of pay and conditions of service for senior managers in the NHS. Based on research by the company.
Frequency	Regular
Availability	General
Cost	£300
Comments	First published in March 1995. Produced in association with the Institute of Health Services Management. Specific inquiries answered from Reward's data bank.
Address	Reward House, Diamond Way, Stone Business Park, Stone ST15 0SD
Tel. / e-mail	01785 813566 enquiries@reward-group.co.uk
Fax / Web site	01785 817007 www.reward-group.co.uk

REWARD GROUP

Personnel Rewards

Title	
Coverage	An annual report with details of basic and total pay, company cars and other benefits. Based on research by the company.
Frequency	Annual
Availability	General
Cost	£275
Comments	Produced in association with the Institute of Personnel and Development (IPD). Published in October. Specific inquiries answered from Reward's data bank.
Address	Reward House, Diamond Way, Stone Business Park, Stone ST15 0SD
Tel. / e-mail	01785 813566 enquiries@reward-group.co.uk
Fax / Web site	01785 817007 www.reward-group.co.uk

REWARD GROUP

Regional Comparisons

Title	
Coverage	Cost of living comparisons for the main regions of the UK covering various products and services, income levels, and lifestyles. Based on Reward's own survey in key centres. Historical data back to 1973.
Frequency	Twice yearly
Availability	General
Cost	£290
Comments	Reports published in March and September. Specific inquiries answered from Reward's data bank.
Address	Reward House, Diamond Way, Stone Business Park, Stone ST15 0SD
Tel. / e-mail	01785 813566 enquiries@reward-group.co.uk
Fax / Web site	01785 817007 www.reward-group.co.uk

767

Title	**REWARD GROUP** **Regional Salary and Wage Survey**
Coverage	Twice-yearly surveys covering 17 local areas with salaries and conditions given for all grades of employees. Based on annual research.
Frequency	Twice yearly
Availability	General
Cost	£225, £90 to participants
Comments	Specific inquiries answered by Reward's data bank.
Address	Reward House, Diamond Way, Stone Business Park, Stone ST15 0SD
Tel. / e-mail	01785 813566 enquiries@reward-group.co.uk
Fax / Web site	01785 817007 www.reward-group.co.uk

768

Title	**REWARD GROUP** **Research and Development Salary Survey**
Coverage	An annual report covering basic salaries, total remuneration, and benefits in the R&D field. Based on research by the company.
Frequency	Annual
Availability	General
Cost	£275
Comments	Published in May. Specific inquiries answered from Reward's data bank.
Address	Reward House, Diamond Way, Stone Business Park, Stone ST15 0SD
Tel. / e-mail	01785 813566 enquiries@reward-group.co.uk
Fax / Web site	01785 817007 www.reward-group.co.uk

769

Title	**REWARD GROUP** **Retail Rewards**
Coverage	Salary information for management, professional, technical, and commercial jobs in the retail sector. Based on the company's own research.
Frequency	Annual
Availability	General
Cost	£130
Comments	Specific inquiries answered from Reward's data bank.
Address	Reward House, Diamond Way, Stone Business Park, Stone ST15 0SD
Tel. / e-mail	01785 813566 enquiries@reward-group.co.uk
Fax / Web site	01785 817007 www.reward-group.co.uk

770

	REWARD GROUP
Title	**Reward - The Management Salary Survey**
Coverage	A management salary report covering over 115 jobs and including advice, forecasts, and comments on salary movements. Based on the company's own research.
Frequency	Twice yearly
Availability	General
Cost	£445 subscription
Comments	Published in March and September. Specific inquiries answered from Reward's data bank.
Address	Reward House, Diamond Way, Stone Business Park, Stone ST15 0SD
Tel. / e-mail	01785 813566 enquiries@reward-group.co.uk
Fax / Web site	01785 817007 www.reward-group.co.uk

771

	REWARD GROUP
Title	**Sales and Marketing Rewards**
Coverage	An annual review of salaries, bonuses, commission, company cars and other benefits. Based on research by the company.
Frequency	Annual
Availability	General
Cost	£275
Comments	Produced in association with the Chartered Institute of Marketing (CIM). Published in October. Specific inquiries answered from Reward's data bank.
Address	Reward House, Diamond Way, Stone Business Park, Stone ST15 0SD
Tel. / e-mail	01785 813566 enquiries@reward-group.co.uk
Fax / Web site	01785 817007 www.reward-group.co.uk

772

	RICHARD HOLWAY LTD
Title	**Holway Report**
Coverage	A two volume report on the software and computing services industry. Volume 1 contains general market data and analysis, including projections for the next four years. Volume 2 has profiles of 800 leading companies. Based largely on research by the company.
Frequency	Annual
Availability	General
Cost	£2,450
Comments	Published in June.
Address	PO Box 183, Farnham GU10 1YG
Tel. / e-mail	01252 781545 holway@compuserve.com
Fax / Web site	01252 781546 www.holway.co.uk

773	RICHARD HOLWAY LTD
Title	**System House**
Coverage	A monthly review of the financial performance of the UK computing service industry.
Frequency	Monthly
Availability	General
Cost	£340
Comments	–
Address	PO Box 183, Farnham GU10 1YG
Tel. / e-mail	01252 781545 holway@compuserve.com
Fax / Web site	01252 781546 www.holway.co.uk

774	RMIF LTD
Title	**Monthly Statistics**
Coverage	Monthly figures for new car sales, in units, with a breakdown between total cars and company cars.
Frequency	Monthly
Availability	Primarily members but other requests considered..
Cost	Free
Comments	RMIF is the Retail Motor Industry Federation.
Address	201 Great Portland Street, London W1N 6AB
Tel. / e-mail	0171 580 9122
Fax / Web site	0171 580 6376 www.rmif.co.uk

775	RMIF LTD
Title	**New Car Sales by County**
Coverage	A regional and county breakdown of new car sales, in units, for the latest year with the percentage change over the previous year. Sales are broken down into total cars and company cars.
Frequency	Annual
Availability	Primarily members but other requests considered.
Cost	Free
Comments	RMIF is the Retail Motor Industry Federation.
Address	201 Great Portland Street, London W1N 6AB
Tel. / e-mail	0171 580 9122
Fax / Web site	0171 580 6376 www.rmif.co.uk

776	ROSS YOUNG'S HOLDINGS LTD
Title	**Frozen Food Retail Market Report**
Coverage	Commentary and statistics on retail sales, market trends, brands, distribution channels, and current issues.
Frequency	Regular
Availability	General
Cost	On request
Comments	–
Address	Ross House, Wickham Road, Grimsby DN31 3SW
Tel. / e-mail	01472 359111
Fax / Web site	01472 240640

777	ROYAL BANK OF SCOTLAND PLC
Title	**Quarterly Survey of Exports**
Coverage	A survey of export trends and prospects in Scotland based on returns from Scottish exporters. Includes a commentary and analysis of the data.
Frequency	Quarterly
Availability	General
Cost	Free
Comments	–
Address	42 St Andrew Square, Edinburgh EH2 2YE
Tel. / e-mail	0131 556 8555
Fax / Web site	0131 556 8555

778	ROYAL BANK OF SCOTLAND PLC
Title	**Royal Bank of Scotland Oil Index**
Coverage	Data on production from North Sea oil fields and the average daily value of oil production based on a telephone survey of oil field operators. An analysis of the statistics is also included.
Frequency	Monthly
Availability	General
Cost	Free
Comments	–
Address	42 St Andrew Square, Edinburgh EH2 2YE
Tel. / e-mail	0131 556 8555
Fax / Web site	0131 556 8555

779	ROYAL BANK OF SCOTLAND PLC
Title	**Summary of UK Business Conditions**
Coverage	Covers production, employment, overseas transactions, prices, wages, industrial investment, banking, short-term money rates and the Stock Exchange. Based on a mixture of bank statistics, Central Government data, and non-official sources. Approximately 50% of the report is text.
Frequency	Monthly
Availability	General
Cost	Free
Comments	–
Address	42 St Andrew Square, Edinburgh EH2 2YE
Tel. / e-mail	0131 556 8555
Fax / Web site	0131 556 8555

780	ROYAL INSTITUTION OF CHARTERED SURVEYORS
Title	**Housing Market Survey**
Coverage	National figures and regional data each month for various types and ages of property. Shows the trends in prices over the previous three months and includes comments on the market situation from estate agents.
Frequency	Monthly
Availability	General
Cost	£10
Comments	–
Address	12 Great George Street, Parliament Square, London SW1P 3AD
Tel. / e-mail	0171 222 7000
Fax / Web site	0171 222 9430

781	RYDEN PROPERTY CONSULTANTS AND CHARTERED SURVEYORS
Title	**Scottish Industrial & Commercial Property Review**
Coverage	A review of economic trends in Scotland, with forecasts, is followed by a commentary on the Scottish property market covering Edinburgh, Glasgow, Aberdeen, and Dundee. Specific sections on shops, and industrial and warehouse property. Based primarily on data from the company.
Frequency	Twice yearly
Availability	General
Cost	Free
Comments	–
Address	46 Castle Street, Edinburgh EH2 3BN
Tel. / e-mail	0131 225 6612
Fax / Web site	0131 225 5766

782

	SALARY SURVEY PUBLICATIONS
Title	**Survey of Appointments' Data and Trends**
Coverage	A generic series title for various surveys of salaries and appointments in a range of sectors including IT, human resources personnel. Most surveys are based on an analysis of advertisements in the press and actual salary data.
Frequency	Regular
Availability	General
Cost	On request - typical prices are £295-£325 per survey
Comments	–
Address	7 High Street, Lambourn RG17 8XL
Tel. / e-mail	01488 72705 ssp@easynet.co.uk
Fax / Web site	

783

	SAMPLE SURVEYS LTD
Title	**Omnicar**
Coverage	A monthly motoring omnibus survey based on a sample of 1,000 motorists. Analysis of purchases, services, DIY, insurance, number of cars in household, engine size, make, model etc.
Frequency	Monthly
Availability	General
Cost	On application
Comments	–
Address	Mount Offham, Offham, West Malling ME19 5PG
Tel. / e-mail	01732 874450 admin@sample-surveys.co.uk
Fax / Web site	01732 875100 www.sample-surveys.co.uk

784

	SCOTCH WHISKY ASSOCIATION
Title	**Statistical Report**
Coverage	Figures on the activities of the industry including production, exports, stocks, and duty paid. Figures for some previous years also given. Based mainly on Central Government statistics with a small amount of original data.
Frequency	Annual
Availability	General
Cost	£25
Comments	A summary of the statistics is available on the web site.
Address	14 Cork Street, London W1X 1PF
Tel. / e-mail	0171 629 4384 london.office@swa.org.uk
Fax / Web site	0171 493 1398 www.scotch-whisky.org.uk

785

	SCOTTISH COUNCIL DEVELOPMENT AND INDUSTRY
Title	**Quarterly Index of Scottish Manufacturing Exports**
Coverage	An index measuring the performance of Scottish exports, based on a survey by the Scottish Council.
Frequency	Quarterly
Availability	General
Cost	Free
Comments	Various other reports on Scottish economic and business trends also produced.
Address	23 Chester Street, Edinburgh EH3 7ET
Tel. / e-mail	0131 225 7911 edinburgh@scdi.org.uk
Fax / Web site	0131 220 2116 www.scdi.org.uk

786

	SCOTTISH COUNCIL DEVELOPMENT AND INDUSTRY
Title	**Survey of Scottish Manufacturing and Exports**
Coverage	Estimates of the value and volume of Scottish manufacturing and exports. Based on a sample of Scottish exporters with a commentary supporting the text.
Frequency	Annual
Availability	General
Cost	Free
Comments	–
Address	23 Chester Street, Edinburgh EH3 7ET
Tel. / e-mail	0131 225 7911 edinburgh@scdi.org.uk
Fax / Web site	0131 220 2116 www.scdi.org.uk

787

	SCOTTISH COUNCIL DEVELOPMENT AND INDUSTRY
Title	**Survey of Scottish Primary Sector Exports**
Coverage	A regular survey of primary sector exports.
Frequency	Annual
Availability	General
Cost	Free
Comments	–
Address	23 Chester Street, Edinburgh EH3 7ET
Tel. / e-mail	0131 225 7911 edinburgh@scdi.org.uk
Fax / Web site	0131 220 2116 www.scdi.org.uk

788	SCOTTISH COUNCIL DEVELOPMENT AND INDUSTRY
Title	**Survey of Scottish Service Sector Exports**
Coverage	A regular survey of service sector exports.
Frequency	Annual
Availability	General
Cost	Free
Comments	–
Address	23 Chester Street, Edinburgh EH3 7ET
Tel. / e-mail	0131 225 7911 edinburgh@scdi.org.uk
Fax / Web site	0131 220 2116 www.scdi.org.uk

789	SCREEN PRINTING ASSOCIATION (UK) LTD
Title	**Survey of Trends**
Coverage	A survey of trends in the previous three months and likely trends in the coming three months based on returns from members. Includes data on costs, sales, orders, margins on sales, capital expenditure, employment, and prices.
Frequency	Quarterly
Availability	Members
Cost	Free to participating members
Comments	–
Address	7A West Street, Reigate RH2 9BL
Tel. / e-mail	01737 240792
Fax / Web site	01737 240770

790	SEA FISH INDUSTRY AUTHORITY
Title	**Household Fish Consumption in Great Britain**
Coverage	Analysis of sales by species for household consumption, split into fresh/chilled and frozen sales. The statistics are taken from a sample survey of households and comparable data for the previous year is given. Some text supports the data.
Frequency	Quarterly
Availability	General
Cost	£75 annual subscription
Comments	Also publishes a regular European Supplies Bulletin with statistics on specific European countries.
Address	18 Logie Mill, Logie Green Road, Edinburgh EH7 4HG
Tel. / e-mail	0131 558 3331 seafish.co.uk
Fax / Web site	0131 558 1442 www.seafish.co.uk

791

SEA FISH INDUSTRY AUTHORITY

Key Indicators

Key statistics on supplies, household consumption, prices, international trade etc. Based mainly on Central Government sources.

Quarterly

General

£35 annual subscription

Also publishes a European Supplies Bulletin with statistics on specific European countries.

18 Logie Mill, Logie Green Road, Edinburgh   EH7 4HG

0131 558 3331   seafish.co.uk

0131 558 1442   www.seafish.co.uk

792

SEA FISH INDUSTRY AUTHORITY

UK Trade Bulletin

Quantity and value of imports and exports of fish intended for human consumption. The latest month's figures with the year to date and comparative figures for the previous year. Based on Central Government data.

Monthly

General

£35 annual susbcription

Also publishes the European Supplies Bulletin with statistics on specific European countries.

18 Logie Mill, Logie Green Road, Edinburgh   EH7 4HG

0131 558 3331   seafish.co.uk

0131 558 1442   www.seafish.co.uk

793

SEWELLS INTERNATIONAL

Franchise Networks

Statistics on car distribution networks, commercial vehicle distribution networks, dealer groups, and petrol retailing.

Annual

General

£145

The 26th edition was published in 1998.

Wentworth House, Wentworth Street, Peterborough   PE1 1DS

01733 467191

01733 467199

794	
Title	**SHARWOOD & CO LTD**
	Ethnic Foods Market Review
Coverage	An analysis of trends in the ethnic foods market with data on total sales, sales by market sector (eg Chinese, Indian etc), sales by type of product, household penetration, and brand shares. Based on research commissioned by the company.
Frequency	Annual
Availability	General
Cost	Free
Comments	–
Address	J A Sharwood & Co Ltd, Egham TW20 9QG
Tel. / e-mail	01784 473000
Fax / Web site	

795	
Title	**SHAWS' PRICE GUIDES LTD**
	Shaws' Retail Price Guide
Coverage	Fair selling prices, recommended by the manufacturers or by the editors, for 13,000 products divided into various categories, e.g. groceries, household, medicines, tobacco,etc. Based on regular surveys carried out by the company.
Frequency	Monthly
Availability	General
Cost	£18.50
Comments	–
Address	Baden House, 7 St Peters Place, Brighton BN1 6TB
Tel. / e-mail	01273 680041
Fax / Web site	01273 606588

796	
Title	**SILK ASSOCIATION OF GREAT BRITAIN**
	Serica
Coverage	Mainly news and comment on the silk industry but it includes some statistics, mainly imports and exports.
Frequency	6 issues per year
Availability	General
Cost	On application
Comments	–
Address	Morley Road, Tonbridge TN9 1RN
Tel. / e-mail	01732 351357
Fax / Web site	01732 770217

797	SILVER FERN RESEARCH
Title	**Silver Fern Omnibus**
Coverage	Regular omnibus survey of general practitioners with a sample size of 50 in 12 areas. Concentrates on prescribing behaviour.
Frequency	Fortnightly
Availability	General
Cost	On application
Comments	–
Address	Gartside House, Harris Way, Windmill Road, Sunbury TW16 7EL
Tel. / e-mail	01932 765751
Fax / Web site	01932 783403

798	SMART CARD CLUB
Title	**The Status of the UK Smart Card Marketplace**
Coverage	A review of the market broken down by applications plus a forecast of card penetration levels for the year 2000. Also includes details of suppliers, the history of the smart card, and technological issues. Mainly text with two main statistical tables.
Frequency	Regular
Availability	General
Cost	
Comments	The first report was produced in 1994 but there are plans for regular updates.
Address	8-9 Bridge Street, Cambridge CB2 1UA
Tel. / e-mail	01223 329900
Fax / Web site	01223 358222

799	SOCIETY OF BUSINESS ECONOMISTS
Title	**Business Economists' Salary Survey**
Coverage	Basic salaries and benefits by employment type, age, and sex. Based on a sample of society members. A commentary supports the data.
Frequency	Annual
Availability	General
Cost	£12.50
Comments	Published in the June issue of the Society's journal, 'The Business Economist'.
Address	11 Baytree Walk, Watford WD1 3RX
Tel. / e-mail	01923 237287
Fax / Web site	

800	SOCIETY OF COUNTY TREASURERS
Title	**Standard Spending Indicators**
Coverage	Statistics on spending on particular services by local authorities in England. Based on returns from the local authorities.
Frequency	Annual
Availability	General
Cost	£300, £50 to local authorities, libraries and universities
Comments	Produced in association with the Society of Metropolitan Treasurers and the Association of District Council Treasurers. Some information can be obtained free from the web site listed below.
Address	Treasurer's Department, Somerset County Council, County Hall, Taunton TA1 4DY
Tel. / e-mail	01823 355295
Fax / Web site	01823 355554 www.local.detr.gov.uk

801	SOCIETY OF MOTOR MANUFACTURERS AND TRADERS (SMMT)
Title	**EIE - UK Export Allocation of Production**
Coverage	A statistical service offering motor vehicle export data.
Frequency	Regular
Availability	General
Cost	Price depends on the nature of the information required.
Comments	Also publishes monthly and annual statistics for other European countries and the world market. Some basic statistics freely available on the web site.
Address	Automotive Data Services, Forbes House, Halkin Street, London SW1X 7DS
Tel. / e-mail	0171 235 7000
Fax / Web site	0171 235 7112 www.smmt.co.uk

802	SOCIETY OF MOTOR MANUFACTURERS AND TRADERS (SMMT)
Title	**PIE - UK Production**
Coverage	A statistical service offering data on UK vehicle production by manufacturer, model.
Frequency	Regular
Availability	General
Cost	On request
Comments	Also publishes monthly and annual statistics for other European countries and the world market. Some basic statistics freely available on the web site.
Address	, SW1X 7DS
Tel. / e-mail	0171 235 7000
Fax / Web site	0171 235 7112 www.smmt.co.uk

803	SOCIETY OF MOTOR MANUFACTURERS' AND TRADERS (SMMT)
Title	**ANON - GB Used Vehicle Sales and in Circulation**
Coverage	A service offering regular statistics on used vehicles sold and total parc.
Frequency	Regular
Availability	General
Cost	Price depends on the nature of the information required
Comments	Also publishes monthly and annual statistics on other European countries and the world market. Some basic statistics on the web site freely available.
Address	Automotive Data Services, Forbes House, Halkin Street, London SW1X 7DS
Tel. / e-mail	0171 235 7000
Fax / Web site	0171 235 7112 www.smmt.co.uk

804	SOCIETY OF MOTOR MANUFACTURERS' AND TRADERS (SMMT)
Title	**MPSS - Motorparc Statistics Service**
Coverage	A service based on the annual census of motor vehicles carried out by the government agency, DVLA.
Frequency	Regular
Availability	General
Cost	Price depends on the nature of the information required
Comments	Also publishes monthly and annual statistics for other European countries and the world market. Some basic statistics on the web site freely available.
Address	Automotive Data Services, Forbes House, Halkin Street, London SW1X 7DS
Tel. / e-mail	0171 235 7000
Fax / Web site	0171 235 7112 www.smmt.co.uk

805

SOCIETY OF MOTOR MANUFACTURERS' AND TRADERS (SMMT)

Title   **MVRIS - Motor Vehicle Registration Information System**

Coverage   Monthly statistics plus individual tailored reports on vehicle registrations. Data available by model, manufacturer, location etc.

Frequency   Regular

Availability   General

Cost   Price depends on the nature of the information required

Comments   Also publishes monthly and annual statistics for other European countries and the world market. Some basic statistics on the web site freely available.

Address   Automotive Data Services, Forbes House, Halkin Street, London SW1X 7DS

Tel. / e-mail   0171 235 7000

Fax / Web site   0171 235 7112   www.smmt.co.uk

806

SOCIETY OF MOTOR MANUFACTURERS' AND TRADERS (SMMT)

Title   **SMMT Monthly Statistical Review**

Coverage   Production and registrations of motor vehicles by manufacturer and model plus imports and exports of products of the motor industry. Less frequent special tables such as forecasts and the annual motor vehicle census. Based on a combination of Central Government data and the society's own survey.

Frequency   Monthly

Availability   General

Cost   £119, £93 members

Comments   Also publishes monthly and annual statistics for European countries and the world market. Some basic statistics on the web site freely available.

Address   Automotive Data Services, Forbes House, Halkin Street, London SW1X 7DS

Tel. / e-mail   0171 235 7000

Fax / Web site   0171 235 7112   www.smmt.co.uk

807	SOCIETY OF PRACTITIONERS IN INSOLVENCY
Title	**Company Insolvency in the UK**
Coverage	Based on returns from members, this report shows the trends in company insolvencies over the last 12 months. The report analyses the reasons for failure and the characteristics of failed companies. Based on almost 3,000 individual cases.
Frequency	Annual
Availability	General
Cost	£50
Comments	–
Address	Halton House, 2-23 Holborn, London EC1N 2DE
Tel. / e-mail	0171 831 6563 gensec@spi.org.uk
Fax / Web site	0171 405 7047 www.spi.org.uk

808	SOCIETY OF PRACTITIONERS IN INSOLVENCY
Title	**Personal Insolvency in the UK**
Coverage	An analysis of personal insolvency trends over the last year based on returns from members. The latest issue is based on over 1,200 individual cases.
Frequency	Annual
Availability	General
Cost	£50
Comments	–
Address	Halton House, 2-23 Holborn, London EC1N 2DE
Tel. / e-mail	0171 831 6563 gensec@spi.org.uk
Fax / Web site	0171 405 7047 www.spi.org.uk

809	SPA (UK) LTD
Title	**Mosaic**
Coverage	Specialising primarily in the retail sector, SPA provides various geodemographic services based on various sources including the 1991 Census, postcode address file, Target Group Index, and the Financial Research Survey (FRS).
Frequency	Continuous
Availability	General
Cost	On application, and depending on the range and nature of the information required
Comments	–
Address	Association House, 7a West Street, Reigate RH2 9BL
Tel. / e-mail	01737 240792 spa-uk@msn.com
Fax / Web site	01737 240770 www.martex.co.uk/spa

810	SPON, E & FN
Title	**Spon's Architects' and Builders' Price Book**
Coverage	Prices of materials, prices for measured work and rates of wages. Based mainly on Spon's own surveys with additional data from other non-official sources.
Frequency	Annual
Availability	General
Cost	£75
Comments	Usually published in August.
Address	Cheriton House, North Way, Andover SP10 5BE
Tel. / e-mail	01264 332424 orders@routledge.com
Fax / Web site	01264 343005 www.efnspon.com

811	SPON, E & FN
Title	**Spon's Civil Engineering and Highway Works Price Book**
Coverage	Prices and costs of building, services, engineering, external work, landscaping etc. Based on Spon's own surveys and other non-official sources.
Frequency	Annual
Availability	General
Cost	£97.50
Comments	Usually published in March.
Address	Cheriton House, North Way, Andover SP10 5BE
Tel. / e-mail	01264 332424 orders@routledge.com
Fax / Web site	01264 343005 www.efnspon.com

812	SPON, E & FN
Title	**Spon's House Improvements Price Book**
Coverage	Prices of house improvement services and materials. Based on Spon's own surveys.
Frequency	Annual
Availability	General
Cost	£42.50
Comments	–
Address	Cheriton House, North Way, Andover SP10 5BE
Tel. / e-mail	01264 332424 orders@routledge.com
Fax / Web site	01264 343005 www.efnspon.com

813	SPON, E & FN
Title	**Spon's Landscape and External Works Price Book**
Coverage	Prices and costs covering hard and soft landscapes and external works generally. Based on Spon's own surveys and some other non-official data.
Frequency	Annual
Availability	General
Cost	£65
Comments	Usually published in August.
Address	Cheriton House, North Way, Andover SP10 5BE
Tel. / e-mail	01264 332424 orders@routledge.com
Fax / Web site	01264 343005 www.efnspon.com

814	SPON, E & FN
Title	**Spon's Mechanical and Electrical Services Price Book**
Coverage	Prices and costs of heating, lighting, ventilation, air conditioning, and other service items in industrial and commercial property. Based on Spon's own surveys plus other non-official sources.
Frequency	Annual
Availability	General
Cost	£77.50
Comments	Usually published in August.
Address	Cheriton House, North Way, Andover SP10 5BE
Tel. / e-mail	01264 332424 orders@routledge.com
Fax / Web site	01264 343005 www.efnspon.com

815	SPON, E & FN
Title	**Spon's Railway Construction Price Book**
Coverage	Annual rail cost information based on Spon's own surveys.
Frequency	Annual
Availability	General
Cost	£125
Comments	Usually published in September.
Address	Cheriton House, North Way, Andover SP10 5BE
Tel. / e-mail	01264 332424 orders@routledge.com
Fax / Web site	01264 343005 www.efnspon.com

816	SPORTS MARKETING SURVEYS
Title	**Sports Syndicated Surveys**
Coverage	Various syndicated surveys on a range of sports including running, football, golf, racing, fitness.
Frequency	Regular
Availability	Participants
Cost	On application
Comments	–
Address	Carlton House, Chertsey Road, Byfleet KT14 7AN
Tel. / e-mail	01932 350600
Fax / Web site	01932 350375 www.sportsmarketingsurveys.com

817	STANDING CONFERENCE OF NATIONAL AND UNIVERSITY LIBRARIES (SCONUL)
Title	**Annual Library Statistics**
Coverage	Expenditure and operational trends based on the annual returns from SCONUL libraries. A small amount of text is included.
Frequency	Annual
Availability	General
Cost	£35
Comments	–
Address	102 Euston Street, London NW1 2HA
Tel. / e-mail	0171 387 0317 sconul@mailbox.ulcc.ac.uk
Fax / Web site	0171 383 3197 www.sconul.ac.uk

818	STATIONERY TRADE REVIEW
Title	**Reference Book and Buyers' Guide**
Coverage	The annual handbook for the stationery industry which includes an overview of the market and trends in the previous year. Includes market information on business machines, social stationery, and office products. Based on the journal's regular survey of manufacturers.
Frequency	Annual
Availability	General
Cost	£45
Comments	–
Address	Nexus Media Ltd, Warwick House, Azalea Drive, Swanley BR8 8HY
Tel. / e-mail	01322 660070
Fax / Web site	01322 667633

819	SURVEY RESEARCH ASSOCIATES
Title	**SRA Omnibus Survey**
Coverage	A multi-client survey covering various topics and based on a sample size of 1,500 adults. Interviews are carried out in the home.
Frequency	Fortnightly
Availability	General
Cost	On application
Comments	–
Address	Tower House, Southampton Street, London WC2E 7HN
Tel. / e-mail	0171 612 0369
Fax / Web site	0171 612 0361

820	SUTHERLANDS LIMITED
Title	**Scotch Whisky Industry Review**
Coverage	A detailed analysis of the sector with data on home and export prices, costs and profit margins, sales, distillers, market shares, brand and company information, exports, and forecasts of future trends. Based on various sources.
Frequency	Annual
Availability	General
Cost	£395 (UK), £415 (overseas)
Comments	–
Address	Lismore House, 127 George Street, Edinburgh EH2 4JX
Tel. / e-mail	0131 527 3000
Fax / Web site	0131 527 3001

821	SYSTEM THREE SCOTLAND
Title	**Scottish Opinion Survey**
Coverage	A regular survey monitoring opinion, marketing, and advertising activity in Scotland. Based on a sample of 1,000 adults.
Frequency	Monthly
Availability	General
Cost	On application
Comments	–
Address	6 Hill Street, Edinburgh EH2 3JZ
Tel. / e-mail	0131 220 1178
Fax / Web site	0131 220 1181

822 TABS LTD

Title **Tracking Advertising and Brand Strength**

Coverage A service specialising in continuous advertising tracking based on a sample of over 1,000 adults. Monitors brand goodwill, advertising awareness, price image, brand awareness, claimed levels of buying/usage etc.

Frequency Monthly

Availability General

Cost On application

Comments –

Address Mulliner House, Flanders Road, London   W4 1NN

Tel. / e-mail 0181 994 9177

Fax / Web site 0181 994 2115

823 TAS PARTNERSHIP LTD

Title **Public Transport Monitors**

Coverage An analysis of trends in three transport sectors - bus industry, rapid transport, and the rail industry - based on various sources.

Frequency Annual with quarterly updates

Availability General

Cost £149.50 each for bus and rail reports, £125 for rapid transit

Comments –

Address Britannic House, 1A Chapel Street, Preston   PR1 8BU

Tel. / e-mail 01722 840268

Fax / Web site 01722 840705

824 TATE & LYLE SPECIALITY SWEETENERS

Title **199- Sucralose Soft Drinks Report**

Coverage Data and commentary on drinks by type, packaging trends, industrial structure, market outlook. Ten years data in some tables.

Frequency Annual

Availability General

Cost On request

Comments –

Address Philip Lyle Building, Whiteknights, Reading   RG6 6BX

Tel. / e-mail 0118 925 2900

Fax / Web site 0118 925 2920

825	TAYLOR NELSON AGB CONSUMER
Title	**AGB Impulse**
Coverage	Monthly omnibus survey based on a sample of 4,300 individuals and covering impulse buying and casual purchases.
Frequency	Monthly
Availability	General
Cost	On request
Comments	Various other research services available.
Address	44-46 Upper High Street, Epsom KT17 4QS
Tel. / e-mail	01372 801010
Fax / Web site	01372 725404 www.tnagb.com

826	TAYLOR NELSON AGB CONSUMER
Title	**Family Food Panel**
Coverage	Monthly omnibus survey of 4,200 homes monitoring food and drink consumption.
Frequency	Monthly
Availability	General
Cost	On request
Comments	Various other research services available.
Address	44-46 Upper High Street, Epsom KT17 4QS
Tel. / e-mail	01372 801010
Fax / Web site	01372 725404 www.tnagb.com

827	TAYLOR NELSON AGB CONSUMER
Title	**Omnimas**
Coverage	Omnibus survey based on a sample of 2,000 adults every week. Face-to-face interviews in the home.
Frequency	Weekly
Availability	General
Cost	On request
Comments	Various other research services available.
Address	44-46 Upper High Street, Epsom KT17 4QS
Tel. / e-mail	01372 801010
Fax / Web site	01372 725404 www.tnagb.com

828	TAYLOR NELSON AGB CONSUMER
Title	**Personal Care Panel**
Coverage	A twice-yearly consumer panel covering purchases of cosmetics and toiletries based on a sample of 4,000.
Frequency	Twice yearly
Availability	General
Cost	On request
Comments	Various other research services available.
Address	44-46 Upper High Street, Epsom KT17 4QS
Tel. / e-mail	01372 801010
Fax / Web site	01372 725404 www.tnagb.com

829	TAYLOR NELSON AGB CONSUMER
Title	**SuperPanel**
Coverage	Weekly omnibus survey based on a sample of 10,000 homes and covering product areas in the packaged groceries, fresh foods, and toiletries markets.
Frequency	Weekly
Availability	General
Cost	On request
Comments	Various other research services available.
Address	44-46 Upper High Street, Epsom KT17 4QS
Tel. / e-mail	01372 801010
Fax / Web site	01372 725404 www.tnagb.com

830	TAYLOR NELSON AGB PUBLICATIONS
Title	**The AGB Cable and Satellite Yearbook**
Coverage	The report includes an overview of the industry as a whole, data on the cable-active and non-terrestrial viewing populations including household penetration by cable and DTH, general viewing trends, average daily hours of viewing per month, advertising data, programming information, and profiles of satellite companies and cable providers.
Frequency	Annual
Availability	General
Cost	£295, £590 combined purchase with AGB Television Yearbook (see previous entry)
Comments	Also publishes various one-off reports on consumer markets.
Address	14-17 St John's Square, London EC1M 4HE
Tel. / e-mail	0171 608 0072
Fax / Web site	0171 490 1550 www.tnagb.com

831	TAYLOR NELSON AGB PUBLICATIONS
Title	**The AGB Television Yearbook**
Coverage	A report containing monthly BARB data on viewing for terrestial television, monthly viewing figures and audience profiles for the top 30 programmes, top programmes by channel and type, advertising spending and impact, demographic analysis, regional breakdowns, and company profiles.
Frequency	Annual
Availability	General
Cost	£395, £590 combined purchase with AGB Cable and Satellite Yearbook (see next entry)
Comments	Also publishes various one-off reports on consumer markets.
Address	14-17 St John's Square, London EC1M 4HE
Tel. / e-mail	0171 608 0072
Fax / Web site	0171 490 1550 www.tnagb.com

832	TAYLOR NELSON AGB PUBLICATIONS
Title	**The Household Expenditure Survey Reports**
Coverage	A series of five reports analysing the detailed results of the government's Family Expenditure Survey by age, wealth, occupation, lifestage, and region. Each report contains data on 300 product categories.
Frequency	Annual
Availability	General
Cost	On application
Comments	Also publishes various one-off reports on consumer markets.
Address	14-17 St John's Square, London EC1M 4HE
Tel. / e-mail	0171 608 0072
Fax / Web site	0171 490 1550

833	TELECOMMUNICATION INDUSTRIES ASSOCIATION
Title	**Telecommunication Statistics**
Coverage	Statistics on the industry based primarily on research by the association.
Frequency	Regular
Availability	Members and selected others
Cost	On request
Comments	–
Address	Douglas House, 32-34 Simpson Road, Fenny Stratford, Bletchley MK1 1BA
Tel. / e-mail	01908 645000 info@tia.org.uk
Fax / Web site	01908 632263 www.tia.org.uk

834 TELMAR COMMUNICATIONS LTD

Title	**Telmar Databases**
Coverage	Telmar has access to various media and consumer databases containing statistics, including the British Business Survey (see other entry).
Frequency	Continuous
Availability	General
Cost	On request, and depending on the nature and range of information required
Comments	–
Address	21 Ivor Place, London NW1
Tel. / e-mail	0171 224 9992
Fax / Web site	0171 723 5265

835 TIMBER TRADES JOURNAL

Title	**Markets**
Coverage	Various statistics on timber and wood consumption, trade, prices etc. Different statistics appear each week and based on various sources.
Frequency	Weekly in a weekly journal
Availability	General
Cost	£98
Comments	–
Address	Miller Freeman Publications Ltd, Sovereign Way, Tonbridge TN9 1RW
Tel. / e-mail	01732 364422
Fax / Web site	01732 361534

836 TIN INTERNATIONAL

Title	**LME Prices/Stocks/Turnover**
Coverage	Prices, stocks, and turnover of tin on the London Metal Exchange plus a general market report.
Frequency	Monthly in a monthly journal
Availability	General
Cost	£120
Comments	–
Address	Tin Magazines Ltd, Kingston Lane, Uxbridge UB8 3PJ
Tel. / e-mail	01895 272406 tinint@itri.co.uk
Fax / Web site	01895 251841 www.itri.co.uk

837 TOBACCO MANUFACTURERS' ASSOCIATION

Title **Tobacco Figures**

Coverage Statistics and commentary on the tobacco industry with tables covering the market, taxes, employment, sponsorship, and advertising. Based on various sources.

Frequency Regular

Availability General

Cost Free

Comments –

Address 55 Tufton Street, London SW1P 3QF

Tel. / e-mail 0171 544 0100

Fax / Web site 0171 544 0117

838 TOP FLIGHT RESEARCH LTD

Title **Exporter Omnibus**

Coverage A regular telephone survey of exporting companies in manufacturing and services aimed at companies offering services to exporters.

Frequency Regular

Availability General

Cost On application

Comments –

Address Weir House, Hurst Road, Hampton Court   KT8 9AQ

Tel. / e-mail 0181 941 2505

Fax / Web site 0181 941 2149

839 TOP FLIGHT RESEARCH LTD

Title **International and Express Users' Panel**

Coverage A regular survey of users of freight and express parcel services, carried out by the above company.

Frequency Regular

Availability General

Cost On request

Comments –

Address Weir House, Hurst Road, Hampton Court   KTA 9AQ

Tel. / e-mail 0181 941 2505

Fax / Web site 0181 941 2149

840 TOP PAY RESEARCH GROUP

Title **Independent Chairman and Non-Executive Directors' Survey**

Coverage Based on over 1,400 interviews per year, a survey of pay for board chairs and non-executive directors.

Frequency Annual

Availability General

Cost £60

Comments Other surveys and services available.

Address 9 Savoy Street, London WC2R 0BA

Tel. / e-mail 0171 836 5831   toppay@atlas.co.uk

Fax / Web site   www.atlas.co.uk/toppay

841 TOY TRADER

Title **Market Surveys**

Coverage Each issue contains a survey of a specific toy market, e.g. electronic toys, board games, dolls, educational toys etc, with commentary and statistics on trends in the market.

Frequency Regular in a monthly journal

Availability General

Cost £60

Comments –

Address Peebles Publishing Group Ltd, Brookmead House, 8 Thorney Leys Business Park, Witney   OX8 7GE

Tel. / e-mail 01993 775545   trdmedia@aol.com

Fax / Web site 01993 778884   www.toy.co.uk/toytrader

842 TRANSPORT 2000 TRUST

Title **Vital Travel Statistics**

Coverage Details of demand for car, motorcycle, cycle, rail, and pedestrian travel based on the National Travel Survey.

Frequency Regular

Availability General

Cost £20.50

Comments –

Address Walkden House, 10 Melton Street, London   NW1 2EJ

Tel. / e-mail 0171 388 8386

Fax / Web site 0171 388 2481

843	TRAVEL AND TOURISM RESEARCH LTD
Title	**Travel Agents' Omnibus Survey**
Coverage	A survey of travel agency staff with a sample of approximately 200 for each survey.
Frequency	Every 2 months
Availability	General
Cost	On application
Comments	–
Address	39c Highbury Place, London N5 1QP
Tel. / e-mail	0171 354 3391
Fax / Web site	0171 359 4043

844	TRAVEL AND TOURISM RESEARCH LTD
Title	**UK Airlines Travel Trade Image Survey**
Coverage	Examines travel agents' images of the main international airlines. Annual report compares latest annual results with some previous years.
Frequency	Annual
Availability	General
Cost	£5,000
Comments	–
Address	39c Highbury Place, London N5 1QP
Tel. / e-mail	0171 354 3391
Fax / Web site	0171 359 4043

845	TREBOR BASSETT LTD
Title	**199- Confectionery Review**
Coverage	Figures for recent years on the confectionery market with data on specific sectors, e.g. chocolate, sugar, seasonal sales etc. Data on key brands, trade sector performance, advertising, retailing, the consumer. Includes a supporting commentary.
Frequency	Annual
Availability	General
Cost	Free to the trade, £10 to others
Comments	–
Address	Hertford Place, Denham Way, Maple Cross WD3 2XB
Tel. / e-mail	01923 896565
Fax / Web site	www.cadburyschweppes.com

	UK STEEL ASSOCIATION
846	
Title	**The UK Steel Industry**
Coverage	Review of the industry with statistics on output, consumption, trade. Also regional distribution of steel companies.
Frequency	Annual
Availability	General
Cost	On request
Comments	The web site also contains some basic statistics freely available.
Address	Millbank Tower, 21-24 Millbank, London SW1P 4QP
Tel. / e-mail	0171 343 3150 enquiries@uksteel.org.uk
Fax / Web site	0171 343 3190 www.uksteel.org.uk

	ULSTER MARKETING SURVEYS
847	
Title	**UMS Northern Ireland Omnibus**
Coverage	A regular survey of 1,100 adults in Northern Ireland based on face-to-face interviews in the home. Covers consumer markets for both products and services.
Frequency	Monthly
Availability	General
Cost	On application
Comments	Also carries out specialist surveys of the Northern Ireland motoring market and a regular readership survey.
Address	115 University Street, Belfast BT7 1HP
Tel. / e-mail	01232 231060 ums@ni.onyxnet.co.uk
Fax / Web site	01232 243887 www.pandora.co.uk/ni/ums

	UNITED KINGDOM AGRICULTURAL SUPPLY TRADE ASSOCIATION LTD (UKASTA)
848	
Title	**Feed Figures**
Coverage	Livestock numbers, output of compounds, compound production by region, use of raw materials, prices etc. Also some European data. Based on a combination of official and non-official sources.
Frequency	Annual
Availability	General
Cost	Free
Comments	–
Address	3 Whitehall Court, London SW1A 2EQ
Tel. / e-mail	0171 930 3611
Fax / Web site	0171 930 3952

849		UNIVERSITY OF DURHAM BUSINESS SCHOOL
	Title	**Small Business Trends**
	Coverage	Detailed analysis and statistics on SMEs with sections on general trends, SMEs by industrial and service sector, and future trends. Based on an analysis of various sources.
	Frequency	Every 2 years
	Availability	General
	Cost	On request
	Comments	–
	Address	Mill Hill Lane, Durham DH1 3LB
	Tel. / e-mail	0191 374 2211
	Fax / Web site	0191 374 3748

850		UNIVERSITY OF NOTTINGHAM BUSINESS SCHOOL, CENTRE FOR MANAGEMENT BUY-OUT RESEARCH
	Title	**Management Buy-Out Quarterly Review**
	Coverage	A market overview and commentary on recent market trends with some statistics on buy-outs.
	Frequency	Quarterly
	Availability	General
	Cost	£100
	Comments	The centre was founded by Deloitte & Touche and Barclays Private Equity Ltd.
	Address	University of Nottingham, University Park, Nottingham NG7 2RD
	Tel. / e-mail	0115 951 5493 mike.wright/kenneth.robbie@nottingham.ac.uk
	Fax / Web site	0115 951 5204 www.ccc.nottingham.ac.uk

851		UNIVERSITY OF READING, DEPARTMENT OF AGRICULTURAL ECONOMICS AND MANAGEMENT
	Title	**Farm Business Data**
	Coverage	Based partly on a survey carried out by the university and summaries of other surveys, the report analyses performance trends in the farming sector.
	Frequency	Annual
	Availability	General
	Cost	£10
	Comments	–
	Address	4 Earley Gate, Whiteknights Road, Reading RG6 6AR
	Tel. / e-mail	01734 875123
	Fax / Web site	01734 756467

852	UNIVERSITY OF READING, DEPARTMENT OF AGRICULTURAL ECONOMICS AND MANAGEMENT
Title	**Horticultural Business Data**
Coverage	Analysis and statistics for three business groups - glasshouse holdings, vegetable and mixed horticultural holdings, and fruit holdings. Based largely on the university's survey supplemented by some Central Government data.
Frequency	Annual
Availability	General
Cost	£10
Comments	–
Address	4 Earley Gate, Whiteknights Road, Reading RG6 6AR
Tel. / e-mail	01734 875123
Fax / Web site	01734 756467

853	UNIVERSITY OF WARWICK, CENTRE FOR RESEARCH IN ETHNIC RELATIONS
Title	**National Ethnic Minority Data Archive**
Coverage	A database of statistics on the UK's ethnic minority population, largely based on the 1991 population Census. Various reports are published from the database on specific topics, e.g. economic activity, age/sex characteristics, households, demographic distribution etc.
Frequency	Continuous
Availability	General
Cost	On request
Comments	–
Address	University of Warwick, Gibbett Hill Road, Coventry CV4 7AL
Tel. / e-mail	01203 523607 CRER@Warwick.ac.uk
Fax / Web site	01203 524324 www.warwick.ac.uk/CRER

854

UNIVERSITY OF WARWICK, INSTITUTE FOR EMPLOYMENT RESEARCH

Title	**Review of the Economy and Employment: Labour Market Assessment**
Coverage	A regular report on labour market trends and general economic trends with features on specific aspects of the labour market. Includes regional, sector data and some forecasts of employment trends. Specific issues cover specific topics.
Frequency	Regular
Availability	General
Cost	£80
Comments	–
Address	University of Warwick, Gibbett Hill Road, Coventry CV4 7AL
Tel. / e-mail	01203 523708 iesal@ice.csu.warwick.ac.uk
Fax / Web site	01203 524241

855

UNIVERSITY OF YORK, CENTRE FOR HOUSING POLICY

Title	**JRF Index of Private Rents and Yields**
Coverage	Statistics on average rents and yields with regional data and data for local authority areas. There is also a Valuations Index and a Transactions Index.
Frequency	Quarterly
Availability	General
Cost	On request
Comments	Published in partnership with the Association of Residential Letting Agents and other agents, Halifax, and the Rent Officer Service.
Address	University of York, York YO10 5DD
Tel. / e-mail	01904 433691
Fax / Web site	01904 432318

856

VENTURE CAPITAL REPORTS

Title	**The Venture Capital Report Guide to Venture Capital in the UK and Europe**
Coverage	General review of the venture capital sector with statistics on total trends and details of specific companies.
Frequency	Annual
Availability	General
Cost	£106
Comments	–
Address	Boston Road, Henley-on-Thames RG9 1DY
Tel. / e-mail	01491 579999
Fax / Web site	01491 579825

857	**VERDICT RESEARCH LTD**
Title	**Book Retailers**
Coverage	Analysis and statistics on market trends and value, consumer spending, key players, and the issues affecting the sector. Based on a combination of published data and original research.
Frequency	Annual
Availability	General
Cost	£990
Comments	Also publishes monthly newsletters on retailing in the UK, USA, and Europe.
Address	Newlands House, 40 Berners Street, London W1P 4DX
Tel. / e-mail	0171 255 6400 retail@verdict.co.uk
Fax / Web site	0171 637 5951 www.verdict.co.uk

858	**VERDICT RESEARCH LTD**
Title	**Children's Retailing**
Coverage	Analysis and statistics on market trends and value, consumer spending, key players, and the issues affecting the sector. Based on a combination of published data and original research.
Frequency	Annual
Availability	General
Cost	£990
Comments	Also publishes monthly newsletters on retailing in the UK, USA, and Europe.
Address	Newlands House, 40 Berners Street, London W1P 4DX
Tel. / e-mail	0171 255 6400 retail@verdict.co.uk
Fax / Web site	0171 637 5951 www.verdict.co.uk

859	**VERDICT RESEARCH LTD**
Title	**Clothing Retailers**
Coverage	Analysis and statistics on market trends and value, consumer spending, key players, and the issues affecting the sector. Based on a combination of published data and original research.
Frequency	Annual
Availability	General
Cost	£990
Comments	Also publishes monthly newsletters on retailing in the UK, USA, and Europe.
Address	Newlands House, 40 Berners Street, London W1P 4DX
Tel. / e-mail	0171 255 6400 retail@verdict.co.uk
Fax / Web site	0171 637 5951 www.verdict.co.uk

	VERDICT RESEARCH LTD
860	
Title	**CTNs**
Coverage	Analysis and statistics on market trends and value, consumer spending, key players, and the issues affecting the sector. Based on a combination of published data and original research.
Frequency	Annual
Availability	General
Cost	£990
Comments	Also publishes monthly newsletters on retailing in the UK, USA, and Europe.
Address	Newlands House, 40 Berners Street, London W1P 4DX
Tel. / e-mail	0171 255 6400 retail@verdict.co.uk
Fax / Web site	0171 637 5951 www.verdict.co.uk

	VERDICT RESEARCH LTD
861	
Title	**Department Stores**
Coverage	Analysis and statistics on market trends and value, consumer spending, key players and the issues affecting the sector. Based on a combination of published data and original research.
Frequency	Annual
Availability	General
Cost	£990
Comments	Also publishes monthly newsletters on retailing in the UK, USA, and Europe.
Address	Newlands House, 40 Berners Street, London W1P 4DX
Tel. / e-mail	0171 255 6400 retail@verdict.co.uk
Fax / Web site	0171 637 5951 www.verdict.co.uk

	VERDICT RESEARCH LTD
862	
Title	**DIY Retailers**
Coverage	Analysis and statistics on market trends and value, consumer spending, key players, and the issues affecting the sector. Based on a combination of published data and original research.
Frequency	Annual
Availability	General
Cost	£990
Comments	Also publishes monthly newsletters on retailing in the UK, USA, and Europe.
Address	Newlands House, 40 Berners Street, London W1P 4DX
Tel. / e-mail	0171 255 6400 retail@verdict.co.uk
Fax / Web site	0171 637 5951 www.verdict.co.uk

	VERDICT RESEARCH LTD
863	
Title	**Electrical Retailers**
Coverage	Analysis and statistics on market trends and value, consumer spending, key players, and the issues affecting the sector. Based on a combination of published data and original research.
Frequency	Annual
Availability	General
Cost	£990
Comments	Also publishes monthly newsletters on retailing in the UK, USA, and Europe.
Address	Newlands House, 40 Berners Street, London W1P 4DX
Tel. / e-mail	0171 255 6400 retail@verdict.co.uk
Fax / Web site	0171 637 5951 www.verdict.co.uk

	VERDICT RESEARCH LTD
864	
Title	**Electronic Shopping**
Coverage	Analysis and statistics on market trends and value, consumer spending, key players, and the issues affecting the sector. Based on a combination of published data and original research.
Frequency	Annual
Availability	General
Cost	£990
Comments	Also publishes monthly newsletters on retailing in the UK, USA, and Europe.
Address	Newlands House, 40 Berners Street, London W1P 4DX
Tel. / e-mail	0171 255 6400 retail@verdict.co.uk
Fax / Web site	0171 637 5951 www.verdict.co.uk

	VERDICT RESEARCH LTD
865	
Title	**Footwear Retailers**
Coverage	Analysis and statistics on market trends and value, consumer spending, key players, and the issues affecting the sector. Based on a combination of published data and original research.
Frequency	Annual
Availability	General
Cost	£990
Comments	Also publishes monthly newsletters on retailing in the UK, USA, and Europe.
Address	Newlands House, 40 Berners Street, London W1P 4DX
Tel. / e-mail	0171 255 6400 retail@verdict.co.uk
Fax / Web site	0171 637 5951 www.verdict.co.uk

866	VERDICT RESEARCH LTD
Title	**Furniture and Carpet Retailing**
Coverage	Analysis and statistics on market trends and value, consumer spending, key players, and the issues affecting the sector. Based on a combination of published data and original research.
Frequency	Annual
Availability	General
Cost	£990
Comments	Also publishes monthly newsletters on retailing in the UK, USA, and Europe.
Address	Newlands House, 40 Berners Street, London W1P 4DX
Tel. / e-mail	0171 255 6400 retail@verdict.co.uk
Fax / Web site	0171 637 5951 www.verdict.co.uk

867	VERDICT RESEARCH LTD
Title	**Grocers and Supermarkets**
Coverage	Analysis and statistics on market trends and value, consumer spending, key players, and the issues affecting the sector. Based on a combination of published data and original research.
Frequency	Annual
Availability	General
Cost	£990
Comments	Also publishes monthly newsletters on retailing trends in the UK, USA, and Europe.
Address	Newlands House, 40 Berners Street, London W1P 4DX
Tel. / e-mail	0171 255 6400 retail@verdict.co.uk
Fax / Web site	0171 637 5951 www.verdict.co.uk

868	VERDICT RESEARCH LTD
Title	**Health and Beauty Retailers**
Coverage	Analysis and statistics on market trends and value, consumer spending, key players, and the issues affecting the sector. Based on a combination of published data and original research.
Frequency	Annual
Availability	General
Cost	£990
Comments	Also publishes monthly newsletters on retailing in the UK, USA, and Europe.
Address	Newlands House, 40 Berners Street, London W1P 4DX
Tel. / e-mail	0171 255 6400 retail@verdict.co.uk
Fax / Web site	0171 637 5951 www.verdict.co.uk

869	VERDICT RESEARCH LTD
Title	**Home Shopping**
Coverage	Analysis and statistics on market trends and value, consumer spending, key players, and the issues affecting the sector. Based on a combination of published data and original research.
Frequency	Annual
Availability	General
Cost	£990
Comments	Also publishes monthly newsletters on retailing in the UK, USA, and Europe.
Address	Newlands House, 40 Berners Street, London W1P 4DX
Tel. / e-mail	0171 255 6400 retail@verdict.co.uk
Fax / Web site	0171 637 5951 www.verdict.co.uk

870	VERDICT RESEARCH LTD
Title	**Housewares and Home Furnishings**
Coverage	Analysis and statistics on market trends and value, consumer spending, key players, and the issues affecting the sector. Based on a combination of published data and original research.
Frequency	Annual
Availability	General
Cost	£990
Comments	Also publishes monthly newsletters on retailing trends in the UK, USA, and Europe.
Address	Newlands House, 40 Berners Street, London W1P 4DX
Tel. / e-mail	0171 255 6400 retail@verdict.co.uk
Fax / Web site	0171 637 5951 www.verdict.co.uk

871	VERDICT RESEARCH LTD
Title	**Jewellery Retailing**
Coverage	Analysis and statistics on market trends and value, consumer spending, key players, and the issues affecting the sector. Based on a combination of published data and original research.
Frequency	Annual
Availability	General
Cost	£990
Comments	Also publishes monthly newsletters on retailing in the UK, USA, and Europe.
Address	Newlands House, 40 Berners Street, London W1P 4DX
Tel. / e-mail	0171 255 6400 retail@verdict.co.uk
Fax / Web site	0171 637 5951 www.verdict.co.uk

872	VERDICT RESEARCH LTD
Title	**Neighbourhood Retailing**
Coverage	Analysis and statistics on market trends and value, consumer spending, key players, and the key issues affecting the sector. Based on a combination of published data and original research.
Frequency	Annual
Availability	General
Cost	£990
Comments	Also publishes monthly newsletters on retailing in the UK, USA, and Europe.
Address	Newlands House, 40 Berners Street, London W1P 4DX
Tel. / e-mail	0171 255 6400 retail@verdict.co.uk
Fax / Web site	0171 637 5951 www.verdict.co.uk

873	VERDICT RESEARCH LTD
Title	**Out of Town Retailing**
Coverage	Analysis and statistics on sector trends and value, consumer spending, key players, and the issues affecting the sector. Based on a combination of published data and original research.
Frequency	Annual
Availability	General
Cost	£990
Comments	Also publishes monthly newsletters on retailing in the UK, USA, and Europe.
Address	Newlands House, 40 Berners Street, London W1P 4DX
Tel. / e-mail	0171 255 6400 retail@verdict.co.uk
Fax / Web site	0171 637 5951 www.verdict.co.uk

874	VERDICT RESEARCH LTD
Title	**Retailing 200-**
Coverage	Forecasts of retailing trends with overviews and details of prospects for specific sectors.
Frequency	Annual
Availability	General
Cost	£1,250
Comments	Also publishes monthly newsletters on retailing in the UK, USA, and Europe.
Address	Newlands House, 40 Berners Street, London W1P 4DX
Tel. / e-mail	0171 255 6400 retail@verdict.co.uk
Fax / Web site	0171 637 5951 www.verdict.co.uk

875 WALLCOVERING MANUFACTURERS' ASSOCIATION OF GREAT BRITAIN

Title	**Members' Statistics**
Coverage	Data on the UK wallcoverings sector based on an analysis of returns from member companies.
Frequency	Regular
Availability	Members
Cost	Free
Comments	–
Address	James House, Bridge Street, Leatherhead KT22 7EP
Tel. / e-mail	01372 360660
Fax / Web site	01372 376069

876 WATSON WYATT WORLDWIDE

Title	**Employment and Salary Surveys**
Coverage	Various surveys of employment and earnings in sectors such as corporate services, architecture, IT etc.
Frequency	Regular
Availability	General
Cost	On request
Comments	–
Address	Park Gate, 21 Tothill Street, London SW1H 9LL
Tel. / e-mail	0171 222 8037
Fax / Web site	

877 WEATHERALL GREEN AND SMITH

Title	**London Office Market**
Coverage	Details of rates for premium offices in areas of London. Based on data collected by the company.
Frequency	Twice yearly
Availability	General
Cost	Free
Comments	–
Address	22 Chancery Lane, London WC2A 1LT
Tel. / e-mail	0171 493 5566
Fax / Web site	0171 430 2628

878 WEATHERALL GREEN AND SMITH

Title	**Regional Office Rent Survey**
Coverage	Details of rates for prime offices in the main regional town centres and business parks. Based on data collected by the company.
Frequency	Twice yearly
Availability	General
Cost	Free
Comments	–
Address	22 Chancery Lane, London WC2A 1LT
Tel. / e-mail	0171 493 5566
Fax / Web site	0171 430 2628

879 WHITBREAD BEER COMPANY

Title	**Whitbread On-Trade Market Report**
Coverage	Commentary and statistics on the on-trade market for alcoholic drinks. Based primarily on commissioned research.
Frequency	Annual
Availability	General
Cost	Free
Comments	–
Address	Porter Tun House, Capability Green, Luton LU1 3LW
Tel. / e-mail	01582 391166
Fax / Web site	01582 397397

880 WHITBREAD BEER COMPANY

Title	**Whitbread Take-Home Market Report**
Coverage	Commentary and statistics on the take-home market for alcoholic drinks with data on market size, brands, outlets, and current trends. Based primarily on commissioned research.
Frequency	Annual
Availability	General
Cost	Free
Comments	–
Address	Porter Tun House, Capability Green, Luton LU1 3LW
Tel. / e-mail	01582 391166
Fax / Web site	01582 397397

881	
	WILLIAMS DE BROE
Title	**Weekly Economic Indicators**
Coverage	Weekly data on UK economic trends with regular forecasts for the main economic indicators.
Frequency	Weekly
Availability	General
Cost	On request
Comments	–
Address	6 Broadgate, London EC2M 2RP
Tel. / e-mail	0171 588 7511
Fax / Web site	0171 588 8860

882	
	WOOL DEVELOPMENT INTERNATIONAL LTD
Title	**Wool Figures**
Coverage	Statistics covering raw fibres, net domestic availability, the manufacturing process, end products, and consumption. Historical data in most tables and based on various sources.
Frequency	Annual
Availability	General
Cost	£20
Comments	–
Address	Development Centre, Valley Drive, Ilkley LS29 8PB
Tel. / e-mail	01943 603376
Fax / Web site	

883	
	WORLD TEXTILE PUBLICATIONS
Title	**The Wool Market**
Coverage	Statistics on the prices of wool based on data collected by the journal.
Frequency	Monthly in a monthly journal
Availability	General
Cost	£80
Comments	–
Address	World Textile Publications Ltd, Perkin House, 1 Longlands Street, Bradford BD1 2TP
Tel. / e-mail	01274 378800 104470.3070@compuserve.com
Fax / Web site	01274 378811 www.vitalo.com / worldtextile

884	WORLD TEXTILE PUBLICATIONS
Title	**Weekly Market Report**
Coverage	A weekly summary of prices and news relating to the wool market.
Frequency	Weekly
Availability	General
Cost	£175
Comments	Published every Thursday.
Address	World Textile Publications Ltd, Perkin House, 1 Longlands Street, Bradford BD1 2TP
Tel. / e-mail	01274 378800 104470.3070@compuserve.com
Fax / Web site	01274 378811 www.vitalo.com / worldtextile

Part II
Title Index

Part III
Subject Index

A

Accountants - Salaries 6, 434, 448

Actuaries - Salaries 743

Adhesives 82

Advertising 8, 9, 10, 506, 672, 822

Advertising - Complaints 14

Advertising - Costs 346

Advertising - Employment 505

Advertising - Expenditure 5, 12

Advertising - Forecasts 11, 13

Advertising - Internet 390

Advertising - Media 346

Advertising - Outdoor 518, 683

Advertising - Poster 518, 683

Aerosols 83, 597

Aggregates 737

Agricultural Machinery 84

Agricultural Machinery - Overseas Trade 16

Agriculture 239, 728, 851

Agriculture - Feed 848

Agriculture - Investment 515

Agriculture - Land 375

Agriculture - Omnibus Surveys 517

Agrochemicals 85

Airlines 279, 844

Airlines - Punctuality 277, 278

Airports 56, 57, 58, 226, 234, 280

Alcoholic Drinks 79, 424, 784, 820, 879, 880

Alternative Investment Market 537, 563

Aluminium 20

Architects 24, 25, 661

Architects - Opinion Surveys 190

Archives 235

Arts - Sponsorship 3

Audio Equipment 141

Audio Software 141, 142

Automatic Vending 55

Automotive Data Services 802

Automotives 774, 775

Automotives - Company Cars 623

Automotives - Prices 284

B

Baby Foods 324

Baby Products - Omnibus Surveys 749

Bakery Products 379

Banking Staff - Salaries 448

Bankruptcies 337, 807

Banks 59, 62, 93, 95

Banks - Clearings 28, 29, 560

Banks - Corporate Sector 62

Banks - Lending 96, 401

Banks - Mortgages 94

Barley 80

Beer 79

Benefits - Housing 249

Biscuits 72, 73

Board 171, 690, 691, 694, 695, 696, 699

Board - Energy Use 689

Board - Overseas Trade 692

Boating 130, 131

Books 74, 75, 76, 103, 734

Books - Prices 75, 548

Books - Retailing 77, 857

Bottled Water 155, 281

Bottles - Glass 122

Bread 393

Brewing 590

Bricks 81

Brown Goods 147, 227

Budgets - Libraries 552

Budgets - Public Libraries 552

Builders Merchants 179

Building 67, 81, 178, 179, 180, 183, 184, 193, 643, 647

Building - Builders Merchants 179

I

Importers - Opinion Surveys 64
Independent Education 481
Independent Schools 481
Industrial - Property 535
Industrial Property 532
Industrial Property - Rents 523
Industrial Robots 151
Industry 297, 298, 372, 601
Industry - Finance 338
Industry - Forecasts 208
Industry - Opinion Surveys 1, 100, 297, 298, 327
Industry - Scotland 786
Information Staff - Salaries 499
Insecticides 85
Insolvencies 337, 807, 808
Institutional Funds 511
Insurance 30, 32, 33, 36, 37, 38, 39, 41, 669
Insurance - Claims 40
Insurance - Computers 584
Insurance - Motor Vehicles 31, 34
Insurance - Overseas Earnings 35
Insurance Staff - Salaries 45
Internet 313, 314, 339, 391, 392, 656
Internet - Advertising 390
Investment 49, 50, 51, 68, 169, 511, 703, 856
Investment - Agriculture 515
Investment - Chemicals 270
Investment - Land 515
Investment - Property 202, 534
Investment - Retailing 205
Investment Fund Managers - Salaries 444
Iron 127, 128, 129, 519, 520, 521

J

Jewellery 754, 755

Jewellery - Prices 754, 755
Jewellery - Retailing 871
Journals 650, 711
Journals - Circulation 54
Journals - Prices 553
Juices 326
Justice 233

L

Land - Agriculture 375
Land - Investment 515
Land - Prices 375
Lawnmowers 395
Lawyers - Salaries 447
Leasing 388
Leasing - Motor Vehicles 167, 168
Leather - Prices 544
Leisure 614, 657
Leisure - Costs 253
Leisure - Finance 252
Leisure - Forecasts 546
Lending - Banks 401
Libraries 75, 262, 549
Libraries - Budgets 552
Libraries - Expenditure 817
Libraries - Finance 261
Libraries - Healthcare 550
Libraries - Services to Schools 551
Life Insurance 39
Lighters 197
Livestock - Prices 606
Local Government 254
Local Government - Capital Payments 236
Local Government - Debt 236
Local Government - Expenditure 80(
Local Government - Finance 245, 263
Local Government - Superannuation Funds 264
Local Government Staff - Salaries 445, 761

London 802

London - Business Conditions 559

London - Economy 558

London - Floorspace 492

London - Hotels 686

London - Offices 200, 335, 877

London - Opinion Surveys 559

London - Property 199, 343, 492, 533

M

Machine Tools 586, 609

Machine Tools - Overseas Trade 587, 588

Malting 80, 590

Management Accountants - Opinion Surveys 231

Management Buyouts 538, 539, 850

Management Consultants 21, 591, 592

Management Consultants - Prices 593

Management Consultants - Salaries 594

Managers - Readership Surveys 137

Managers - Salaries 439, 442, 444, 472, 474, 618, 621, 742, 764, 770

Managing Directors 52

Market Data 207, 211, 219, 220, 334, 357, 361, 367, 368, 417, 419, 420, 426, 431, 432, 433, 468, 471, 490, 530, 531, 599, 600, 615, 632, 654, 671, 834

Market Data - Forecasts 598

Market Data - Regions 676

Market Research 48, 132, 134, 135, 136, 471, 530, 531, 599, 615, 632

Marketing 232

Marketing - Direct 330, 331

Marketing Staff - Salaries 603, 740, 771

Matches 197

Meat - Prices 606

Mechanical Engineers - Salaries 510

Media 8, 10, 134, 135, 136, 334, 471, 672

Media - Advertising 346

Media - Circulation 54

Medical Practitioners - Omnibus Surveys 721

Metal Packaging 608

Metals 138, 152, 519

Metals - Overseas Trade 520, 521

Metals - Prices 403, 562, 607, 836

Mobile telephones 315

Money Supply 59, 60

Mortgages 321, 322, 626, 653

Mortgages - Banks 94

Mortgages - Building Societies 194

Motor Vehicles 547, 623, 627, 628, 629, 631, 774, 775, 793, 803, 804, 805, 806

Motor Vehicles - Components 651

Motor Vehicles - Electric 341

Motor Vehicles - Fleets 168

Motor Vehicles - Insurance 31, 34

Motor Vehicles - Leasing 167, 168

Motor Vehicles - Overseas Trade 801

Motor Vehicles - Prices 284

Motor Vehicles - Rental 167

Motorcycles 627, 628, 629

Motorists 547

Motorists - Omnibus Surveys 610, 783

Mushrooms 634

Music 635

N

National Health Service Staff - Salaries 764

Neighbourhood Retailing 872

New Issues 540

Newspapers 650

Newspapers - Circulation 54, 522

North Sea - Petroleum 715, 778